How to CONNECT with Your iTEEN

a parenting road map

Susan Morris Shaffer
and Linda Perlman Gordon

New York   Chicago   San Francisco   L̶i̶s̶b̶o̶n̶
Madrid   Mexico City   Milan   New De̶l̶h̶i̶   San Juan
Seoul   Singapore   Sydney   Toronto

1 2 3 4 5 6 7 8 9 0   QFR/QFR   1 9 8 7 6 5

ISBN 978-0-07-182421-7
MHID   0-07-182421-9

e-ISBN 978-0-07-182412-5
e-MHID   0-07-182412-X

McGraw-Hill Education books are available at special quantity discounts to use as premiums and sales promotions or for use in corporate training programs. To contact a representative, please e-mail us at bulksales@mheducation.com.

To our grandchildren,
Julian Vuong Shaffer,
Levi Henry Miller and Sari Juliet Miller,
who make life magical

Contents

There are two lasting bequests we can give our children.
One of these is roots, the other, wings.

—JOHANN WOLFGANG VON GOETHE

ACKNOWLEDGMENTS

Like our earlier books, we couldn't have written this book without the encouragement, support, and enthusiasm of so many people. We particularly want to give thanks to those parents, teens, friends, and family members who so generously shared their personal stories with us.

We wish to express gratitude to our agent, Joelle Delbourgo, for bringing us creative and significant opportunities, and to Christopher Brown and Peter McCurdy, our editorial team at McGraw-Hill.

Susan

To Mark, who shares my life, and endless hours of collaboration, always with love.

Special thanks to my children, Elizabeth and Seth, who provide boundless charm, humor, originality, and more joy than any mother could hope for. To my son-in-law, Josh, and daughter-in law, Linh, for their great kindness to me and love and support of my children.

To my team at the Mid-Atlantic Equity Consortium—for their constant support, willingness to assist, and devotion to promoting academic excellence for all children. My heartfelt thanks! A very special thank you to Noelle Terefe Haile and Nora Morales for their contributions to this book.

To Phyllis Lerner, for her candor, keen eye, and ongoing encouragement.

To Susan Wechsler—who is always willing to talk through ideas and provide me with her insightful perspective. Most importantly, I am grateful for our incredible friendship.

To my cousin Steven Glick—I would be remiss if I didn't acknowledge his life long support of my work and his own commitment to educational excellence as a consummate educator at San Francisco City College. He is never far from my thoughts.

Linda

To Arnie, who is my loving partner, my anchor and my tranquility.

To my daughter Emily and son-in-law David who provide me countless treasured moments while they are perfecting life's most important juggling act; pursuing their careers while joyously parenting Levi and Sari, the next generation of iTeens.

To my son Zach, whose honesty and expertise about teenagers offered me a collaboration I cherished.

To Kimberly Kol—for her contributions and expertise on eating disorders.

To Kerry Perlman—for her insightful knowledge about popular culture and teen life.

To Donna Shoom Kirsch—for her friendship, generosity of time, professional wisdom, and loving support.

To Mickie Simon and Lisan Martin, who provide unlimited support, wisdom and an endless amount of laughter.

Introduction: Whose Life Is It Anyway?

You cannot tell always by looking
what is happening.
More than half a tree is spread out
in the soil under your feet.

—Marge Piercy, "The Seven of Pentacles"

Teenagers have always been a challenge. One parent observes, "Life with a teen can be compared to wrestling with an octopus." Some have suggested sending them on a prolonged six-year camping experience. If only it were that easy. People often say that the first step toward recovery is to admit that you have a problem. Your problem is that there is no simple escape plan. You will raise your teenagers, and with a little luck, you and your teens will live to tell about it.

For many of us who have survived these years, the dread of adolescence dominates any discussion about parenting. Only after the ritual commiserating do we share the joys of adolescence. In fact, as parents of our now-adult children, we continue to talk about our own parenting skills. We admit that we might be sharing too much information (TMI) about what we didn't know then, couldn't quite

— 1 —

understand, and should have (in our offsprings' opinion) done differently. And now two of our children are raising their children, our grandchildren. But that's a topic for another book.

While the challenges of parenting teens are nothing new, today's context looks drastically different. Teens are growing up in a landscape where they are digitally connected every single moment of every single day and night, fully justifying our name for them: *iTeen*. iTeens are buried under their web of digital networks. These digital connections not only redefine how to maintain emotional connection with your kids, but also redefine privacy. For iTeens, there is very little privacy in the way that we historically have defined it. At the same time, parents are expected to set protections and rules around social media. We somehow have to help our teens to understand that, without boundaries, the information they so easily share lasts forever. Their data are like plastic bottles; they never go away.

iTeens may appear sophisticated because they are digital natives, yet they are unsophisticated in many ways because they have been so sheltered. Their play has been monitored and overscheduled. They aren't on their own, and they have little unscheduled downtime without a screen. This can have an impact on imagination, problem solving, and the ability to deal with free time, which they too often label as boredom.

This new tech reality presents a fundamental shift that separates the experience of today's teens from that of previous generations. It is difficult for parents to maintain authority and stay connected emotionally to their teens with the onslaught of unfiltered information, constant stimulation, and instant access iTeens thrive on. It is difficult for parents to have face-to-face conversations in this world of longer work hours, shortened attention spans, and 140-character tweets and texts. Deep relationships don't develop and can't be sustained in a millisecond. Parents and teens try to connect during a series of transitions, interrupted conversations, and planned activities. For these reasons, parenting during these times can seem a daunting task.

The iTeens we discuss in this book are millennials, people born between 1980 and 2000, more than 80 million in all, according to data from the U.S. Chamber of Commerce Foundation (2012). They are also known as the click generation (click on it); all growing up during the technology age. They are the children of baby boomers, the Me Generation. Their mothers and fathers include yuppies, soccer moms, and helicopter parents, adapting to the age of technology—some better than others. Together the two generations (kids and their parents) are coping with stagnant wages, the shock of having seen the worst recession since the Great Depression, and concerns about whether economic recovery can ever bring the return of enough middle class jobs. Some teens may not be able to live the lifestyle they were fortunate to have lived as children. Their parents are coming to terms with the possibility that they may not be able to retire but will just get progressively more tired. This combination of events often creates a fragmented world for teens. We suspect they are growing up less optimistic than their parents were.

Raising children has always been about teaching meaningful values and skills and about providing opportunities for children to be self-confident, self-reliant, and resilient. In the past, the slow pace of social evolution made these tasks easier. Values, skills, and the basis for self-confidence were somewhat static. Teenagers have always challenged authority, which is part of their developmental "job," but family and community have traditionally kept them in check. Only in the past 150 years has the pace of change become rapid enough to notice in real time.

Today parenting has become less about teaching children what is genuinely important for them to learn and more about trying to ensure their happiness. What teens want in the moment has become more important than what they need to become productive and resilient adults. In some ways, the balancing act of the relationship has tipped away from the parent to the child. Many parents currently want to be friends with their children, and this new desire dilutes the essential and unique role parents play.

We learned many lessons from the first books we wrote about teens and, subsequently, from the books we wrote about parenting adult children. Combining our careers—one of us is a clinical social worker, the other an educator —we have been analyzing successful and challenging parenting for, between us, 80 years. We have focused on teenagers for over half of that time, beginning with our own children. (We each have an adult son and an adult daughter.) We have learned that, although the global and American societies are changing rapidly, many parenting tasks remain mostly unchanged. The *what* remains the same; the *how* is different.

What are the lessons we have learned? We believe communication and connection are essential to creating a lasting and loving relationship with our children; you can't be friends with your children when they are teens. This doesn't mean you can't enjoy the same things and share much in common, but parenting is very different from a friendship. A friendship requires being on a level playing field. We hope you are never at the same stage of development as your teen.

We also believe in a long view of parenting, which means you have to pace yourself—when you can. All of the research indicates that teens are not fully developed until their midtwenties, so what was once a discrete developmental stage now goes into adulthood, 6 to 10 years later than anticipated. We have learned that overparenting (hovering over kids' every move and shielding them from difficulties) can sustain dependency and hinder self-esteem, prolonging this already-extended period of adolescence. Growing up is an incremental journey—a marathon and not a sprint!

We have learned that you can use some characteristics of adulthood as a framework for parenting teens. These characteristics require tools that can be intentionally taught so that teens can become resilient adults.

We have also learned the hard way that our job is not to make kids happy; that's their job. However, we provide an important safety net for children to be able to make mistakes, learn from them, and develop a deeper, more authentic self-confidence. Teens need to know that we are there and that we love them unconditionally, but our job is not to fix everything for them. Our job is to give them increasing responsibility so they can become self-reliant. Unfortunately, and typically, our job sometimes degenerates into a fight of wills, and teens don't feel supported, they feel nagged. Duct tape seems to be the only answer. The mother of 14-year-old Henry remembered how this goes, starting with her attempt at a helpful reminder:

> "Henry, don't forget to call Grandma to thank her for your birthday present." Henry sulked and shrieked, "Mom, you've reminded me three times this week about calling Grandma. Let it go already! You don't think I'm responsible, so you bug me about the same things over and over again." Before I could utter a word in my defense, Henry gave me the silent treatment and then continued to lash out angrily that he was perfectly capable of remembering to call his grandma. It's amazing how quickly an innocent interaction ignites into a full-scale war. And do you think he called Grandma?

Once they become adolescents, teens think we become dumber by the minute. It's hard for us ever to be right. At the same time, teens want and need our approval. This need evokes contradictory messages, because our children believe adults are clueless about the things that matter most to teens; parents' experiences are outdated, and their interest is suspect. Even though adolescents perceive their parents to be Neanderthals, parents have to keep their messages coming. As often attributed to Mark Twain, "When I was a boy of 14, my father was so ignorant I could hardly stand to have the old man around. But when I got to be 21, I was astonished at how much the old man had learned in seven years."

Long View of Parenting

Society once looked at the teen years as an isolated period of development. But this is no longer true. The teen years are currently described by mental health professionals and sociologists as part of the continuum of children growing up. The teen years blend into the pre-adult years, which then lead to children becoming emerging adults. At some point, they ought to carry the title "adults" without any extra descriptors. However, many conditions in society stand in the way of an easy transition into adulthood.

These shifts in family life have resulted in significant societal changes. For example, the Affordable Care Act now allows children to be covered under their parents' health insurance until the age of 26. Same-sex marriage has provided a legal validation for families that once was reserved only for a heterosexual couple and their children. A growing percentage of 20- to 30-year-olds hold poorly paid or unpaid internships or jobs without benefits. Paying off higher education loans, well into middle age, means moving back home, experiencing greater financial dependency on parents, and delaying milestones such as buying a home, having children, and establishing neighborhood roots (Davidson, 2014).

The age at which our children can support themselves, let alone a family, has reached a new high in the last two decades. In fact, an astonishing 85 percent of college seniors planned to move back home with their parents after graduation (Dickler, 2012). This is affected further by high unemployment—nearly 15 percent for those aged 20 to 24—which has made finding a job difficult. Young people also suffer from unrealistic expectations that often don't match their skills and job availability. And without a job, there's nowhere for these young adults to go but back to their old bedrooms, curfews, and chore charts.

Understanding these changes, along with the long view of parenting, creates new expectations for both parents and teens. Parents should expect a prolonged period of adolescence, giving more guidance on an array of issues that earlier generations handled without much parental input. Parents must intentionally teach and provide experiences for teens to develop grit and perseverance, which means allowing them to own their successes *and* failures. Parents also should expect to build with their teens the foundation for a lifelong relationship with mutuality and connection. The perspective we offer in this book is predicated on this long view of parenting, and the new brain research supports this view. Teens don't understand consequences until they reach their midtwenties.

In addressing these new changes, it is helpful to recognize that certain experiences also remain the same during the transition from childhood to adulthood. Some of these common experiences include becoming your own person, forming peer relationships, developing job and career skills, and beginning to determine a purpose and path for future life, perhaps with a partner.

All of us remember that after, during, and immediately preceding our teen years, we expected to cast off childhood and assume an instant adult identity. This, of course, is a fairy tale. iTeens need parents who can help them become the adults they want to become. This is hard when clear markers such as graduation from college or even marriage no longer define the notion of an adult. Teen years are a time, as Carol Dweck (2007) discusses in her research, when mastery takes time and mistakes are good. As parents, we want to be careful not to overly praise or push kids in ways that make them afraid to risk making errors or taking wrong turns. These short-term disappointments are, in fact, perfect opportunities for learning and building resilience. Being a teen means using time to explore what one is passionate about while developing essential skills that will serve throughout one's lifetime.

We will use the characteristics of maturity we have learned from our experiences to give parents of teens a road map to guide their children. This is not a time to opt out. This is a time to support, observe, and be available.

Tools for Building Characteristics of Maturity

Think about the teen years as an apprenticeship. What do teens need in order to become productive and successful adults, however they choose to define success? To identify these characteristics, we have worked backward. We have researched successful adults, held focus groups, talked with and listened to experts, and added our personal experiences as professionals and parents. We have determined that, for a teen to become a productive and resilient adult, the following six behavioral characteristics are essential:

1. Persistence and grit
2. Self-management and impulse control
3. Personal responsibility and self-reliance
4. Empathy and self-awareness
5. Boundaries and setting limits
6. Cultural competence/accepting differences

In this book, we provide strategies and stories to develop these behavioral characteristics as we discuss the issues that confront teens. We provide a *how-to* book rather than a *what-not-to-do* book. Following are some of the topics we address:

* The landscape of teenagers
* Entitlement and its impact on building self-reliance and self-confidence
* The characteristics of maturity that parents of teens can use as a guide in raising healthy, competent, and resilient children
* Current brain research, including the relationship of brain development to teen behavior and risk-taking activities
* The impact of gender differences
* The impact of popular culture on teens
* The impact of social media on teenage behavior
* Teens' experiences and challenges at school
* The relentless and extensive consequences of bullying and harassment
* The importance of friendship for teens
* The qualities of a perfectly imperfect parent
* Building a foundation for healthy connection
* The long view of parenting

Teenage success requires emotional clarity and resilience. Parental success requires knowledge, affirmation, and community. We have used our focus groups to discuss meaningful parenting and to validate its effectiveness. We provide you with strategies to create household and community environments that enable teens to learn to identify feelings and build emotional intelligence. Using these skills inoculates teens so they are better equipped to handle inevitable failure and loss.

Teenagers require substantial resilience to navigate this challenging developmental stage in an increasingly demanding world. Research demonstrates that the ability to be resilient can be learned, and we provide parents with strategies to build resilience. By teaching resilience and providing opportunities to practice it, we can change a child's life trajectory from risk to success, and our children need to learn this ability from the adults in their families, schools, and communities.

Using Fuzzy Logic for Parenting

In the mathematical concept of "fuzzy logic," uncertainties and discrepancies become routine yet clearer and decipherable in time. Parenting teens could be described in similar terms. The process doesn't follow the time frame for the scripted linear logic of a 30-minute TV sitcom. Another analogy is the archetypal discussion with kids about sex: one talk doesn't provide them with all of the information they need to make responsible choices. That goal takes a collection of talks in response to different developmental needs, along with positive role models who help to guide children to responsible decisions. As parents, we have to provide many healthy messages over the span of our children's growing up and hope they incorporate those messages into their perception of the world and decision making. Our job as parents is to communicate our values and beliefs while separating our struggles from theirs; to provide opportunities for our teens to develop what we call "a broader integrated identity," as defined in the next paragraph; and to help them heal when necessary.

A broader integrated identity is one in which a teen's sense of self is not completely dependent on any one interest or thing. Having a more expansive sense of self allows teens to stay centered and more secure in response to having less-than-stellar athletic skills, surviving a fight with a boyfriend or girlfriend, getting a low grade on a history exam, or not being invited to a party. These experiences are part of life; some of them happen to everyone at one time or another.

Barbara, the mother of 22-year-old Alison, explained how she and her husband helped their daughter develop a broader sense of self in the face of academic difficulties:

> Alison struggled so much with reading that in ninth grade they put her in special-education classes in our large, urban high school. When we first discovered her dyslexia, we were relieved, because the discrepancy between the bright girl we knew and the girl in the special-education classes finally made sense. The most important lesson we learned during this period was that the only way to save her self-image was to find something other than academics where she could excel.
>
> For Alison it was dance. When she performed in front of an audience, she came alive. She was a different person—secure, confident, and creative. Alison lit up on the stage. This was an area where she could be competitive, and it provided her with another "self" that she could rely on when she was feeling unsuccessful at school. The self-confidence she gained from dance spilled over into other parts of her life, including, over time, doing well in school. She could draw upon her success in dance to help her define, in a positive way, who she was.

Alison's parents refused to let her be pigeonholed by only one category of her life. They understood the importance of finding their daughter's passion and supporting her. The more opportunities we provide for our kids to experience their own competence, the more resilient they become.

Another important component to raising teenagers is being available to them. Staying close to your child may prevent risk-taking behaviors. The closer you are, the more opportunities you have to empower them. Contrary to the popular belief that little children need their parents more than adolescents do, we know that these years also require attentiveness and close supervision.

What we have learned from talking to many, many parents is that their desire to stay close to their children during the teenage years is universal. They just don't always know how. In writing this book, it is our intent to present parents with a practical guide to further understanding the emotional dimensions of their teens and increasing their children's competence and connection.

Your family has operating principles and values that are unique to you and parenting styles that affect what works and what doesn't. We encourage you to be deliberate about including the principles and values specific to your culture and heritage. Helping your teens develop a strong sense of self requires building confidence and pride in their background. Having self-confidence increases the resiliency of teens and their sense of well-being as they address the trials and tribulations of their age.

Often, you won't know in advance what specific methods will work with your iTeen. However, by remaining engaged and constantly trying, you will become more knowledgeable about what works for them and when. Even with those strategies that do work, you will need flexibility, variety, and a sense of humor to move ahead with your teen during these demanding years. Don't despair; if you stay involved and connected, you will also build your own stories of precious and memorable moments.

Resisting the Entitlement Trend

Could it be that by protecting our kids from unhappiness as children, we're depriving them of happiness as adults?

—Lori Gottlieb (2011)

The Changing American Family

Over the past few decades, we have experienced enormous cultural shifts, which have expanded and altered the definition of the American family. The changes stem from a whole host of factors, including greater career opportunities for women, more divorces, legalization of same-sex marriage, emergence of households with single parents or two working parents, new patterns of immigration from non-European countries, defunding of support programs, and the impact of media, technology, and popular culture.

Just as the definition of family has changed, so have our ideas about what is best for our children. Child-rearing beliefs vary and change over time. Each generation tries to correct the mistakes it believes its parents made. Currently many parents emphasize happiness over temporary childhood discomfort, which can result in our children's increased sense of entitlement. Parenting experts are researching the consequences of praising children regardless of what they do or how they perform and how this leads to a loss of motivation, fear of failure, unhappiness, and a sense of entitlement (Gottlieb, 2011).

Several parenting strategies can encourage a child's sense of entitlement (Mogel, 2010). These include overpraising, overinvolvement, overprotecting, becoming bailout specialists, parental indulgence, and a general absence of rules and clear boundaries. Also significant is a child's expectation of instantaneous gratification, fueled by technology and 24/7 social media. This chapter takes a closer look at what causes entitlement and why it is a problem. It also identifies parenting strategies that are more appropriate and can correct the problem. Finally, it introduces some principles for taking a "long view" of parenting, which is required by the changes in society and shifts in parenting philosophy that together have stretched adolescence beyond the teen years to the early twenties.

Excessive Praise and the Courage to Fail

Many experts express concern that when parents demonstrate approval that isn't really authentic, it robs their teens of incentive and motivation. Kids know when approval is meant to make them feel good but isn't based on real accomplishments. It's important for teens to feel that they actually have earned approval. iTeens may give up because in trying just a little, they feel they have done enough. In fact, some teens have learned to expect praise for even the smallest effort. When these teens encounter obstacles, they often give up rather than fail. We have all heard the conventional wisdom that failure is an opportunity to learn and to try harder next time. There is, however, a real consequence in never trying for fear of failure. When you frame your life around success alone without experiencing failure, you stifle growth and the endless possibilities of new opportunities and experience.

Many parents fall into the trap of giving their children the star treatment by excessively complimenting their talent and intelligence. Parents have been guided for decades by the conviction of mental health professionals and educators that praising children will create confident kids, and that this confidence in turn will enable kids to tackle difficult tasks. These parents believe that telling children they are smart and capable will be an automatic self-fulfilling prophecy and help build their children's sense of self. They worry that if they don't give their children enough positive feedback and attention, the kids will become insecure and unhappy. But in fact, overpraising and neglecting to let our children fail is being done at the expense of facilitating self-reliance and motivation.

Will, a high-school freshman, decided not to try out for the junior varsity football team after he dropped the ball twice in the first practice. He was used to success, and initially he had taken it for granted that he would be on the team. When he didn't play his best during the first day of tryouts, he couldn't tell himself that one bad day is just that: one bad day. Instead of focusing and practicing more, he gave up and decided he wasn't good enough. This is the dark side of too much unwarranted praise and not enough persistence to try harder. It creates a child who gives up too quickly when things get tough. Fifteen-year-old Mark described a similar feeling about his performance in school: "I feel the pressure of having to live up to the label my family puts on me. I am the 'smart one.' I find myself looking for shortcuts to succeed, for fear of falling short. I have too much to lose if I get a bad grade, and I want to please my parents, even if it means cheating."

Too often parents treat their children as if the kids are the sun, moon, and stars combined. Consequently, their kids begin to believe it. Because many parents expect their kids to be outstanding in everything, anything less than stardom becomes unacceptable for both the parents and their children. In fact, according to an editorial in the *New York Times*, "Some high schools have 10, 20 or 30 valedictorians, along with bloated honor rolls and a surplus of graduation prizes. Many kids at all grade levels are 'bubble-wrapped' in a culture that doesn't praise effort nearly as much as it does accomplishment" (Bruni, 2013). As a result, the students have an unrealistic and inflated sense of their own success.

This widespread emphasis on kids being special and maintaining this unrealistic expectation of success contributes to what Madeline Levine, author of *The Price of Privilege*, calls the "mass delusion" of communities in which parents assume their child is destined to be in the Ivy League. Levine lectures to high-school parents, telling them, "A majority of your children are average," pausing as a chorus of sharp inhalations drain the air out of the room. "And, guess what? So are you" (Shulte, 2014).

Lisa, now a mother of a 12-year-old, revealed, "I was mortified when my parents wanted to include a highlight film of my tennis career with my college applications. I was a good player, but no Serena Williams. My parents believed I was so gifted that I never really developed a realistic sense of my playing ability. Living under their microscope made me hesitant to try other sports." Lisa's experience makes sense. When you're expected to be special, it's hard to accept making mistakes, which in turn prevents you from trying new things.

Some parents engage in excessive approval because their identities are tied to their children's performance and achievements. Parenting is not an alter-ego sport. As psychologist Wendy Mogel likes to caution, "Our children are not our masterpieces" (Gottlieb, 2011). Too many parents confuse their own needs with their children's.

Constant praise and inauthentic approval do not necessarily result in self-confident children. When the value of hard work is not reinforced, genuine self-confidence and self-reliance are difficult to attain. Parents who praise every activity, every piece of writing, and every drawing do their children a disservice. Frank Bruni wrote in the *New York Times*, "There are sports teams and leagues in which no kid is allowed too much more playing time than another and in which excessive victory margins are outlawed. Losing is looked upon as pure trauma, to be doled out gingerly" (2013). A middle-school basketball coach said,

> This season my team started out like the *Bad News Bears*; they were just not very good. But after a month of hard work and practice, they

finally jelled as a team and played their hearts out every time they had a game. The last game of our season we were up by a significant amount of points, and the other coach asked me to tell my best shooters to go easy in order for his team to save face. It put me in a tough position and went against everything I taught my players. What kind of message is that for my students and the ones on the opposing team?

The "everyone gets a trophy" philosophy is based on empty praise and the false notion that kids are so fragile they could be damaged by not feeling special. Often, kids are rewarded for just participating without any greater reward for determination, resolve, or actual achievement.

As a result of parents' excessive praise, teens may either pursue perfection or avoid challenge. In pursuing perfection, they are constantly trying to get it right, to stand out and to be considered special. Parents' goal for their children should be to have a realistic sense of themselves and their skills and abilities, which allows them to learn what it takes to succeed and how to do it. This doesn't mean that you don't encourage your children or provide them with opportunities to demonstrate their skills. Rather, it means that children will benefit when parents can accept them for who they are.

However, not all praise is bad. What works is to applaud effort and actual accomplishment. When you say things like "You really tried hard at that" and "That was such a good idea," you are praising the effort and real achievement. Praising effort is good because it rewards children for staying involved and trying hard. But unwarranted praise comes with unintended surprises and consequences.

Hovercraft Parenting and Overinvolvement

Hovercraft parenting is overly vigilant and hovers overhead like a drone. Parents swoop down in an attempt to protect their teens from hitting bottom or failing at an activity. The paradox of showering your teens with attention in this way is that it doesn't allow them to learn to be accountable for their behavior. It bears repeating: kids need to fail. When we protect our children from natural consequences, we ultimately increase their sense of powerlessness and sense of entitlement. Alicia, a high school freshman, said:

> Frankly, I'm scared of my shadow, and I blame my parents. They see danger everywhere. My friends take the bus to the mall, but my parents won't let me go with them. This summer I want to be a mother's helper, and they think caring for a neighbor's child is too much responsibility. I feel like a shrink-wrapped kid. If their surveillance doesn't let up, I'll start lying and say I'm at my friend's house when I'm somewhere else.

Hovering and overdoing prevents the development of self-reliance in teenagers, even though it sometimes stems from a real threat and from efforts to keep a child safe. The mother of 17-year-old Megan recalled,

> When Megan was younger, she had awful stomach cramps, and I dragged her to doctors until she was diagnosed with celiac disease. It broke my heart to see her doubled over in pain, and I did everything I could to make her comfortable. Since her diagnosis, I've been as vigilant as a hawk, not only making sure that her diet is gluten free, but using a separate toaster for bread with wheat to prevent cross-contamination. My husband is telling me to back off and let Megan be in charge of what she eats. He believes that she's been old enough to take charge of her diet for quite some time and should have this experience before she leaves for college. While I know he's right, I continue to struggle to hold back, especially when Megan smiles and says, "Mom, you make it best; can you do it?"

Years before the college application process begins, some parents place tremendous emphasis on building an effective résumé for college. These parents put together their child's college application very early and intentionally. College admissions officers report being able to spot applications that reveal that parents had their child spend every summer in a program geared to wow the admissions officer. As a result, too much time is spent curating a résumé, and too little is spent on developing life skills. Consequently, teens are anxious about whether they can take care of themselves, yet at the same time, they enjoy the benefits of their parents overdoing for them.

A mother with a different perspective offered, "I want to make sure that when my daughter starts college, she is not one of those 'bat-out-of high-school' kids, the ones who had everything arranged and scheduled for them. These kids are massively unprepared for living on their own." Remember, if you're hovering, you're not allowing your children to learn how to take care of themselves. Development is an incremental process. Teens have to build the base skills before they can excel. The analogy here is a baby learning how to crawl and then walk. The effort progresses one movement or one step at a time.

Another catchy term for overinvolved parents who try to eliminate every barrier from their teen's path is "snowplow" parents. These parents respond to the increasing educational demands by taking responsibility for the work. Science projects are now produced by PhD parents, and term papers are cowritten with journalist parents. One father said,

> Andrew attends a private school that attracts international students. For his eighth-grade science fair, Andrew did a great job of demonstrating electrical charges by making puffed cereal jump in the air. My wife and I thought this was a great idea; it met the requirements of the fair, and most importantly, he could do it himself. One of his classmates was the grandson of a high official in Kuwait. The palace engineer completed his science project. It was no surprise when he won first prize. The parents all remarked, "Our kids didn't lose to an eighth-grade classmate; they lost to the country of Kuwait!"

When parents are overinvolved, it's no wonder that grown children have difficulty making their own choices and accepting the consequences of their mistakes. Author of *The Blessings of a Skinned Knee* and parenting expert Wendy Mogel observes, "The extended adolescence results in college deans referring to overprotected kids without the ability to handle their problems with roommates or laundry as *teacups* and burned out, dazed survivors of bewildering boot camp as *krispies*" (2004). Because the effect of parental overinvolvement may stifle teenage development and growth, we need to understand fully how parents can foster maturity during the teenage years.

Many parents who thought they'd have more self-control feel a lot of pressure from other parents to jump on the hovercraft. Have you experienced a pang of insecurity when listening to your friends talk about what they've planned for their kids? Kate, the mother of a high-school junior, revealed her anxiety:

> I'm not an overly anxious mother, so I wasn't prepared for being so intimidated by the number of college visits my friend had scheduled for her son. I thought my son would just make arrangements with some of his buddies that were already attending schools, hang out with them, get a sense of the place, and apply to those that were most appealing. Now I have discovered that parents have made elaborate plans to do multiple trips with prearranged interviews. I began to wonder, Is he going to college, or are *we* going to college? If I'm going, I'd prefer a school in a big city, but I digress. I've already been to school; now it's his turn! I think I'd better get a grip, because staying grounded is going to be hard when surrounded by my friends!

Another parent offered these insights:

> The best advice I got in the fall of my daughter's senior year in high school was from the father of twins already in college. He said, "Hold on tight and fasten your seat belt. For the next six months, the anxiety from other parents will throw you off balance. Their fear spreads through other senior parents like a virus. Remember, this

year will pass, and your daughter will probably be happy with the school she gets into."

Bailout and Fix-It Specialists

We fix everything, because we can. Parents are still under the illusion that they can control and influence their children's health and success. But failing is underrated! In fact, teenagers learn from disappointments. Dan Kindlon, a child psychologist and lecturer at Harvard, in an interview with Lori Gottlieb for *The Atlantic*, warns against what he calls our "discomfort with discomfort." He believes that if kids can't experience painful feelings, they won't acquire "psychological immunity." "It's like the way our body's immune system develops," he explains. "You have to be exposed to pathogens, or your body won't know how to respond to an attack. Kids also need exposure to discomfort, failure, and struggle" (Gottlieb, 2011).

We need to let them grieve and be heartbroken when they fail to make the team or when they lose their first girlfriend or boyfriend. Feeling let down, hurt, and discouraged is part of life. To become resilient, teens need to know they can survive pain and how to do it. Our job is to provide support and help them develop the coping skills to get through the difficult times, rather than making life momentarily easy by doing everything for them. None of us is comfortable when our kids are frightened, sad, or unhappy; however, we're doing them a disservice if we deny them the opportunity to develop self-reliance and life skills. We are most effective as parents when we expect them to use their own resources to confront their fears, cope with adversity, and achieve their goals.

This approach means we take a backseat and limit our involvement to support and coaching. By doing so, we encourage teens to handle and learn from discomfort and difficult situations and show them that we have confidence in their abilities. Teaching them how to deal effectively with uncomfortable feelings actually protects them from seeking unhealthy ways to escape. Teenagers who can't tolerate emotional discomfort often use sex, porn, alcohol, or drugs because they haven't learned to self-soothe. Unless we want our children to turn to less healthy ways of self-regulating, we need to let them fix and bail out for themselves as much as possible. Entitlement undermines their ability to begin the task of taking care of themselves as they are able.

Parents, writers, and mental-health professionals are increasingly talking about entitlement and its negative effect on our children. American children are incredibly indulged, writes Elizabeth Kolbert in the *New Yorker*. We have showered them with technology, video games, and other things, along with giving them too much influence and power. In Kolbert's article, she quotes Sally Koslow, author of *Slouching Toward Adulthood: Observations from the Not-So-Empty Nest*: "Our offspring have simply leveraged our braggadocio, good intentions, and overinvestment," and our children "inhabit 'a broad savannah of entitlement that we've watered, landscaped, and hired gardeners to maintain.' She recommends letting the grasslands revert to forest: 'The best way for a lot of us to show our love would be to learn to un-mother and un-father'" (Kolbert, 2012).

One of the moms in our focus groups told us about her daughter. Jenny became interested in collecting quarters from each state when she was eight years old. To encourage her, Jenny's dad sensibly bought her a beautifully bound book to hold the coins. But Jenny eventually grew impatient with the amount of time it was taking to collect the whole set and started to lose interest. Jenny's father's instinct was to complete the book by going to the bank and buying $20 in quarters at one time. Fortunately, her mom intervened and said, "If you do this, it will rob Jenny of the opportunity to find the coins for herself. She won't get the joy of discovery as she accumulates each coin." Mom was right to take the long view. If Dad had simply bought the coins, Jenny would have learned that she could reach her goals by complaining, giving up, and waiting for Dad to make it happen. She wouldn't have felt a sense of accomplishment in completing the task on her own. Nor would she have had the opportunity to simply enjoy the process of collecting, which in and of itself can be rewarding. When we rush in to fix things, we squash our children's motivation and deny them the ability to develop skills that foster confidence, grit, and self-reliance.

So Why Do We Parent This Way?

We parent this way because we are overly invested in our children's success. Too often parents' motivation to take charge is largely tied to their pride in their children's successes and accomplishments and how these reflect on them. When parents jump in and do things for their children, it's often more a reflection of their own anxiety and needs. This potentially deprives their kids of the opportunity to develop competence and a strong sense of self. When parents too frequently push and direct children, their children are less likely to develop internal motivation and persistence or take pride in their own accomplishments (Bronson, 2007).

We parent this way because we are uncomfortable setting limits and sitting with our children's unhappiness and frustration. The father of a 16-year-old son said, "Josh tells me he's sad and that it confuses him because he knows so well how good he has it. In fact, the worst part of his angst is his guilt about being depressed." This dad isn't alone. Several therapists we interviewed describe their teenage patients talking about anxiety and emptiness that they can't attribute to clinical depression or absent parents. When nearly a third of seniors at McLean High School in Virginia say they've been depressed for more than two weeks because of feeling empty, unworthy, and under too much pressure, it's a sign that parents have to stop hovering and start setting boundaries for the mental health of their kids (Shulte, 2014).

We parent this way because setting limits for teens requires more time and energy than many parents have to give at the end of a long workday. And no one wants to feel like a "mean" mom or dad. In the short term, it is often easier to surrender than to face a screaming fight with a teen. As one father put it, "I saw each disagreement as a potential tiresome battle requiring too much energy, so I rarely took a stand . . . whether it was just one more bedtime snack or extending curfew. Now my son is sure he can convince me to give in on anything. I understand why he thinks he has the power to sway me on any given demand, because I caved in over the years and lost the parenting war." Only when parents can project forward and understand how the short-term compromises of today fuel the battles of tomorrow can they find the strength to set more limits and to say no.

This overly involved parenting style places a higher priority on harmony and momentary happiness. Parents who avoid this kind of conflict miss opportunities to teach the skills necessary for success and future adulthood. Children will always push against their parents' rules, but they need the rules to bump up against so they can learn and develop. Without limits, children feel anxious and rudderless, lost at sea. When parents defer to their children, the children suffer because they fail to understand reality.

When adolescents have few limits, they have a hard time exercising control. The ability to show restraint is critical to self-discipline and maturity. It is a parent's responsibility to provide limits. In fact, parents who don't set boundaries may do harm. One parent commented, "I know that I'm guilty of coddling my children. My fear is that I'm preventing them from going out into the world and acquiring the basics of life for themselves. I see an unprecedented level of entitlement showing up as a lax attitude toward self-development, literacy, and the challenges they face." Parents are often unsure how to draw the line between being too soft when their children need tough love and too withholding when their children need time-limited parental support. Limits are the antidote to misplaced entitlement.

And finally, we parent this way because we feel pressure from juggling work and family. We sometimes respond to the hectic pace of life by failing to set and enforce boundaries and rules. We don't want to spend the limited time we have with our children teaching rules of behavior and setting limits and boundaries. Instead, we tend to avoid conflict by focusing on doing for our children and giving them what we think they want to make them happy. Philosopher Jean-Jacques Rousseau wisely said, "Do you know the surest way to make your child miserable? Let him have everything he wants; . . . his wants increase in proportion to the ease with which they are satisfied" (Bartleby, 2001).

Why Do We Need a Long View of Parenting?

Currently, launching our teens into adulthood is more circuitous than it was in previous generations. The journey is not as fast, nor is the path as clear as it was when today's parents were in their teens. This sociological change has developed, in part, from parents who confuse overinvestment with loving their kids. We understand that this is a difficult balancing act for parents. However, short-term parenting solutions are not necessarily going to get teens where they need to be to become mature adults.

As a result, we have identified some characteristics of maturity that will provide you, as parents of teenagers, with a road map for raising persistent, motivated, gritty, and resilient teens who are less afraid of making mistakes. The information in this book is intended to fill an information gap and help parents to see the long view of parenting. These characteristics can help parents guide their children toward adulthood so they can adapt more effectively to crisis and change. Persistent effort is a learnable skill, and to better prepare teens for the challenges ahead, parents need to shift from praising the product to praising the effort. Having a clearer understanding of where you want to go will help you become more consistent in your responses to the inevitable surprises, shocks, and potential bombshells you will encounter during adolescence. Most important, this practical guidance will better prepare your teens for the inevitable surprises, shocks, and bombshells *they* will encounter throughout their lives.

Follow the Yellow Brick Road: Laying the Groundwork for Adult Maturity

Children learn to have self-confidence by internalizing the healthy parts of the relationships they have with their parents and other caregivers. Successful parenting during the teen years may not be readily apparent until the teens become adults. However, the foundation you build is critical to your children becoming more independent over time.

It's difficult to measure maturity, so we need standards to guide us. In *Emotional Intelligence: Why It Can Matter More than IQ*, Daniel Goleman states that emotional intelligence consists of qualities that include self-awareness, impulse control, persistence, self-motivation, empathy, and social deftness. These characteristics enable people to become competent, mature adults.

Understanding the characteristics needed to build maturity gives parents a framework to help their teens negotiate their own lives more effectively. Demonstrating these characteristics and providing opportunities for teens to develop them is one of the great challenges of twenty-first-century parenting.

What are these behavioral characteristics?

1. Persistence and grit
2. Self-management and impulse control
3. Personal responsibility and self-reliance
4. Empathy and self-awareness
5. Boundaries and setting limits
6. Cultural competence/accepting differences

Let's take a closer look at each of these characteristics.

Persistence/Grit

While all teenagers experience anxiety and self-doubt when confronted with a difficult task, some will give up, and others will push through their discouragement. The difference between the teens who quit and those who persevere is their ability to tolerate frustration before achieving their goal or to understand why the goal can't be achieved. People with persistence and grit have the ability to respond to failure by trying again with more effort and focus. According to psychologist and mother of four boys Donna Shoom-Kirsch,

Parents should support and encourage their children as they learn to navigate their world. If one path doesn't lead to a successful outcome, parents should offer alternatives and demonstrate that there are always other paths. When kids are very little, they impulsively run ahead and a parent's role is to rein them in. As they get older, however, parents need to gradually give them more lead, even if they run into a little trouble. Our job is to say it's okay, even if it doesn't work, just go out there and try again. Children have to learn from their failures. (Personal communication, 2014)

This lesson remains equally important for teenagers. Fifteen-year-old Alyssa shared her experience:

> When I have a computer problem, I'm like a dog with a bone and don't give up until it's solved. Last week I had trouble with my word processor. I desperately needed to finish a paper for the next day and couldn't get the program to cooperate. After threatening to throw my laptop across the room, my mom told me to call Microsoft, which sent me to Apple, which sent me back to Microsoft, but I just kept asking my questions until I was satisfied. Eventually, the support person helped me figure it out. It took hours, but now it works, and I know how to deal with this problem if it ever happens again.

When parents show interest, and/or make suggestions to help teens meet a new challenge, they provide a framework or "scaffolding" that enables the young people to tackle new things without fear of failure. Patience and interest provide a safety net without parents' taking over and doing it for them. This strategy often takes more time than parents doing the task for their teens, but this investment allows teens to develop persistence, a necessary tool for adulthood.

While frustration is part of the development of persistence, there is a balance between having too much frustration, which can lead to giving up, and enough frustration to foster tenacity and grit. Some teens respond to obstacles with insolence or rebellion. Others project the blame from their failures onto others, and many just act blasé, pretending they don't care. Don't be fooled, however; they care.

Teens may better learn the value of persistence if parents define success as making an effort and demonstrating improvement (putting a bit less emphasis on the end product). Sam, father of 13-year-old Lindsay, said,

> Lindsay has a learning disability, and math is virtually impossible for her. We got her a tutor, and she is now working harder on math than on any other subject. But still she can't get a B. We often let her know that we are just as proud of her C in math as her A in history, because she puts in so much effort. I believe that our pleasure in her persistence and determination keeps her from giving up. From my perspective, even if she never receives a grade higher than a C, she's succeeded.

Fifteen-year-old Lily said it best: "My mom always told me the secret of her own academic success came from my great-grandparents, who said, 'Everyone is about the same in terms of innate intelligence. The difference is how hard you work.'"

Letting our kids make mistakes or even fail is one of the most difficult challenges for a parent. But to do otherwise is a disservice because it denies them the opportunity to develop self-confidence. Persistent and resilient people treat failure as an opportunity to try again and do better. This is a tough lesson to learn, and it takes time and reinforcement. Children know these skills instinctively. For example, tenacity combined with intelligence teaches children to ask to be fed, to cry when their diapers are wet, to walk, to entertain themselves with toys, and to read. When children reach the age of socialization, there is a paradigm shift as they start worrying about how they look to other people and how others feel about them. This is a time when parents can make a difference. Parents can teach their children perseverance and grit by supporting them to extend themselves and take reasonable risks and allow their children to rebound from mistakes and failure.

When reasonable, allow teens to do for themselves rather than doing it for them. Resist fixing everything, because that disables them. Success is more about grit and managing disappointment than anything else. Older teens and young adults still want your approval, so they want to do things right. Approval should be more about the quality of their effort and perseverance than the outcome or product.

Self-Management/Impulse Control

Teen brains are not fully developed, and many young people don't know how to control their impulses, so they can't really grasp the concept of delayed gratification. They are very reactive and may not succeed at controlling their impulsivity until their midtwenties. "As any parent knows," wrote Justice Anthony Kennedy, "youths are more likely to show 'a lack of maturity and an underdeveloped sense of responsibility' than adults. . . . These qualities often result in impetuous and ill-considered actions and decisions" (Ritter, n.d.).

When teenagers are anxious, passionate, or under stress, they often don't examine the consequences of their actions. One mom gave this example:

> At midnight I was awakened by a phone call from the police, and you can imagine my immediate reaction was terror. "Is this the Francis house?" the officer asked, and I answered, "Yes," with panic in my voice. "We have a house full of underage drinkers, and your daughter is one of them." "Thank God!" I said, so happy that my

daughter Carly wasn't found dead on the side of the road. But the officer countered with, "Ma'am, this is serious!" I picked up Carly along with her citation. They were drinking beer, laughing loudly, and blasting music in the backyard and never thought a neighbor would notice and complain. I said, "Carly, what were you thinking?!" And the real truth of the matter was that she wasn't.

Teens are emotionally volatile, open to taking risks, aggressive, reactive to stress, and vulnerable to peer pressure. Teenagers who don't learn to self-regulate and manage their impulses have a more difficult time reaching their potential. Middle school is the most difficult time. Things can settle down as teens move through high school, but if teenagers don't have ways to metabolize and express their angst, they may choose to self-medicate instead.

This is a great opportunity for you and other adults in your teen's life to be positive role models. Check in with yourself and do an honest assessment. Are you reactive? If so, be more conscious of how you behave and control your own impulses.

Also, some behavioral approaches can help your teen to have more impulse control. One of the easiest and most accessible tools for self-regulation is exercise. Exercise has been proven to help elevate mood and ease the symptoms of attention deficit hyperactivity disorder (ADHD), which makes it an invaluable resource for our teens. You can also offer stress-reduction strategies such as meditation and/or visualization to give your teens ways to self-soothe when they are stressed.

Make sure to tell your children that what feels good today may feel awful tomorrow. Although impulses are powerful, acting on all of them is not necessary and could be harmful. One mother said, "Every time I go back to the fridge for another spoonful of ice cream, I think of that old phrase: a minute on the lips is a pound on my hips. But the pleasure in that moment has a tough pull. This must be what it's like for my son when he confronts a moment of pleasure and can't think about the consequences."

Be clear about your expectations for your teen, and explain why you believe they are reasonable. We recommend setting rules that make sense to your children, such as establishing a curfew that is reasonable and normal for your community. Psychiatrist David Fassler suggests that teens may display poor impulse control or negative behaviors because they don't truly understand what's expected of them (Miller, 2014). Rules provide opportunities for teens to develop their ability to control impulses and to create important boundaries. Without these skills, teens may feel less comfortable and able to set their own limits. Rachel, an 18-year-old, reflected on the challenge:

> I think I must have been a tyrant. My parents rarely said no to me, and I always knew that I could use my baby voice and flash my dimples to get anything I wanted. Now that college is so much on my mind, I worry about how I will be able to handle living on my own. Will I be able to live on my monthly allowance and pass up a cute pair of shoes without charging them to my mom and dad? Trust me, I'm often stuck between my impulse to indulge and my fear that I have no restraint. I hope that when I have children, I'll figure out when to say no as well as yes.

Rachel's parents didn't do her any favors by giving her everything she asked for, even though they apparently were financially able to do so. Their inability to balance when to indulge and when to restrict made Rachel fearful about her dependency on them and about her ability to control her own impulses.

Sometimes an important approach for practicing self-regulation is to be quiet and just listen. Listening allows for a moment of self-reflection that may let you know how you feel. Once you understand how you feel, you can better know how to cope with your emotions effectively. When parents take the time to listen and reflect on what their teens are saying, they can teach them to identify, understand, and tolerate complex feelings. By resisting the impulse to fix your children's feelings, you can give them the room necessary to learn to self-control.

Personal Responsibility/Self-Reliance

One of the basic principles of maturity is learning to be responsible for one's choices and actions. Accepting personal responsibility results in a more independent, competent, and self-sufficient adult. Responsibility is a process through which rights and duties become internalized, and a sense of commitment to truth and concern for others is displayed. Guiding your children toward self-sufficiency is incremental. Your role is to identify the issues and use those teachable moments so your children develop an internal moral compass and increasing awareness of the impact and consequences of their actions.

Personal responsibility is influenced by many factors, such as age, peer influences, and parental practices. Demonstrating a sense of responsibility includes the following behaviors:

* Realizing one's own unique strengths and experiences
* Believing in doing more than just enough to "pass"
* Recognizing the importance of behaving responsibly
* Making choices through thought and reflection
* Owning up to mistakes and failures
* Attempting to make better choices as they become available

Parents should emphasize and reinforce to teens that they are ultimately responsible for their own lives. With this awareness, teens will avoid blaming others for adverse life experiences and the associated feelings of uncertainty and powerlessness. Parents should seek out opportunities to foster critical thinking, encourage reflection, build more self-awareness, and better understand the impact of behavior on others. To feel more responsible for their own lives, teenagers need opportunities to practice making choices, to reflect on the outcomes, and to be held accountable for their behavior.

Teens benefit from clear expectations. Familial tasks such as doing the dishes, taking out the garbage, shoveling the driveway, mowing the lawn, doing laundry, or carpooling younger siblings all provide opportunities for teenagers to feel pride in their contribution. The objective of these responsibilities is to demonstrate that the family operates as a team with each member carrying some part of the load. Providing your children with household assignments allows them to demonstrate competence and personal responsibility. Having them fulfill their obligations, and holding them accountable, builds confidence.

Empathy/Self-Awareness

During adolescence, the brain is still developing, and the accompanying changes have a major effect on teenagers' cognition (thinking and reasoning), impulse control, and executive functioning (the mental processes that enable planning, focus, remembering instructions, and managing multiple tasks). During this period, teenagers develop "cognitive empathy," the ability to put themselves in someone else's shoes. They are able to see things from another perspective, which in turn creates the social skills required for understanding how their behavior affects others. This explains why antisocial behaviors such as bullying should diminish as teenagers gain empathic skills (Shellenbarger, 2013).

Empathy usually is associated with sympathy, warmth, and compassion. Acquiring empathy does include these characteristics. However, empathy is actually a more comprehensive concept: awareness of the impact of one's behavior on others and a sense of ownership of the consequences of one's actions. Empathy is the foundation for mature relationships and promotes connection by inviting understanding. When 16-year-old Michael was young, he frequently visited his grandfather in a nursing home. Including Grandpa Harry in family holidays required carefully transporting him by wheelchair from his nursing home. Throughout his early childhood, Michael watched his parents lovingly integrate his grandfather into their daily lives, and this sensitivity for the well-being of another had a profound impact on Michael.

Recently, Michael's friend Peter found out that his mother had a serious illness. Peter told Michael about his mom on New Year's Eve.

Rather than celebrating with his friends at the annual holiday party, Michael arranged to have dinner alone with Peter. Michael said he knew Peter appreciated his comfort and support, illustrating perfectly the concept of empathy. Michael knew that his desire to party and have fun with his friends was not as important as providing support for his friend. His mother always told him, "Michael, you reap what you sow." Michael understood from his parents the importance of empathy, and should Michael ever find himself in a similar situation, his actions are likely to be reciprocated.

Another way to teach empathy is to help your teen better understand the family's circumstances. Many of today's teens lack a real understanding of what their parents actually do on a day-to-day basis to support their lifestyle, and few teens ask. Parents, regardless of income, don't want to burden their children with the stress and pressure associated with maintaining their standard of living. Parents fear that this information will make their teenagers feel guilty. In their effort to protect their children by withholding the details, parents are missing a rich opportunity to teach compassion. In Ron Taffel's words, "This leaves children disconnected not only from their parents' common work struggles, but also from the perseverance and determination that daily survival requires" (2006). It's hard to raise thoughtful, empathic, and compassionate children if parents don't give them opportunities to demonstrate their understanding and appreciation.

An equally critical way to foster empathy is to seek opportunities to be quiet and listen. Gottman and DeClaire (1997) refer to this skill as "emotional coaching." An emotional coach will elicit or draw out a range of emotions, including sadness, anger, and fear. Parents who function as effective emotional coaches can train their children to identify, understand, and tolerate complex feelings, which will have a lifelong application. Emotional coaches are more successful at setting and maintaining healthy boundaries, and they are patient in permitting children to express their emotions. The emotional coach doesn't try to fix the feeling, but mirrors the emotion back to the child and, by doing so, facilitates the child's growth and sense of self.

By asking questions rather than providing answers, you are demonstrating confidence in your teens' ability to solve problems and better understand how their actions affect others. Asking questions such as "So what do *you* think she should do?" or "How do you think you'll feel if you don't go to the party?" or "What will happen if you do break up with her?" will better equip your teenagers to get in touch with their feelings and their impact on others. By guiding and coaching your teens in their decision-making process, you are giving them opportunities to develop skills in empathy to practice now, as well as building their confidence to handle similar situations in the future.

We have all come across children who do not demonstrate strengths in traditional academic environments but clearly have intuition, compassion, and wisdom. One mother talked about her son Noah, who has serious learning difficulties and couldn't wait to be finished with high school. Of her three children, Noah is the one who always knows what she is feeling, knows the right things to say, and asks how her day went. She said, "Noah not only asks about work, he actually listens to what I have to say. Noah can tell how I am feeling when I walk into the house after work. His interpersonal skills are superior, and I know they will carry him in good stead for the rest of his life. My sweet Noah is an old soul."

Emotional intelligence (ability to identify and manage your own feelings and the feelings of others) provides the skills to label and understand feelings, which leads to greater self-awareness and the ability to establish and maintain positive relationships. Parents can foster the healthy growth of emotional intelligence by supporting and encouraging the development of their children's internal compass. Teaching teens to listen to their inner voice rather than responding to the conventional wisdom and/or being swayed by prevailing attitudes creates emotional intelligence. A psychotherapist mom remembered, "I'll never forget a professor saying, 'If you only have a hammer in your toolbox, then everything you see had better be a nail!'" We all require a full set of tools to cope with adult life. When people place too much emphasis on achievements and material gain, they are often surprised as adults at the emptiness they feel even when they have acquired all the desired trappings. Emotional intelligence provides the tools to give adults a more balanced, connected, and gratifying life.

Boundaries/Setting Limits

Developing boundaries begins early. As soon as toddlers start to explore the world, parents realize that their children have lives of their own. This aha moment reappears with spectacular clarity when our children become teenagers, when they close their bedroom doors, keep secrets, and challenge all limits. During this developmental stage, teachers, parents of teenage friends, and, yes, the local police department beer party squad may know more about your children's social life than you do!

One of the best ways to learn how to respect boundaries is by learning to cooperate with siblings. In the past, there were more opportunities for sharing; houses were smaller, and the norm was for more than one person to share a bedroom. So much is learned from sharing a bedroom. The mother of three teenage boys said, "As kids, I was neat, and my sister was a slob. Her clothes lived on the floor, and she would dive into the pile to dress every morning. I finally divided the room in two and declared my half the neat zone, totally off-limits for her." It wasn't long ago that homes had one TV with few stations, requiring the entire family to share the resource. As recently as 20 years ago, there were few personal computers in individual homes, and everyone in the family used the ones that were there. In many middle-class communities today, kids have their own bedroom, and their homes have multiple TV screens and digital devices. There are fewer opportunities for kids to share, a skill that requires negotiating boundaries and setting limits.

Parents can model good boundaries by behaving with integrity, setting protective limits, and engaging in appropriate behavior. In dysfunctional families, boundary violations can produce teenagers who make poor choices, either in relationships or by hurting themselves by cutting and or self-medicating with drugs, sex, or alcohol. Seventeen-year-old Zach has seen this:

> I can always tell whether my father's been drinking by how he enters the house. If the door closes quietly, then I know it should be a good night. But if he bursts in like Kramer on *Seinfeld* and slams the door, we're in for trouble. I try to disappear into my bedroom, but sometimes there's no escaping his wrath when he's out of control. In middle school, I vowed I'd never drink, but now that I'm seventeen, I have to be honest and say I often want to escape, and I'd be lying if I didn't tell you that I can't swear I don't drink and smoke weed myself.

Robert Frost said, "Good fences make good neighbors." Finding that balance and setting limits can be tricky. Appropriate boundaries permit us to voice our wants and needs without self-reproach. When teens don't know how to set limits and protective boundaries, they may be unable to say no without guilt. Tara, an 18-year-old senior, said:

> I always feel responsible for everyone else. Sometimes I purposely say my phone is out of power to avoid receiving texts from friends. When I have plans for an evening, I feel guilty excluding anyone who calls me. I actually avoid people because I can't say no without feeling selfish. I wish I didn't obsess about how the other person feels. It's not that I want to be rude; I just want to be able to spend my time with whomever I want.

Parents can guide their teens to maintain healthy boundaries by showing them when it is OK to say no and modeling appropriate boundaries. There are many good examples of teens setting boundaries for themselves. Cameron, an eighth-grader, said:

> My mom and dad have been divorced for a few years. And recently, my mom has started dating. My brother and I think my dad still

hopes they will get back together, because Dad has been asking me all kinds of questions about Mom's social life. When they got divorced, they always said they didn't want to put me and my brother in the middle, so I was proud of myself when I told my dad to stop asking about mom.

Dana, a 10th-grader, said to her boyfriend, "I feel pressure when you act disappointed because I have to study instead of hanging out with you. It's not fair to make me choose between doing well on my math test and making you happy. You should want me to do well!" This boundary is one that sets the stage for a healthier relationship.

Trevor, a high-school freshman, said, "The first semester of high school, my buddies were talking trash to impress the older kids. They freely made antigay jokes that infuriated me. I told them how I felt and said I didn't want to be with them when they acted like jerks. The good news is they took it in and stopped making offensive comments in my presence."

For teens, boundaries define what they will and won't accept from others. For parents, boundaries help everyone in the family take responsibility for his or her own behavior. Boundaries are the limits that create safety and empower us.

Cultural Competence/Accepting Differences

Today's children are growing up in the most diverse society in our history. Cultural competence is the essential ingredient that allows children to interpret and appreciate their own culture, and then use this knowledge to understand others.

Many parents we interviewed commented on their teens' comfort with diversity. According to one father, "My son just downloaded a CD by a comedian, Hari Kondabolu, titled *Waiting for 2042*, named for the year when the U.S. Census Bureau projects that white people will become the minority in America." One immigrant mom whose three daughters were born in America said, "When I voiced my opposition to gay marriage, my daughters were appalled and said, 'Mom, in this country we don't feel that way. Don't be prejudiced!'"

These examples provide us with important lessons regarding the culture in which teens are growing up and the problems we will cause them by imposing dated assumptions. While teens are more accepting of diversity, parents can best help them by demonstrating their support for cultural respect, inclusiveness, and tolerance. One mother told the following story:

> I was sitting at a Pacers basketball game, and a homophobic television sports reporter walked in shouting distance from me, my son, Ryan, and his girlfriend. I hate heckling, so when I could sense my son getting ready to shout something, I braced myself. He yelled, "Don't be a homophobe; gay people have rights, too!" Ryan knows screaming makes me uncomfortable, and he defended his behavior by saying, "Mom, this reporter uses his show as a bully pulpit to spew hate. I think he should be embarrassed and held publicly accountable." While I might not have enjoyed hearing Ryan confront this reporter, I am proud of his beliefs and feel like I taught him well!

Parents can best demonstrate positive attitudes toward people from different cultures by their words and actions. One father said, "My son's kindergarten teacher told the parents to think about how what we say at home may have an unintended effect on our children's relationships at school. She asked us to avoid making harshly judgmental comments in front of our children about people who are different. She's right; we are our child's most powerful role model."

Cultural competence is also a crucial ingredient in building self-esteem. Pittsburgh Steeler Heinz Ward, born in 1976, has talked about growing up with shame because he was bullied based on his Korean and African American heritage. As a child, Ward struggled to find an identity between two cultures. He felt like a lost child who didn't fit with either the Korean or African American culture. However, when he visited Korea, he finally acknowledged his roots and has subsequently become a powerful model for other biracial children (Wiseman, 2006). Understanding and embracing your family history gives you a context and demonstrates how to treat people.

Most of us did not grow up in a world as culturally and racially diverse as our children are experiencing today. The assumptions that many of us grew up with are no longer valid. Our challenge as parents, therefore, is to grow and change with the times by modeling tolerance and speaking out against discrimination. Cultural competence is an essential skill for living and working in today's diverse world and global economy. The ability to get along with people and appreciate differences is essential to adulthood in the twenty-first century and allows us to enjoy the richness of the world we live in. Our children's appreciation for and comfort with diversity will help them take advantage of all the opportunities available to them and contribute greatly toward their future success.

The Way We Are as Parents

Three of the most important parenting objectives are to have our kids (1) ready for college and (2) able to function independently while (3) maintaining healthy connections with family and friends. However, we sometimes act in counterproductive ways. These actions can take a toll on our teens and make meeting these objectives more difficult. We want to fix things for them, but we also want them to learn to take care of themselves. When teens appear to be sophisticated, we may expect them to understand more than their life experience permits. Parents who sanitize their children's environment during the teen years delay the development of their kids' decision-making skills and deny them the ability to become self-reliant and tolerate consequences. These skills, if underdeveloped, may make their next stage of life more challenging than it needs to be. In recent years, colleges have backed away from the role of surrogate parent, and students are left to parent themselves before many of them are actually ready to do so. This combination of almost unlimited personal freedom and the expectation of self-reliance create anxiety if teens are unprepared.

The earlier parents start to cultivate and lay the foundation for maturity, the more likely children are to develop into healthy and resilient adults. We need to ground our children in reality and give them opportunities to master their own lives incrementally. A parent of a high-school senior observed, "Having just completed college tours, I was surrounded by anxious parents who asked all the questions and gave us the feeling that they wanted to pick their kid's courses, roommates, and majors." Colleges not wishing to alienate prospective parents and/or students enable this behavior when they should simply convey, "Please have your children ask the questions." Some colleges separate parents from their children during college tours so prospective students can ask their own questions. Several years ago it was unheard of years for parents to call professors or school administrators to try to manage their children's educational experience. Now, on occasion, parents are calling law schools about their children.

Parents who both micromanage their children's lives and raise them to feel entitled sabotage their children's development of self-confidence, grit, and skills necessary to successfully navigate adult life. These teens and young adults often find themselves unable to cope with performance expectations, prioritizing, scheduling, limits, disappointments, challenges, and rejections. To manage adult life effectively, teens need to have opportunities to practice making and learning from their own mistakes. Where teens have lacked encouragement to develop these critical skills, parents will be unpleasantly surprised to discover that they will be teaching these skills when their children are well into their twenties and beyond.

There Is a Silver Lining

Teaching teens these skills is a matter of moderation. Combining coaching and providing teens with the freedom to implement these skills allows them to learn what works, what doesn't, and why. Parents can remain close and still maintain their role as mentor and supporter. A secure attachment and the lack of a generation gap have generally increased the connection between children and parents, which continues into adulthood. This silver lining is reflected in many stories from parents who told us that they feel closer to their children than they did to their own parents. Some parents of today's teenagers are more pragmatic than their boomer parents who focused on a more democratic family and lacked the time necessary to teach their children the adult life skills they had developed for themselves. One mom shared this description:

> I grew up in a home that was more democratic than my home now. My brother and I had a lot of power. If we didn't want to go to a restaurant, we'd just complain to get our way. My brother and I were intolerable, yet it didn't seem to register with my parents. They were ever so patient. It's not that way in my family. The hierarchy is clear: I am the mother, and they are the children. They don't have an equal vote. I have less tolerance for back talk, and I believe my expectations, coupled with consistency, provide a sense of safety and comfort for my kids.

Many parents understand their role and are raising their children differently from their own upbringing.

Connection is still essential to building resiliency in our teens. However, this connection has to be aligned with the developmental age of our children. Little by little, we have to let go. If we provide our teens with appropriate boundaries, emotional intelligence, cultural competence, and the other qualities of a mature adult, they will be able to make better choices and rebound from challenging situations. We see these better and more appropriate decisions when we hear from employers about employees' requests to take time off to attend teacher interviews. Pediatric nurses are now seeing both mothers and fathers learning how to diaper and feed their infants. On any beautiful Sunday, you can see fathers with babies on their backs walking with other dads, a more common sight than it was 20 years ago. Many of today's parents can remain involved while also being confident in setting limits. This is the balance required to set the stage for healthy development.

Parents can monitor the extent to which their children have internalized desired characteristics by observing whether their children have established personal identities, have developed reasonable and rational judgment, have begun to make independent decisions, behave in a purposeful and responsible manner, and are self-reliant and self-confident. These measures of maturity generally emerge incrementally over time.

2

Psychology: Lost in Translation

Adolescence is not about letting go. It's about hanging on during a very bumpy ride.

—Ron Taffel (2006)

Have They Lost Their Minds?

If you're reading this chapter, you've reached those dreaded teenage years. In the words of one mother, "I remember my friends with older kids saying, 'You think the terrible twos are bad; just wait till adolescence!' Now I'm here and feel both overwhelmed and clueless." It's a turbulent and confusing time when your child may still conform at school but acts out and resists the rules at home. The child your teacher says is a delight has developed a major attitude, and you find yourself in conversations where you inevitably end up saying the wrong thing. These are the years when you have a foot permanently in your mouth.

While you feel a loss of control, so do your teenagers. Life for your teens is moving very fast, with hormones raging, physical appearance changing, friendships shifting, and new expectations emerging. As information seeps out over the airwaves, your children are being shaped more by forces outside of the family, and your influence is lessened significantly. Child expert Ron Taffel states, "Decades ago, most kids carried parents around inside, whether they wanted to or not. . . . Parents constituted a deeply felt, internal presence, however neurotic and oppressive it might sometimes have been. Millennium kids live in a context of fragmentation . . . cool and cruel on the surface while they hide surprisingly healthy passions beneath" (2006).

What Psychologists Say about Becoming Your Own Person While Staying Connected

Adolescence is the continuation of a long process of development, and reaching maturity takes significantly more time for teenagers today than it did for previous generations. Currently, the process of becoming an autonomous adult continues into one's late twenties. When we consider that our children are experiencing puberty earlier and are no longer launching their careers immediately after college, we are looking at a new extended period of adolescence, with the later years referred to as "emerging adulthood."

Children's temperament and personality gradually emerge through the early years, but it is only during the teen years that a coherent sense of self emerges and their unique personality is truly formed. While this process starts at the beginning of adolescence, it's a gradual and uneven process, which varies from child to child. In fact, at any one moment in time, teens may be at different stages in their intellectual, social, moral, and/or emotional development—and that is why *you* may sometimes feel confused by inconsistencies in your children's emotions and behaviors. Your children may be similarly caught off guard and surprised by their feelings and reactions.

The primary task of adolescence is to establish an identity, which is often attained through social and moral development. Social development can be reflected in your teens' ability to form supportive and close friendships. Moral development can be seen as your teens' capacity to internalize a sense of right and wrong and to be caring and empathetic persons. During these years, teens will begin to see that there is a world beyond family and school. This is when teenagers look to each other for a better understanding and clarification of their values, a process that helps them individuate and separate from their families. Since Erik Erikson wrote *Childhood and Society* in 1950, much of the discussion about adolescence has centered on his theory of psychological development. According to Erikson, the crux of adolescence is "identity versus identity diffusion." In plain talk, this can be interpreted to mean answering two questions: "Who am I?" individually and "How can I remain me, connected to others, without being subsumed by them?" (1994).

Attachment

Attachment refers to your child's emotional connection to you. Feeling close to a loving caretaker in infancy is fundamental because it creates the foundation for security. The secure bond built through closeness gives your children the ability to separate from you but also to return to seek comfort when they are upset. Healthy attachment allows for individuation. This attachment is very important because it provides the foundation for positive growth throughout life. David J. Wallin, author of *Attachment in Psychotherapy* (2007), observes that our attachments shape us because they form our concept of *self*, identity, character, abilities, and attitudes.

Therefore, parents should aspire to give their children a secure attachment, which helps them establish a balance between finding reassurance and connection to others and developing the capacity for exploration. The significance of creating a healthy attachment can't be overstated, because it lays the foundation for children's ability to connect to and trust others throughout their lives. Children thrive when they can enjoy warm and intimate relationships. Teens who have a secure attachment with a loving adult from infancy make healthier choices in relationships and are able to trust that the world is safe. A securely attached adult is comfortable trusting others and is able to form lasting relationships.

Unfortunately, our culture suggests that being too close to our teens produces a stifling, symbiotic, and enmeshed relationship. This undermines and conflicts with the actual importance of staying connected to our children. This is especially true in America, where we enshrine the independent spirit of "Go west, young man."

Finding the balance between attachment and individuation is a high-wire act because people grow best when they experience a balance between support and challenge. It is our job to support our teens' independence without pulling away, despite the inevitable confusion and tension we may feel when our teenagers appear to be invaded by another personality.

Misreading Psychological Cues

Further complicating the process, society and many parents have very different expectations for girls' and boys' adolescence. Our society encourages parents to help boys become men by pushing them away so they can learn to resolve issues on their own. At the same time, our culture gives parents permission to maintain a deeper connection with daughters.

If we give too much weight to those assumptions, we often misread the psychological needs of teens. We tend to think boys are doing well when they could actually be struggling, because they generally don't give much verbal feedback. It's easy to assume our sons are fine, even when they could benefit from our attention and assistance. With our daughters, we can misinterpret that they are in agreement when it is more likely that they are uncomfortable with voicing a dissenting opinion. A core dilemma for adolescent girls is their struggle for balance between their need for self-expression and their need to please others, while boys struggle with exposing any vulnerability.

Do We Push Our Sons Away?

The popular conception has been "Boys will be boys." Instead of promoting connection, our society dictates that separation be the primary focus for boys' psychological development. Parents have followed the tradition of pushing boys to separate from them, in order to become "healthy" male adults. In fact, many parents believe that remaining too connected to family inhibits the development of the autonomy boys need to be masculine. Independence is almost enshrined in the American culture for American males. We stop nurturing our sons earlier than we do our daughters, because we fear we are emasculating our boys by making them too soft. Despite research demonstrating that at birth male babies are actually more expressive than female babies, one mother remembered how the day after her son was born, she felt scared because she was so bonded but worried whether she could pull away from him to make him strong. Through many conversations with mothers, we found that they hear warnings about boys needing to be tough to survive and fit in.

Based on these traditional cultural pressures, mothers of boys often give their sons much more space than they give their daughters, almost tiptoeing around them. One mother reported, "It's so hard to get any details from Matthew. He likes to talk when he has a good day, but not when he's upset or when I initiate a conversation." Another mother lamented, "If he [her son] is in a bad mood, I stand back. Why should I feel like that?" A teacher told a story of working with boys in her photography class: "When the lights go out, they start to talk. I'm always surprised by how much they self-edit when the lights are on." Another mother said, "Jacob was telling me about his first day of high school, and my nose started to run. I reached for a tissue, and the box was empty, so I just stood there listening with a nose running, wiping it with my sleeve. I knew that once I left the kitchen to get a tissue, the magic moment would be over!" Parents know that boys determine when they will talk and when they won't.

However, our need to focus on independence has been in conflict with our sons' basic human needs for love, support, and emotional encouragement. Boys are as relational as girls. A middle-school counselor we spoke to said, "When I think of the boys I work with and other men and boys I know, they actually place a very high value on relationships and develop powerful and lifelong, unconditional bonds. I believe the way in which boys express their connection is different from girls and women, but the bonding itself can be equally powerful."

Most teenage boys are preoccupied with social media, sports, and friends. While boys often may seem uninterested in being close, they still cherish and want a close relationship with their parents. Even though adolescence is a time when boys are attempting to strike out on their own path, they still seek their fathers' approval. It's important for a father to appreciate his son's choices, especially when those choices differ from his own. This is how a father can demonstrate respect and support for his son. One father told us how he struggled when his 16-year-old son chose to stop playing baseball:

> I was on my high school baseball team and still found time to play on a rec league with my friends. Baseball kept me away from drugs and drinking. I never realized how much I wanted this for my son Ben until he decided to quit. I'm honestly confused. Ben says he's sure he's done with the sport and wants to concentrate on lacrosse. I know zero about lacrosse and feel like I have nothing to offer him. Right now I'm struggling with faking enthusiasm, but I know I should get behind his decision. Ben's choice is about him, not me!

This father is right. Fathers shouldn't personalize the choices their sons make. Boys want to measure up to their dads and need to know that their choices have value.

Each adolescent boy, and particularly an older teen, feels he is expected to make his own way in the world. Many parents we spoke with, regardless of race, class, or ethnicity, talked about how they often abdicate parenting their boys during adolescence. For example, fewer parents reported that they required their sons to inform them of their whereabouts on weekend evenings; in contrast, all of the parents of daughters required them to call if their plans changed during the course of an evening.

We need to broaden the scope of acceptable behaviors for boys to give them alternatives to the aggressive and competitively driven behaviors typical of them during adolescence. For example, it is fundamentally unfair to discount the role of girls as friends in the lives of our sons. Our sons need interpersonal skills to have successful relationships as partners and parents. One dad reflecting on his son's college experience told us, "Perhaps there has been a shift with co-ed dorms resulting in boys and girls developing more meaningful friendships more often than in our generation." It is no longer a cultural norm that boys and girls can't be friends. Boys can now express a wider range of emotions without being perceived negatively. Keeping this in mind, parents should take into consideration the needs of the individual, instead of relying on expectations and responses based on gender stereotyping.

Do We Hold Our Girls Too Close?

In contrast to what we have observed in boys, adolescent girls do not construct an identity by establishing personal boundaries between themselves and others. Girls do, however, construct their identities through their relationships with parents, friends, and significant others such as teachers, camp counselors, and other supportive adults. This can makes it more difficult for girls to establish healthy boundaries in romantic and friend relationships.

Women form their identities in a context of the mother-daughter relationship. According to Nancy Chodorow, "Mothers tend to experience their daughters as more alike, and continuous with, themselves" (Gilligan, 1982, p. 7). We, mothers and daughters, are mirrored from head to toe, replicated by common genes, sexual makeup, and social experiences. Mothers provide a genetic and emotional road map for their daughters.

In our focus groups, many mothers expressed feeling "tethered" to their daughters. One mother revealed, "Maggie can push my buttons more than anyone. It's as if we merge together as one person. It's different with my son, David, whose biology makes it clear that he isn't me." This bond is particularly strong during adolescence, a period that offers an opportunity for both mothers and daughters to rediscover their identities. While a shared biology can contribute to an increased potential for empathy and closeness, it may also inhibit the process of differentiation and individuation. This powerful connection creates complex relationships in which mothers and daughters often project and ascribe feelings to each other that aren't helpful to growth and development.

Physician and author Nancy Snyderman reports in *Girl in the Mirror* that for a mother, the "past, present, and future collide when we look into our daughters' faces. All of our dreams—those we've realized and those we consider beyond our grasp—are in the room with us" (2002, pp. 12–13). For a mother, raising a daughter is like going back to the future, and watching herself while watching her daughter. Observing our daughters reminds us of experiences we had as young girls. This identification with our own past can provide us with greater empathy and understanding, but it can also resurrect childhood pain and cause us to react in a negative way.

Healthy mother-daughter attachments can foster positive self-esteem and self-affirmation. However, this intense, close relationship can also be a breeding ground for conflict, resulting in the typical example of the "push-pull" nature of the mother-daughter relationship. It was evident that the mothers in our focus groups experienced this paradox. They raved about their daughters in one sentence and expressed hurt, frustration, and pain in the next. In discussing her daughter, one mother said, "I'm surprised at how in one moment I feel so close to her and then just minutes later, I want to strangle her." The psychological connection between mothers and daughters often creates an environment in which they are overly sensitive to each other. This can result in both mothers and daughters vacillating between demonstrating appropriate empathy and behaving with insensitivity or callous indifference.

Our daughters, unlike our sons, begin to separate and individuate in the everyday, mundane moments, not just around the big life decisions. One mother we spoke with bought herself a jean jacket and showed it to her daughter, Becky, to see if she approved. This mother said, "All I wanted was a simple yes or no. However, Becky looked at me with a sneer on her face and said, 'Is that for me or for you?' 'For me,' I answered, and then Becky rejected my choice of jacket by spitting out one carefully dismissive word: '*Trendy.*' I thought to myself, 'My own mother never belittled me like this.'" This type of nasty behavior comes out when our daughters experience not-alikeness or when they experience too much alikeness. For example, when mothers buy jeans that their daughters would like for themselves, their daughters may perceive that their territory has been invaded. Taylor, a 15-year-old, said, "My best friend's mother just bought platform sneakers with rhinestones. I want to barf. I feel terrible for my friend. She must be humiliated."

When parents come to understand that this is a normal process of development, it is easier to accept this type of reaction and see it not just as insensitive and callous. It may simply be an example of their daughters beginning to form their own identities. Daughters very often are judgmental only because their relationships with their mothers are so important and loom so large over their lives.

Another mother told us, "We're like a mixture of oil and water. We're always on the verge of an argument; something could explode at any moment. If I tell my daughter her hair looks good curly, she'll ask me why I didn't like her hair blown straight. I always feel that I'm dancing on a pin and can tip over any second. Every comment I make has the capacity to be misunderstood. Our conversations are just so loaded."

This mother was acutely aware that her words have the ability to evoke feelings and emotions in her daughter that the situation may not warrant. Even though we may think our comments are innocuous, our daughters often interpret our words differently from what we intend or actually mean to say. And even when mothers try to be nonjudgmental and supportive, their conversations are often loaded because the present is infused with the past.

Daughters seem to have fewer everyday struggles with their fathers because they are not trying to establish their independence from their dads. Fathers and daughters often have less stormy relationships because fathers have a built-in ability to see their daughters as separate from themselves. This perspective allows dads to be less reactive and daughters give them different feedback.

According to one father, "My daughter, Madison, is my best audience. She laughs at my corny jokes and thinks whatever I do and say is OK, just because it's me. It drives my wife crazy. It's definitely a double standard, and I am the beneficiary of her unconditional acceptance. I've escaped living under Madison's microscope, which she expertly uses on her mother. I have it easy compared with my wife, Julie." Daughters don't share the same hot buttons with their fathers as they do with their mothers. For this reason, gender definitely affects how you may parent your daughters and how they react to you, which then affects how your daughters feel about themselves.

Time spent with her father can have critical benefits to a daughter's self-esteem, because a positive relationship indicates to her that she is both interesting and worthy of his attention. Fathers also have an important role in encouraging their daughters to set high expectations for their social and professional lives. When a father demonstrates his comfort in relating to his daughter both as a young woman with a developing body and as a whole person, she becomes more comfortable with herself.

Let's Get Physical: Brain Research and the Plastic Years

Children's brains are very pliable and are not exclusively programmed at birth. The fact may seem pretty daunting, but parents can actually affect the circuitry in their children's brains. Each experience in a child's life leads to new neurological connections. The ability of the brain to mature and change throughout childhood, adolescence, and young adulthood is called plasticity.

The brain grows to 90 percent of its full size by the time we are 6 years old. Later, between the ages of 12 and 25, our brains undergo a massive reorganization, pruning away unused connections and strengthening those that remain. Also, because the brain acts like a sponge, teenagers can make room for new skills and interests. This explains why we may store our memories from adolescence better than we do during times of less change in our brains. One mother of two teenage sons said, "I still have a soft spot for the cheesy, bubblegum music I loved in high school. Unfortunately, my taste in music never got more sophisticated." When you consider it, most of us retain a fondness for the sounds of our adolescence. The teenage years are vitally important because the brain's plasticity can also help teens pick up new skills. It's a perfect time for learning language, sports, music, etc.

In addition to the brain's transformation, hormonal changes affect teens. Hormones explain some of teenage behavior, but they hardly account for all of it. The new field of cultural neuroscience helps us understand gender differences in our sons and daughters, and this growing knowledge can help teens develop a wider range of acceptable behaviors. For example, looking at the current research, neuroscientists are saying that the scans of brains in boys and girls are more similar than their behavior would have us presume. Girls and boys adapt to the culture they are born into.

We are just beginning to understand how the different experiences and environments our teenagers encounter in their lives will affect their brain development. In the past, the nature-versus-nurture question was usually framed as an either/or question, pitting biology against culture and heredity against environment. The new research changes how we view the age-old question of nature versus nurture. It is increasingly impossible to view either nature or nurture as mutually exclusive, because the brain changes through life experience. Rather, nature and nurture are exquisitely intertwined.

When we seek to understand adolescent development, a more productive goal than choosing between nurture and nature is to understand how heredity and environment interact. Until teen brains complete the phase of reorganization and development that occurs between ages 12 and 25, their behavior may be erratic and confusing, and their bodies can be awkward and clumsy. A mother of a 16-year-old daughter said, "When Sophie enters the room wearing sandals with her three-inch platforms, she towers over me. I'm not used to looking up to speak to her. Her growth spurt seemed to happen overnight. One day Sophie was short, and now I feel like Gulliver's mother. What must it be like to be in that rapidly changing body?" Although your children's physical changes in height and sexual development may be obvious to everyone, the less apparent changes in teenagers' brains are just as dramatic.

With techniques such as magnetic resonance imaging (MRI), we now understand that the brain overproduces cells and connections twice in our lives: first when we are babies, and then again during adolescence. Dr. Jay Giedd, chief of brain imaging at the Child Psychiatry Branch of the National Institute of Mental Health, reported that during adolescence the brain is very busy pruning and eliminating unneeded connections (Giedd, 2000). The teenage brain undergoes a transformation in adolescence that alters the nature of thinking in profound ways.

Adolescents rely heavily on the area of their brain called the amygdala, the part of the brain that is involved in processing emotions such as rage, fear, and sexuality (Hedaya, 2010). In adolescence, the amygdala is well developed, while the frontal lobe, which is responsible for judgment, is still relatively immature. Since the frontal lobe is not strong in adolescents, we know it's less likely to process information accurately. This less-developed frontal lobe results in younger teenagers often acting more impulsively. They regularly misinterpret advice from their parents until they a develop capacity for judgment and abstract thinking skills. In adolescents, the frontal lobe is not well enough developed to override emotions from the amygdala with any reliability, which makes teenagers more inclined to respond immediately to stimuli with gut reactions. This immature development of the adolescent brain explains why teenagers are less able to modulate, inhibit, or understand the consequences of their behavior.

Teenagers don't have the same understanding of cause and effect as adults do. How many times have you asked your daughter with incredulity, "Why did you do that?" and she has answered, "I don't know"? Or how often have you asked your son, "Why did you invite ten kids to the house, knowing that in a millisecond, the situation could explode?" and his answer invariably is "I don't know"? They give you this answer because they honestly don't know. Their judgment is affected by the fact that their brains are not yet fully formed. Specifically, the frontal lobe of their brain, which is responsible for controlling impulses, is still developing. This is why teenagers don't think through consequences as thoroughly as adults. Development of their frontal lobe will enable them to be less impulsive and to understand that every action has consequences.

Experimentation and Risky Business

Most teenagers get pleasure from taking risks and pushing limits. The changes that are under way in the adolescent brain have an important function because they help your child stretch and take risks as a way to get ready to leave the comforts of home. Daniel Siegel, author of *Brainstorm: The Power and Purpose of the Teenage Brain*, says, "As children, we're dependent on our parents for everything, for a sense of security that comes from being seen, being safe, being soothed by our parents. If we didn't have some fundamental change in how the brain was functioning, why would anyone leave the comfort of the home nest?" (2014).

Siegel describes home as a safe base, a launching pad from which teenagers question the familiar and find themselves attracted to things and activities that are new and novel. Behavior during the teenage years creates the "hard wiring" for the adult years. And as one parent said, "Thank goodness, or else we would have more than twentysome-things to contend with; we'd have forty-year-olds living at home!"

This drive to action contributes to the teenage tendency to mini-mize risks and focus on rewards, a quality referred to as hyper-rational thinking. Once parents learn that there is an anthropological reason why their teens won't listen to endless warnings and advice about what not to do, they can focus on giving them the tools they need to keep safe during this period of risk taking.

Siegel suggests that parents can protect their children by helping them to develop an inner compass. "If you teach kids to have an inter-nal compass, they will literally get a 'gut' feeling to influence a decision—'this doesn't *feel* right'—his gut will say something, his heart will say something—he won't listen to the words his mom and dad gave him, but he will listen to his body and his body will influence his brain—this is his internal compass, deciding to not do something because it doesn't *feel* right" (Siegel, 2014). An inner compass or anchor helps teens get in touch with what is right and wrong. All kids need this coping mechanism. Siegel recalls one mother who told her son to pay attention to the feeling he had whenever he felt off-kilter. She wanted her son to become more aware that his inner voice was telling him what was right or wrong.

This gut feeling is exactly what Doug, a high school senior, said he used to prevent himself from driving while drunk:

> I was at a party with my friends playing a drinking game. After downing more shots than I care to count, I knew I was in no shape

to drive myself and my friends home. My friends urged me *not* to call a parent and kept trying to convince me that nothing bad would happen, but I felt funny and decided to go with my gut instinct. So I called my parents. I used my one "get out of jail free" card, and they didn't yell or punish me. My parents warned me about minimizing risks and told me to listen to my gut, and I did.

This story demonstrates how Doug followed his inner compass and decided not to do something because it didn't feel right.

Knowing about the science of the brain may not enable you to change your children's behavior, but it helps you to better accept and respond to their angst, their sense of invincibility, and their risky attraction to experimentation. Siegel (2004) suggests that parents recognize *intent* in behavior and respond to the teen's mind-set (the motivation) rather than the teen's behavior. The intent may be to explore, while the outcome may be destructive. When parents understand that their teens were motivated to investigate, their response may be very different. We want to reinforce and validate exploration.

Your discussions and debriefings with your teens can help establish and reinforce the pattern of listening to their hearts and paying more attention to their inner voices. With this knowledge and greater understanding, you will have more success in reaching your teens at a time when they normally would be resisting, avoiding, and pulling away.

Young teens are a particularly high risk group. Their brains, which are not yet fully developed, make them even more prone to risky behavior, including drug and alcohol use. Teenagers can be very concrete, which is reflected in their black-and-white thinking. They experience mood swings, which makes them generally more reactive and emotional. This combination of emotional instability and risky behavior explains the constant conflict you may be experiencing with your child.

Risk taking is both normal and developmentally appropriate during adolescence, and this puts parents of teens in a difficult position. A natural inclination for many parents is to try to put cotton batting around everything to protect their teens. But there is only so much hovering parents can and should do. Parents would be wiser to recognize that not all risk taking is bad and perhaps even anticipate this behavior. It's precisely this need to push the edge of what's acceptable that helps teenagers mature and grow into healthy adults. Teens take risks to see for themselves what works and what doesn't, who they are and who they aren't, testing limits as a means of creating their own uniqueness. This in turn helps our teens grow into mature, analytical adults. Not all risk taking is dangerous. One father of a 15-year-old daughter recounted a situation where he recognized that fact:

> Liz is normally the one I would refer to as my careful child. I've never had to take her to the emergency room, because generally she doesn't push herself to try anything that's scary. But last summer at camp, she was either too embarrassed to admit her fear or didn't want to miss out, so she did something uncharacteristic for her. She learned to water-ski and was so proud of herself she had the counselor videotape it because she knew we'd be surprised. I know this is no big deal for most kids, but I'm happy Liz overcame her fear. In this instance, she took a chance and succeeded.

Positive risk taking allows teens to make safer choices and reap rewards. Making new friends, exploring new interests, and participating in activities such as sports, plays, and community volunteering all have components of risk taking. The opportunity for success represents the positive aspect of risk taking, while the threat of embarrassment and failure represents the flip side. With proper encouragement and guidance, parents can help their teens channel the dangerous parts of this developmental stage into positive learning experiences.

However, some of this experimentation can be very dangerous, especially today. Our high tech and sexually provocative world often puts our children in stressful and precarious situations. The following scenario describes how risk can creep into a normal social activity: Your teenage daughter goes to a party with kids she knows, so she thinks she has no reason to be afraid. Someone secretly drops a drug like Rohypnol or ecstasy into her drink. When the drug dissolves, it is colorless and odorless. As she consumes the drug, it takes effect. Under the influence of either one of these drugs, she may experience drowsiness, dizziness, confusion, lack of coordination, loss of inhibition, impaired judgment, and reduced levels of consciousness. This is a chilling scenario.

Some parents totally ignore this reality, while others are overly consumed with anxiety about the dangers that can befall their children. One parent who might belong to the second group is the mother of two high school teens:

> My kids know that I worry. Unfortunately, at the most inopportune moments, I have a tendency to make public service announcements about some information that I believe is important to keep them safe. Yesterday I was with my son, daughter, and a few of their friends who know me well. The subject of drinking came up. I went into automatic pilot and proclaimed, "Kids, you know those red Solo cups you drink from at parties? Well, while you aren't looking, someone else may put some drug in your drink. You have to be very careful." I then blurted out, "Wait! I have a good idea: maybe carry some plastic wrap with you and put it on the rim of your cup to keep your drink safe." As you can see, I was on a roll, lost in my parental paranoia. I thought this was a fabulous idea, and in retrospect, it's just crazy. In response to my overzealous, nutty idea, one of my kids' friends said, "Stacey, why not just send them to college with sippy cups?"

Knowing that this type of risk exists requires you to present information to your teens in a way that strikes a balance between scaring the daylights out of them and teaching them how to be aware of their environment. Doing this without sounding like a caricature can feel like a high-wire act.

Teenagers should be allowed and encouraged to grow up, have a good time, and test limits. We have to acknowledge that experimentation is a normal part of adolescent development. Yet if you suspect your child is excessively using drugs and alcohol, then, of course, you need to step in. Knowledge is power, and to gauge how your teens are handling their lives, you have to be aware of what's out there.

One father told us how his daughter, who had been invited to a party at a friend's house, cried and pleaded with him not to call the friend's parents before the party. He said, "Through her sobs, she cried, 'Dad, I'll die if you call! No one's parents call; it will be the kiss of death. I won't go. Just don't call!' And she's right. I've asked around; after a while, most parents stop calling."

Many parents had personal stories that rivaled the plot of the movie *Risky Business*. One mother said,

> Your house is a bull's-eye if you aren't home. Imagine how fast the news of your absence spreads with cell phones and e-mail. My son, Josh, invited a few of his friends to our house when my husband and I were going to be away for the weekend. Josh, in his naïveté, thought he could put up tape to block off the newly decorated living room, believing that a masking tape barrier would protect my new furniture from two hundred of his "closest" friends. We were lucky in that we learned about the party through a friend who had placed her ear next to the bathroom door, listening to the plans being formed.
>
> Even though we knew about the plans for a party, we decided to go away because of our friends' willingness to house-sit. They parked their car in front of the house to prevent kids, who came in droves, from entering the house. Our friends observed a *Field of Dreams*–like line of car headlights for the entire block and around the corner. My son learned that there were going to be hundreds of kids after one friend posted the address on Twitter!

Many other parents echoed this reasoning. One mother said of her daughter, "During Steph's first high-school party, she had the largest boy, a defensive tackle, guard the food while the jewelry upstairs was left unguarded. Did she think the milk and American cheese were more valuable than my engagement ring?" That's how naive they are. Consequences seem less important than the attraction of doing something they know they aren't supposed to do. No matter how smart your son or daughter is, you can't anticipate how convoluted their reasoning can become. As we discussed earlier in this chapter, your teens' judgment and ability to forecast consequences are not fully developed.

As a parent, you must recognize that incidents can get out of hand in a flash, and you have to be prepared to protect your children and yourself from the potential consequences of these occurrences. These years take a kind of parental vigilance the military would be proud of.

What's a Parent to Do?

While teenagers are hardwired to take risks, we can steer them toward more appropriate activities that will boost their self-confidence. Think of your role as building the scaffolding that supports your teens until they build their own sturdy sense of self. Parents are so important during this period. Be around, not like a hovering drone, but more like a safety net, and when your teenager royally screws up, make the punishment fit the crime. One dad said, "If he can't get home before his curfew on Friday night, he doesn't get to use the car Saturday. I don't take it away for a month; that will just be overkill and probably make him more oppositional. My thinking is a small offense gets an equally small punishment." Freaking out never gets your point across; take a breath, think, and then talk to your teens. They all mess up, and those who took risks as younger children may develop personalities and temperaments that lead them to take more risks as teenagers. Be aware and be ready and open to discussion. After all, teenagers eat and breathe risk.

It's confusing when our teenagers often make it very clear that they don't think we have much to offer them during adolescence, yet they still want and need our attention. Time and again, teenagers say they want and need their parents, even though parents are surprised to hear this. One mom said, "My daughter is constantly treating me with such disregard that it makes my blood boil." A dad said, "My son, Josh, is always sleep-deprived; his sleep has been pushed into a slice of time between midnight and dawn, so he's working with absolutely no reserve." Another dad said, "Jenny feels that no one understands her, and you know, she's not so wrong." In fact, during adolescence many parents say they don't quite know their kids, and it throws them off balance. Our teenagers are sleep-deprived, give us mixed messages, and feel misunderstood; it makes sense that we have no idea how much they want and need us. But they do!

So Much to Do and So Little Time

Today's world puts our children under too much pressure. With so many competing demands, parents need some perspective themselves to know when to step in and provide some relief for their teens. Years before the college application process, parents and teens worry about creating a résumé worthy of somebody who has already been in the workforce for a while. They feel compelled to pursue many time-consuming interests at the same time. The pressure to be multitalented can result in overscheduling and burnout. Teens feel tremendous anxiety and stress from doing so much in so little time, as well as from failing a test, not being chosen for the sports team or getting a part in the school play, or losing a boyfriend or girlfriend. The mother of a 17-year-old high-school junior offered this example:

> Jed had his heart set on getting a lead in his high school play. He had a callback for one of the parts, and I could feel how nervous he was, waiting for the selection. The day the cast list was posted in school without Jay's name on it, he was devastated. Not only was he embarrassed, but he was devastated. I was concerned because Jay

didn't seem to have any ability to make himself feel better about this disappointment.

We had a real heart-to-heart, and I said, "Jed, usually you can handle disappointments and you can bounce back. What's going on?" And that's when he broke down and sobbed. He said that he had so much on his plate, so much to do between the school-required community service, his soccer practice and games, and his schoolwork. He absolutely couldn't figure out how to get it all done, nor could he decide how to cut back. When I tried to reassure him that his dad and I would sit down with him and see how to help him prioritize, he cried and said, "But what about college, what about college?" I just felt so bad because we had been putting so much pressure on him to achieve without being sensitive to the fact that he is just a kid. At 17 years old, he felt the burden of his entire future on his shoulders.

Many teens do not have the skills needed to handle their stress and the anxiety that comes from stress. Parents have an opportunity to help buffer their children during these stressful years. This is where parents can have such an impact, not only psychologically but in their children's brain development. When adults help buffer a teenager from stress, this sets the stage for children's optimal brain development. Parents who create a safe, loving, and supportive environment for their children help ensure healthy brain development. Just knowing there's someone to talk to when they're desperate or overstressed is very reassuring to teenagers.

A New Vision

Societies are capable of creating intimate and fruitful human relationships that nurture the best of the female and male brains. The brain's plasticity is the reason gender stereotypes are diminishing as we respond to the enormous societal changes that have been going on since the 1970s.

Cultural and social changes driven by technology, together with discoveries in brain research, redefine how we think about raising strong, confident, and healthy children. You don't have to separate for your children to become autonomous. They can be connected while becoming individuals. You don't need to disconnect from your children for them to grow into independent adults.

We want our children to develop a secure sense of self, which is why it's so important for them to maintain a deep connection with parents. Having a parent or parents who want to remain competent and close does not diminish our children's maturity. Instead, it's helpful to view this period of adolescence as a *change* in your relationship with your teen rather than a separation from you.

We believe that connection is realistic and compatible with today's mothers, fathers, and caretakers. There is a balance to strike between the interaction of children's unique biology and their life experiences. Our behavior is not predetermined by biology; it is more determined by how we love our children and how connected they are to friends, their community, and us.

As they age, teenagers begin to see themselves in relation to the world. As teens develop a greater and solid sense of self, they ask themselves: What kind of an adult do I want to be? What impact can I have on the world? This maturity comes from feeling worthy and believing that they have the ability to effect positive change. For parents, the teen years are part of the continuing cycle of letting go while continuously giving our children the tools to make their way in the world.

3

Reality Check: How Do We Raise Our Sons and Daughters?

Parent modeling that includes the unspoken as well as the spoken word is the most powerful force in shaping a child's life.

—A Focus Group Parent

Raising Boys and Girls Is Sometimes the Same and Sometimes Different

There are two schools of thought when it comes to gender differences. There are those who insist that all differences are biologically hardwired. And there are those who believe that differences are fostered and nurtured. While inborn differences do exist, they are developed, cultivated, and/or exacerbated by the way society treats boys and girls.

Teenagers confront stereotypes daily, promoting assumptions that strong boys are assertive but strong girls are aggressive and "bossy." Sensitive boys are weak, but sensitive girls are empathetic. Because adolescence is a time of conformity, these expectations limit boys' and girls' interests, skills, behavior, and pursuits. This is the insidious nature of stereotyping. Even though there is some evidence that many gender stereotypes have been eliminated or diminished, teens continue to be bombarded by media and marketing campaigns that perpetuate gender bias and stereotyping (Day of the Girl–US, 2013).

While plenty of parenting books are available, there is not one single manual explaining how to be a boy or how to be a girl. Yet our culture(s) dictate and promote accepted gender roles and behaviors. This socialization leads most of us to adopt approved gender-based behaviors, characteristics, and attitudes. Today, some young women aspire to and become pilots and soldiers. Some young men aspire to and become elementary school teachers and nurses. Some young men are comfortable expressing emotion and nurturing others. Some young women are comfortable in leadership roles and being outspoken. The twenty-first century certainly provides more choices and acceptance, yet during their teens, most children struggle with their need to fit in. Experts and parents are left to wrestle with these traditional expectations and, at the same time, new and more expansive definitions of gender.

Girls, more than boys, often struggle to develop autonomy because of pervasive gender role stereotyping. Both traditional psychological literature and the gospel according to Madison Avenue ascribe adjectives such as *logical, rational, objective*, and *competitive* to males. Communal adjectives such as *intuitive, emotional, subjective, cooperative*, and *nurturing* are ascribed to females. Only in recent years have we come to acknowledge that independence is equally important to everyone, and learning the language of feelings, self-sufficiency, and connectedness is important to both genders. Guiding children to define themselves requires overcoming gender role stereotyping.

Parents typically consider themselves the primary influencers of their children, along with a little help from traditional sources like schools or religious institutions. Today they compete with smartphone apps, friends, popular culture, and Madison Avenue. These added influencers compete to control the development of stereotypical thinking for the purpose of creating markets to sell products and make money. This competition begins with the pink and blue baby hats given out in hospitals. Noah's dad said, "Noah was hell-bent on staying clear of pink from very early on. I remember wearing a pink polo shirt when he was three years old, and he said, 'Daddy, take that off. It's a girl color. Boys don't wear pink.' Now, where did he get this idea? I wear pink, and I'm very careful not to categorize something as only for girls or for boys. Frankly, I'm a bit surprised; he must get it by osmosis." This "osmosis" starts very young and continues throughout life in the form of beauty and cosmetics advertisements in magazines like *Teen Vogue, Discovery Girls*, and *Seventeen*, fashion and articles about "How to Catch and Keep a Boyfriend," rappers, ESPN, and video games such as *Madden NFL* and *Grand Theft Auto*. As a result, marketing in large part drives gender stereotypes.

A parent of a young teen was thrilled that both of her children were interested in soccer. In looking to equip them, she went to a local toy store. In addition to the typical black-and-white balls, she noticed balls in pink and blue. She perceived in the colors a marketing objective: dissuading her from buying one ball for both of her children and persuading her to buy one ball of each color, doubling the expense. No one can say that this marketing ploy isn't about money.

In response to the popularity of *The Hunger Games, Brave*, and *Divergent*, toy makers continue to capitalize on gender stereotypes. Instead of Ariel, the mermaid princess, the new heroines carry bows and arrows "in a swirl of pink, purple, white and gold plastic, with names such as Heartbreaker and Pink Crush" (Stout & Harris, 2014). Even Mattel has a new Barbie doll that comes with a bow and arrow. Regardless of the progress we have made, marketing may be the primary agent of what it means to be a boy or a girl. Responding to new role models for young girls, in this Stout and Harris *New York Times* article, psychologist Sharon Lamb says,

I don't see this [e.g., new toys for girls with weapons, including guns and arrows] as making girls more aggressive, but instead as letting girls know that their aggressive impulses are acceptable and they should be able to play them out (as we have with boys). But, what I don't like is the stereotyped girlifying of this. Do they have to be in pink? Why can't they be rebels and have to be re-BELLES [one of Hasbro's pink archery sets]? Why do they need to look sexy when aggressing, defending the weak or fighting off bad guys? (Stout & Harris, 2014, p. 20)

And so the debate continues, as do the stereotypes.

Socialization is complex and deeply rooted in our families, schools, and cultures. These social pressures have a more pernicious impact on young teens when they drive youngsters to experience unnecessary and harmful losses. As boys and girls are socialized into their appropriate gender roles, they are often asked to trade off personal strengths. For example, girls are encouraged to be compliant and accommodating and to focus their energy on being attractive. They also are warned to take fewer risks and are criticized for being too outspoken, having too many opinions. This trade-off can drive them to diminish or hide their competitive spirit, assertiveness, and power (Sandberg, 2013). Boys are encouraged to pursue power in the outer world. While being strong is an important tool for success, stereotypes can pressure boys to deny genuine feelings of fear, vulnerability, pain, and sadness. They might then trade off skills such as networking, communication, self-expression, and empathy. We believe that gender-affirming parenting expands the way our children look at, approach, and experience the world.

Moving Beyond Stereotype Constraints

The conventional wisdom is that it's harder to raise daughters than it is sons because daughters have too much angst and drama in their lives. We hear you. Boys often present less drama, but their emotional issues are just as loaded. They both present challenges. It's just hard to raise teenagers.

Our cultural values include protecting daughters by keeping them close. In contrast, we are persuaded to help boys become men by pushing them away and encouraging them to learn to solve their concerns and problems on their own. We suspect that both boys and girls occasionally need protection. They also need encouragement to explore the world and learn to address challenges, failures, and consequences on their own. While gender stereotypes put many teens at risk, those who question their gender or express their individuality beyond gender stereotypes may be ridiculed or criticized by adults and their peers. Or worse, they may "silence" or harm themselves. This face-saving silence or risk of rejection means teens often stop expressing their true feelings honestly. This loss of voice sacrifices the necessary development of relationship skills and a strong self-identity. Nate, a 13-year-old, said this:

> I'm not athletic and was always the last boy picked for any athletic team. It's probably the reason my father coaches my baseball team this year. I'm sure he knows I'd never get on a select team if he wasn't the coach. He thinks he's doing the right thing, but I feel awful knowing I'm just a charity case. I don't deserve to be on the team. Every time I miss a ball in the outfield or make the third out in an inning, leaving friends on base, I want to die. But what can I say? I'd feel like a wimp if I quit, and yet I feel like a loser for playing.

The truth is that both girls and boys face similar challenges as teenagers, whether it's in the stereotypical universe or transcending gender stereotypes. Growing up and developing a strong personal identity is hard work and greatly benefits from parental and other adult support.

We have learned that discussions about gender do not need to have a "battle of the sexes" tone, implying that attention to one group has to be at the expense of the other. We don't need to discount the unique needs of girls to address the unique needs of boys. Pitting boys against girls hurts us all.

We also have learned that when there is only one child of each gender in a family, there may be a greater tendency to slip into gender stereotypes. When a family has two sons and/or two daughters, parents can more easily see that *all* girls and *all* boys are not *all* the same. Our goal is to better understand the genders' similarities and differences and work to stay connected with our teens as they discover themselves.

For Girls: The Holy Grail for Fitting In Is to Conform to the Social Order

Teens want to be accepted and fit in. For boys, acting "feminine" is a line that, when crossed, can result in unwanted consequences. Girls toe a different line. To fit in, they can conform to a broader range of prescribed behaviors but still must attend to their female social group's pecking order. This Holy Grail for teenage girls drives their behavior.

Part of changing from being a young girl to a young woman involves meeting cultural demands that idealize and exploit youth, thinness, and sexuality. At puberty, girls begin to be much more aware of outside influences, particularly those that stress the importance of looks, weight, clothes, and friendship. Focusing on acting and looking the "right" way to be part of a group may cause girls to fail to see their uniqueness. Many teenage girls become so focused on their differences, frequently internalized as imperfections, that they never feel they quite measure up. Being part of a group often trumps being an individual.

One mother shared with us her experience with her daughter, who always tried to look different (purple hair, grunge clothes). At first, her mother was proud of her daughter because she thought she was asserting her individuality, but as her daughter became more and more isolated, the mother realized that she looked different from other kids because she *felt* different. The mother was clueless about how to help her daughter. She was reluctant to share her concerns with other parents, because she was embarrassed that her daughter didn't fit it, and the mother didn't want her labeled as odd. The mom feared being judged because she couldn't control her daughter's appearance. This mother would be comforted to know how many other parents have similar stories.

Understanding the need to belong, remembering what it was like to be a teen, will help you to be better able to identify your daughter's expectations and challenges. This knowledge gives you an entry into many conversations that can help your daughter sort through and make sense of her feelings to find her own voice and make good choices. This understanding will allow your daughter to begin to know and appreciate who she is, identify what she stands for, and determine what her values are, and it will help her to set boundaries. Your daughter's stories (especially if she's actually speaking to you) and endless information may distract you, but this period requires looking beyond the actual words to fully comprehend the subtext of her experience.

For Boys: The Holy Grail Is to Avoid Failing or Showing Weakness

A boy also needs peer acceptance to feel good about himself. While the rules don't appear as rigid, except when it comes to hiding emotions for fear of being labeled as weak, they are just as limiting. Boys are expected or must learn to be masculine, stoic, tough, competitive, goal oriented, driven, and invincible. Being masculine may include not being a good student, not expressing feelings, and not being empathetic or sympathetic. This set of standards is frequently enforced by accusations of homosexuality in response to any departure from expected behavior or the slightest failure. One mother articulated her confusion about this issue when expressing her feelings about her son. She explained that she valued his sensitivity but worried he was too nice and not tough enough. However, she understood that if he were a girl, she would value, indeed prefer, the daughter's easygoing behavior and temperament.

Living in a culture that doesn't support boys' emotional expression puts pressure on them not to talk. They don't talk because they don't want to reveal their vulnerabilities and be perceived as weak. They don't talk for fear of being misjudged and permanently labeled. Without guidance that is flexible and accepting of differences, boys must protect themselves by dismissing their emotional lives. This produces an aloof veneer and bravado that boggles parents. Boys live by the code of toughness and present a macho facade, thinking they are protected and will survive. They see emotional connection as unsafe, because it threatens to disclose weakness. As parents, we are forced to spend time and effort to see behind their male facade, hiding emotions with sometimes false or at least the overstated posture that everything is "just fine." This makes it difficult for us to pinpoint problems. As a result, one father told us, "I feel like I'm Sherlock Holmes trying to find information [about my son]." Another father lamented, "I feel I can't get to his core; we can't deal with big issues." Boys learn that to be masculine and fit in, they must deal with life's challenges themselves and not fail.

To better equip our sons, we can begin to teach them the language of feelings when they are young and the discussion is not emotionally loaded. A classic and fascinating study by Robin Fivush (1989) shows that mothers use fewer words, particularly words that describe feelings, with their sons than they do with their daughters. After an outing to the zoo, Fivush took a video of the mothers talking to their sons or daughters about the experience. The recording showed a distinct difference between the way mothers recapped the experience with their daughters and the way they recapped it with their sons. Picture this: A mom takes her daughter to the zoo, holding her hand firmly when they approach the lion's den. The mother asks, "How does it feel when the lion roars? Isn't it scary to hear such a big noise?" Nearby, another mother asks her son, "Wow, the lion is loud! Can you make a sound like the lion?" When describing an encounter with a loud lion, the mothers used richer and more descriptive language with their daughters than with their sons. With their sons, the language was sparse and didn't inquire how the boys felt about the lion roaring. With their daughters, they were much more apt to ask feeling questions. This encounter teaches the daughters how to link a word with how they feel if they are frightened. These seemingly simple questions give girls the message that feeling fear is expected and OK. It also helps to expand their emotional and cognitive vocabulary, which serves them well when they have to label and describe how they feel about other life experiences (Eliot, 2009).

By not teaching boys the language of feelings, parents place them at a disadvantage. Without the ability to articulate and label emotions, boys are less able to process them. Indeed, by failing to ask questions that allow a boy to express fear, parents give their son the nonverbal message that it is unacceptable for him to acknowledge or express a feeling of fear. Parents omit many feeling words when they talk to their sons, and what we don't say can be as powerful as or more powerful than what we do say. The absence of a vocabulary describing a range of feelings makes it tough for our sons to decipher their feelings. It also makes our attempts to talk to them more difficult.

In our focus groups with teenage boys, the discussion often started with pat answers: "No problem." "No, that never bothers me." "I don't worry about it." "I can handle it." We would ask questions such as "How do you handle it when a girl breaks up with you?" At first, we would get answers such as "No big deal; I just move on." Their answers were so convincing that we were continually fooled. However, after the initial bravado and appearance of total competence, the boys' answers became more complex, more thoughtful, more nuanced, and more revealing. As the focus groups proceeded, boys became more animated and engaged. At the end of the session, boys often commented that they had enjoyed the opportunity to talk, share opinions and feelings, and be heard. Their genuine appreciation was often revealed by their desire to extend the hour-and-a-half meeting and continue the discussion. The boys would tell us that they didn't get to talk like this too often.

One boy who had not expressed or revealed anything particularly earth-shattering or private commented that he had never talked this much to his parents and he enjoyed the experience. As a result of these types of responses, we began to appreciate how powerful our simple focus group format was and how few opportunities boys have to share their opinions and feelings.

As parents, we must teach our boys the lesson that understanding their inner lives and emotions empowers rather than weakens them. After they gain this understanding, we can help them create a road map of their inner life. With this self-awareness, boys are better able to differentiate anger from sadness or frustration. When boys have the skills to understand their feelings, they can channel their feelings more easily into appropriate behavior.

Differences and Similarities in the Ways We Parent Our Sons and Daughters

Our experience shows us, and research supports our understanding, that we treat our sons differently from our daughters. The majority of the boys with whom we spoke agreed that their parents and other adults treat them differently because they are boys. For example, we give our boys more freedom than we give our girls. One girl remarked, "If you're a girl, your parents will be much more protective of you. My parents have a lot of trouble with my growing up and being more independent." Parents tolerate more distance from sons than we think is healthy, and the opposite may be true for daughters.

Parents deal differently with misbehavior, often depending on the child's gender. Boys are punished more frequently, and girls receive an explanation of why the particular conduct is inappropriate. Some boys even said that their parents seem more suspicious of their conduct, often assuming they are misbehaving without trying to learn the full story. One mother confirmed this perception: "When I see my son in trouble, to me it would be trouble that he caused." When this happens at school (see Chapter 6) and at home, the message is solidified. Boys in our focus groups reported how they were treated differently from their sisters. As one boy observed, "When my sister gives my parents her sugary sweet face, she can get exactly what she's asking for." According to these boys, their parents "let her [the sister] do what she wants." Other comments included "They always tell me no, and they tell her yeah," and "They give her what she wants when she asks for it." Although it's hard to admit, we more often expect our sons to solve their own problems themselves, but we readily jump in to protect and fix our daughters' problems.

Another area in which many of us treat our sons and daughters differently concerns physical affection. Many parents remember the moment when their little boy began to stiffen when hugged or kissed in public. In a focus group, one mother recalled this turning point with her son. When he turned 10, he said to her, "I just can't hug you now. I know I will again one day." As early as age 5, boys begin announcing to parents that kisses are no longer acceptable, particularly in public. One mother told us about saying good-bye to her son. When she carpools her 9-year-old, Ben, and his friends to school, he waits for his friends to walk away from the car and then comes around to the driver's side to kiss his mother good-bye. Because hugging and kissing are a normal part of greeting and expressing love and friendship between men and between parents and children in other cultures, the restraints boys feel about showing affection in American culture cannot be blamed entirely on biology.

The Paradox of Aggression

We also see major differences in the ways girls and boys express anger. In our focus groups, a mother told us about her daughter's struggle with explosive anger. One night her daughter, Morgan, asked for a new hoodie. When her mother said it wasn't necessary with summer coming on, Morgan flew into a fit of rage and started to scream. Morgan's mom had long been worried about similar outbursts and her daughter's seeming inability to handle frustration. The next day, during a quiet moment, the mother tried a little probing.

With encouragement, Morgan revealed that the girls in her peer group had been taunting her for being "fat." Morgan desperately wanted to avoid being picked on and explained that the hoodie was her way of hiding her body. "Buy this for me" actually meant, "Help me to deal with my friends and body image."

Morgan's mom practiced direct, gentle, supportive communication to determine the underlying cause of Morgan's outburst. This mom didn't get caught up in the words her daughter was using; instead, she listened to the tone of Morgan's voice, which revealed that something else was going on. Eventually, Morgan and her mom became very effective at communicating without yelling and, indeed, often with a mere glance or eye message. This breakthrough created a more trusting and satisfying relationship for both of them. In fact, Morgan's self-esteem was boosted because she subsequently felt good about how well she could handle her anger.

Morgan's way of coping is not unusual. Girls use compensation techniques to mask the true reasons for their behavior. Parents of boys know they use techniques for avoiding detailed verbal communication to protect themselves from criticism. Boys may not show or share their angst. While girls may communicate many details, they redirect their feelings to protect themselves from the risk of someone thinking they're doing something wrong. Girls learn to disagree in indirect and less confrontational ways. A snarky eye roll or running off to text a friend is a typical response.

Boys can express anger, and sometimes it seems that is the only emotion they are allowed to express. They learn to express anger when they are frustrated, disappointed, and sad. By believing the myth that "boys will be boys," boys feel that anger and violence are two of the very few avenues by which they can express their emotions. Without the skills and vocabulary of emotion and developing empathy, boys can turn to anger and violence to prove their competence. We train boys to think of themselves as "winners or losers," and those who are labeled as losers can become dangerous to themselves and others. We have seen evidence of this in the rapid escalation of shootings in our schools and our homes. As James Garbarino states in *Lost Boys: Why Our Sons Turn Violent and How Can We Save Them*, "If we understand the sadness in boys, we'll deal with that sadness and not have to wait to have to cope with their aggression" (1999, p. 16).

Psychologist Susan Wechsler worries about "how easy it is for some boys to disconnect themselves from others. It seems more than simple independence and has a more negative feel to it" (personal communication, September 23, 2013). Another psychologist, Donna Shoom-Kirsch, believes that "this alienation permits disrespect and the blaming of others. It also fuels apathy and lack of empathy, and may contribute to the increase of violence in schools" (personal communication, May 29, 2014). If we raise our boys to have a lack of empathy, it makes sense that they won't be averse to inflicting violence on or harassing others. We see the results in schools, at work sites, and the movie theater, malls, and Navy Yard killings, all perpetrated by men. As therapists tell us, one of the most important things that we as parents can do is to increase our children's capacity for empathy, and to help them understand what it's like to be in the shoes of the victim whom our children or others are harassing.

Boys, Girls, and Everybody Else: Gender Diversities

Not every child fits easily into male and female categories. Because female and male are on a spectrum, other identifiers are used across adolescent development. Those teens who do not fit into these discrete categories are referred to as nonconforming sexual or gender minorities. Today's young people across the gender spectrum often are more aware of their own and their peers' sexual identity, expression, and orientation. Many have changed from "this is appalling to, you know, what is wrong with that?" (Kepple, Page, & Gainer, 2012). However, their parents are often less accepting of these differences and expect that their children will "grow out of it" and/or struggle with sexual orientation issues.

The sea change is that many teens are more comfortable and open about their own sexual orientation and much more accepting of it in friends and family members than their parents are. One mother recalled telling her 14-year-old daughter about her brother: "I told Ashton that her dad and I had something important to discuss. We took a walk on the beach to let her know about my brother, who recently came out. Ashton responded, 'Is that all? I thought you were going to tell me that you and dad were getting a divorce or that one of you was sick. I know Uncle Bob is gay.'" While this acceptance and "no big deal" are true for some teens and their families, we have to remain vigilant advocates for those who still require support.

Despite increased awareness of and more positive media attention to nonconforming sexual minorities, they continue to face many challenges. These challenges include feeling different from peers, feeling shame about sexual orientation, worrying about parents' response, and being rejected and harassed by others. The fear of rejection from both society and parents is very strong. Many teenagers know to keep their sexual orientation secret, because coming out in an unwelcome climate can be fatal (Greytak, Kosciw, & Diaz, 2009).

Just as children are often confounded by their parent's or parents' sexual relationships, many parents are likewise uncomfortable with their adolescents' growing romantic and sexual interests. The same kids who may have turned their heads away during a romantic interlude in a movie will now have natural curiosities about their own and others' bodies. Having a child who doesn't conform to society's heterosexist norms becomes even more challenging.

One 13-year-old daughter expressed to her parent that she was attracted to all people, not a specific gender. Today this is called pansexuality. The girl's mother later recalled her reaction:

> Although I accept and love Taylor, it has taken me time to get here.
> I feel I am on a journey, trying to figure out as I go how to best

support Taylor. I have some guilt, when I think to myself that I wish Taylor was different. But I put those feelings aside, and I am at a place that I can tell Taylor, "Whatever makes you happy." But I would be lying if I didn't say it is an adjustment. I live in the world, and the world is hetero-normative. I don't want my kid to be a target. We take for granted the acceptance that is given to heterosexuals. I need a category to better understand where Taylor fits. I can handle gay, and I can handle straight, but I struggle with this category.

Parents do not have the power or control to cause their children to become lesbian, gay, bisexual, transgender, queer (LGBTQ) or straight. James, 14, reported, "I went through hell because there was no one for me to talk to. I had these feelings, and I couldn't explain them . . . but they hurt, and I needed someone to talk to. I never got that, and I needed it." If your child identifies as LGBTQ, you must listen to him or her with respect and avoid dismissing the child by saying that he or she is going through a temporary phase. Support is available for parents who feel confused, angry, or unhappy about their children's sexual orientation. Groups such as PFLAG (formerly known as Parents, Families and Friends of Lesbians and Gays), whose contact information is available on the Internet, can provide you with the support of other parents who will share their own experiences and wisdom.

Gender Identity

The language about gender continues to evolve as we gain more awareness and understanding. We're sure there will be new terms by the time you read this chapter. According to the American Psychological Association, awareness about one's sexual identity starts very young. *Gender identity* refers to one's sense of self as male, female, or transgender. When a child's gender identity and biological sex are not congruent, the person may identify as transsexual or as another transgender category (American Psychological Association, 2011). *Sexual orientation* is different from sexual identity. Sexual orientation refers to the sex of those to whom one is sexually and romantically attracted. Categories typically include gay or lesbian (homosexuals), straight (heterosexuals), and bisexuals. Research suggests that sexual orientation doesn't always appear in such definable categories and, instead, occurs on a continuum.

Gender identity may be fluid for some people (American Psychological Association, 2011). Thus, to understand the complexities of gender identity, we must explain the concepts of *gender solid* and *gender fluid*. One mother's story offers an example:

> When I was six, in the early fifties, I knew three things: if you told me I was a boy, I would have been happy because I could have been a ball boy at Fenway Park; my dad had more power than my mom; and my brothers had fewer chores. At six, being a ball boy was the height of my six-year-old ambitions. They told me I was a girl, I grew up as a girl, my parts are a girl, and I am OK with this. My ideas of clothes are jeans and a T-shirt, even though I dress more traditionally for work.

This mother's story is an example of a girl who is gender fluid. She's comfortable accepting her identity as a girl and comfortable expanding the options available to her as a girl and as a woman. She also said, "My husband, on the other hand, served a term in the Marines and came out of the womb playing with toy soldiers. If you had said at the age of six, 'Mark, you're not really a boy, you're a girl,' he would have been horrified and said something like, 'Oh no, cooties!'" Mark's reaction is consistent with someone who is gender solid. His body and society's expectations of him match perfectly.

Finally, *gender expression* refers to the way a person acts to communicate gender within a given culture, such as through clothing and interests (American Psychological Association, 2011). Some children call themselves *gender queer*, and some professionals refer to transgender teens as *gender variant*. Girls and boys who realize they are gender variant often are aware early on that they don't fit in, but they're not sure why. Catherine Hyde, Transgender Coordinator, PFLAG Colum-bia-Howard County, MD, and Regional Director, Mid-Atlantic, PFLAG National, calls these children *gender creative*. She asks that we keep the definition as broad as possible: *trans steric* covers transsexual, transgender, and the entire trans community (personal communica-tion, November 13, 2013).

Some people are very gender fluid and can move back and forth across the male-to-female spectrum. *Trans girls* are children who were born with male genitals yet identify as girls, and *trans boys* are children who were born with girl parts yet identify as boys. Often young boys who exhibit interest in wearing tutus and enjoy typically girl activities get extra pushback, which creates a greater disconnect for them, whereas we tolerate a little more gender fluidity with girls. So if girls want to play with trucks and be superheroes, we are more likely to accept that behavior. In her article "When Kids Play Across Gender Lines," Emanuella Grinberg says, "Boys are more likely to get picked on for stepping outside of the box to play with dolls or wear a pink backpack than girls are for playing with cars or wearing jeans" (2012). Because of these stereotypes, girls don't run into opposition as early as boys; they often experience this opposition beginning in puberty.

The Risks Facing LGBTQ Teens

Some LGBTQ teens exhibit signs of depression, manifested by isolating themselves socially and having lower self-esteem and lower school performance. These signs of distress should not be ignored, because LGBTQ youth are two to six times more likely to attempt suicide than straight teens are (Kosciw et al., 2012). According to the American Academy of Child and Adolescent Psychiatry's website, they account for 30 percent of all completed suicides among teens (Kosciw et al., 2012).

LGBTQ teens who do have the courage to come out risk being teased mercilessly. A young lesbian teen told us, "Going through the halls, I'd get called names and pushed. There was never any end to people laughing at me. Some of the girls wouldn't be friends with me because they thought I would always be coming on to them. Do they come on to every boy? I don't think so. Why wouldn't I want to be just friends like everyone else?" With this response to their sexual orientation, lesbian and gay teens are forced into isolation at a time when they need connection and support.

Integration of a positive adult identity is a challenge for all teens and especially LGBTQ teenagers because they learn from a young age that being anything besides straight carries a stigma. Lauren, a high school junior, said this:

> I have a hard time around my girlfriends because they often say things about queers, fags, and dykes, and it cuts through me like a knife. I haven't told anyone at school that I'm a lesbian, because I'm just not ready. And the more offhand comments I hear, the less secure I get. It's starting to get in the way of my relationships, and I find myself being alone more. It's simpler to hide in my room and stop going to parties than to listen to all the insensitive comments and judgments that make me feel worthless.
>
> This summer I worked at a day camp with a counselor who started a support group for lesbians at her school. I wish I had a group of friends that I could be real with. Maybe it would make me feel secure enough to open up to my straight friends.

Life for LGBTQ teenagers is even more difficult than for other teenagers, so their need for their parents' help and support is even greater than that of their peers.

Lauren's friend at camp is one of many teenagers who do not shy away from the subject of sexual orientation. Many brave teens are part of an emerging LGBTQ youth agenda that addresses safe schools, suicide prevention, and AIDS prevention. Other teens are taking their girlfriends or boyfriends to the prom and refusing to hide their orientation from other teenagers. At T. C. Williams High School in Alexandria, Virginia, a gay student ran for prom queen and won. Other teens have also shared more positive experiences when coming out. Megan, 15, said, "I had a totally welcoming experience, although boys are still curious about what we do when we're alone. I finally bought a shirt with a saying that reads, "Yes I am, and no you can't watch."

High school girls also talked about their gay friends. "Tyler is one of my best friends," said Alexis. "We talk about everything. He's one of the strongest people I know, and I'm so proud of him every day. He still faces teasing from the jocks, but he is still hopeful that even that will change. I can't imagine ever not being friends with him." This acceptance is in alignment with the sea change that has taken place nationally about LGBTQ. According to a *USA Today*/Gallup 2012 poll, there is rising optimism among LGBTQ Americans that issues involving homosexuality will one day no longer divide the nation. This optimism is due in part to the increasing acceptance of same-sex marriage (53 percent of poll participants) and the increased acceptance of LGBTQ Americans in their communities (91 percent of poll participants) (Kepple et al., 2012).

Even with this progress, we found that boys have, to a greater or lesser degree, significant fear of stepping outside the box. Homophobia is still so profound; the concept extends to any emotion or feeling that is considered to be feminine. In today's schools, students think there is nothing more demeaning than to be called gay or fag; antigay harassment is not just directed at gays and lesbians, it's the most common form of harassment among all teenagers (Kosciw et al., 2012). While we have reason to be optimistic, it is still a struggle for teens to be different. We are fortunate to have federal and state-level policies (California and Connecticut, for example) protecting LGBTQ teens until the rest of our society catches up (Kosciw et al., 2012).

In a focus group, some boys said that although they can accept homosexuality as a valid sexual orientation, they prefer not to spend much time with overtly "feminine" boys for fear of such boys "coming on" to them. Some girls in our focus groups confirmed this self-consciousness. One girl told us that when boys participate in traditionally feminine activities, such as dance and drama, they risk being labeled gay. In fact, more than 60 percent of the high school students in the 2011 National School Climate Survey said they had heard negative remarks about gender expression—frequently or often not acting "masculine enough" or "feminine enough" (Kosciw et al., 2012). The pressure not to disclose sexual orientation makes many gay, transgender, and bisexual teens more likely to attempt suicide and take risks, sexual and otherwise, that endanger their health (Kosciw et al., 2012).

Another target of attack is a boy's competence. Boys' fear of failure and discomfort with intimacy also come from needing to avoid being labeled a "wuss," "pansy," "fag," "loser," "sissy," "dork," or "mama's boy," and from needing others to affirm his competence. Now calling someone "gay" can also mean stupid. The consequence is that boys may feel embarrassed at showing any soft or emotional attributes or behaviors, including intimacy. When you talk to your teens about homophobia, it is important to discuss how this bias confines people to rigid sex roles. Such roles prevent our girls and boys from being themselves.

Many of these kids have found solace on the Internet, making it their lifeline. A parent of a gay 16-year-old teen saw this: "The most vulnerable teenage group before were gay kids, right? They had no community that they could come out to. When the Internet came, before you even had the openness you have now, I think the Internet is a lifesaver for so many kids." This can be especially true for gay teens who live in small towns and may feel like the "only one."

Providing Space and Support for LGBTQ Teens

A 2010 study by San Francisco State University found that LGBTQ adolescents with accepting parents not only were more confident, but also were at much lower risk of depression and substance abuse (Sadowski, 2010). Caitlin Ryan, director of the Family Acceptance Project at San Francisco State University, says, "We found that parents and caregivers can modify rejecting behaviors when they understand how their reactions to their LGBT children—their specific words, actions, and behaviors—affect their children's health, mental health, and well-being" (2010). Dr. Diane Ehrensaft, author of *Gender Born, Gender Made*, wrote,

You listen to the children. Given the space, they will tell you. You also grow to understand that establishing an authentic gender self is a journey that may unfold and change over time. You get help from a trained professional if you are confused and would like someone to think about it with you. The most important thing is to sort out how your child is expressing him or herself now and what s/he needs to feel expansive and good about his or her gender identity and gender behaviors. (2012)

But allowing children to express their own chosen identity, even at a preschool age, can prevent frustration and anger down the line. According to Ehrensaft, "It is not a matter of labeling or projecting into the future, but knowing who your child is right now" (2012). Catherine Hyde writes,

Lots of people believe that children are too young to know that they are really a girl or a boy or that they are attracted to other girls or boys. We have children who tell us that they know from a very young age that they are gay. Not all trans are solid identifiers. So I tell parents, "With any journey one step illuminates the next. Don't jump in by giving your child hormones. Start with one step at a time: 'Sweetie, you can wear any dress you want and I will stand beside you. ''Is this working?''Is this the right thing for you?'" (personal communication, November 13, 2013)

Lynn Mueller, the former coordinated student services specialist for the Maryland State Department of Education, Division of Student, Family, and School Support, confirms this advice: "Go for the ride, just ride with them. It will have ups and downs, like any ride" (personal communication, November 13, 2013). However, Mueller adds that when students are undergoing hormone treatment or puberty blockers, the school community needs to understand that they are transitioning from one gender to the other. The school community can implement the following measures to support LGBTQ students:

* Adopt and implement comprehensive bullying/sexual harassment policies that specifically speak to nonconforming sexual minority youth.
* Support student clubs that provide support for LGBTQ students (for example, Gay-Straight Alliance).
* Provide professional development for school staff so they have a better understanding of how to support LGBTQ students, increase their accountability when they see harassing and bullying behaviors, and recognize the impact on students when they don't have this information.

With these kinds of measures in place, all students will have a greater opportunity to learn and be successful in school and beyond.

Without support, many parents are rightfully frightened, because they know that the world is not a friendly place for those who are different. Parents can't protect their kids from prejudice, but they can have open and honest conversations, teach them how to navigate society, let them know they are not alone, and get support when they need it. These parenting strategies will help their children develop the grit and perseverance to respond to a more hostile world and become resilient.

Protecting the Emotional Life of Teens

While the dynamics of development are somewhat different for boys and girls, the consequences are similar: they disconnect from their true selves and from their families. To minimize this occurrence, we have to provide adolescents with opportunities to develop emotional and moral courage. Each gender can be free from the constraints of cultural straitjackets only when young women and young men break out of strict cultural stereotypes. One gender frees the other. Girls do not grow or benefit at the expense of boys, and boys do not grow or benefit at the expense of girls. Without the pressure to "prove" their manhood or womanhood, boys and girls can grow in ways that are natural and comfortable, rather than in reaction to preconceived ways of being.

The issues associated with giving our children more models for emotional expression are important for both genders. Girls and boys must be able to reach their full potential, with a complete range of emotional expressiveness. We need to value attachment as the primary task of human growth, for both boys and girls, because without community and closeness, we fail to thrive as individuals and as members of society, regardless of our social class, race, culture, or gender. The consequences of repressed feelings for both boys and girls can be unsatisfactory relationships. Gender stereotyping can create health issues, risky behavior, and less authentic communication with family and friends. Whereas girls might turn to starvation or self-mutilation as emotional outlets, boys might drive too fast, drink too much, take drugs, commit vandalism, skip school, and sleep around. The girls' behavior is seen as self-destructive and a plea for help; the boys' behavior is often dismissed as simply "bad."

We agree with parents, researchers, and teens in our focus groups: adolescents still need a strong connection to their parents. Teens need a family relationship that helps them to confront stereotyping and become the best they can be and reminds them that they are not defined by what others expect. Some of our favorite practices to help teens confront stereotypes include giving girls opportunities to find their own voice, use it, and not be derailed by labels; giving boys permission to rely on others when they need to; giving girls permission to own their successes; teaching boys to know what they are feeling by helping to label these feelings, beginning when they are very young;

allowing boys to express a full range of emotions; and allowing all of our children to become who they deserve to be, finding their authentic self.

How should you parent your daughters and sons? We are not aware of any society or culture that treats girls and boys the same way. Unless you live on another planet, you do need to parent boys and girls differently to counteract the negative messages society sends them. But more than that, we think we need to parent each child as an individual. We need to look at each child's personality, strengths, weaknesses, and the way society affects him or her, and then parent accordingly. We want your teens to have the freedom to find out who they are, speak their minds, and have meaningful relationships. Once we give them permission to make mistakes and explore new territory (cognitively, socially, emotionally, and physically), boys and girls will be better able to become resilient adults.

4

Media Takes on Teen Culture

Whoever controls the media, controls the mind.

—Jim Morrison

As boys and girls move from childhood into adolescence, they begin to redefine themselves. This evolution is a complex process that includes creating a new self-image, adjusting to and developing an ethical and moral code, coping with sexuality, understanding gender expectations, and preparing for future lives as men, women, and workers. While girls and boys are exposed to multiple cultural influences during this process of change, the media now have unprecedented influence on their development. In fact, according to *NBC News*, American teenagers spend 31 hours per week watching TV, 3 hours watching movies, and at least 16.7 hours a week online (Weaver, 2013). While the numbers from the polling sources may vary, they all demonstrate that our teens are spending enormous chunks of their day juggling numerous forms of media at a time. Theirs is an ADHD world with multitasking at its core. Unless your teens are living under a rock or unconscious, media seep into every part of their lives.

Now that media have so many delivery systems, our children are inundated by relentless messages that vie for their attention with the intent of making them "good" consumers. These messages sell a narrow vision for social success. They make it clear that being beautiful and sexy are prized values for girls, and boys need to be powerful while seeming strong and in control.

Media and cosmetic corporations study teens carefully to understand how to push their buttons and get them to buy products. Marketing to teens is considered successful when it creates an unnecessary need that didn't exist before. Media's main goal is to sell products or services that solve the very problems they create. Unfortunately these messages do more than sell products; they sell judgments about body image, self-worth, social values, and behavior.

The goal of the advertising industry is to increase insecurity to sell more products. Consequently, advertisers prey on teens' desire to conform. One remedy for this onslaught of manipulation is media knowledge, and both girls and boys can benefit from recognizing the extent to which they are being targeted as a consumer group. It's all about creating need. One mother said, "My daughter, Devin, knows the names of designers and products I can't afford to buy. She's sixteen years old and is saving for a Prada purse. Give me a break! My daughter is considering spending hundreds, all her allowance and birthday money, on one purse because it makes her feel sophisticated. If she needs a label so badly, I should tattoo one on her wrist."

Parents can provide the antidote to the media's manipulation and negative messages by arming their teenagers with critical-thinking skills. Because the media target teens with "pink" and "blue" intent, let's look at this through a gendered lens, beginning with a discussion of teenage girls.

Mirror, Mirror on the Wall

Appearance is one of the primary expressions of self in our culture. The definition of womanhood has varied over time and across cultures. Teenage pudginess was more accepted in the past. According to JoAnn Deak in *Girls Will Be Girls*, "When most of us were this age, prepubescent girls weren't expected to look like glamour models" (2002). However, as in older times, beauty remains a prized attribute. Teenage girls struggle with the sometimes competing standards of beauty and capability. Currently, coming far behind, girls are supposed to be competent, but trust us, the drive to be thin has a staggering lead. Most girls and young women report being unhappy with their bodies. Because they don't like their bodies, they are dissatisfied with *themselves*. In fact, 42 percent of first- to third-grade girls want to be thinner, while 81 percent of 10-year-olds are afraid of getting fat, and 80 percent of 10-year-old American girls say they have been on a diet (The Representation Project, 2014a).

This even happens as early as preschool! Sophie, a vivacious four-year-old, asked her mother, "Mommy, what's that black line on your eyes?" Her mom told her it was makeup, and Sophie smiled and said, "I love makeup; makeup makes you beautiful." Her mom answered, "Oh, Sophie, you're already beautiful, and I'm beautiful, your brother Josh is beautiful, and daddy's beautiful," to which Sophie replied, "Yes, Mommy, we're all beautiful unless you're chubby!" When preschoolers are already focused on body image, it's no surprise that the number one desire of young girls aged 11 to 17 is to be thinner (The Representation Project, 2014a).

In 2004, marketers for Unilever's Dove brand did a study they called "The Real Truth About Beauty: Revisited," on women's relationship with beauty. The study revealed that only 4 percent of women around the world consider themselves beautiful and that the anxiety and preoccupation about looks begins at an early age. In a study of over 1,200 girls aged 10–17, a majority, 72 percent, said they felt tremendous pressure to be beautiful (Unilever, 2011). The study also found that 6 of 10 girls alter some activities because they feel bad about their appearance!

Girls and young women view the image of the ultrathin fashion model as exciting. This has the power to make them feel unworthy, no matter how normal their bodies may be. Failing to achieve physical perfection creates anxiety and insecurity, because most women compare themselves with the impossible standards we see in the media, and we inevitably fall short. Yet what we see in the media is a manipulated, curated image that is often not achievable in nature. In a TED Talk, Victoria's Secret model Cameron Russell (2013) tells us that even most models feel their bodies fall short of the ideal. Russell faults the glamour industry when she says models are not in control of anything, even their own image. Their photos are retouched constructions by professionals who build the image they want. While the resulting photograph may be appealing, it is also very superficial and demonstrates that even some models feel they fall short of our unrealistic standards of beauty.

Hour after hour, American girls receive powerful signals to be thin, beautiful, and sexy. These "spectator sports" are among the most influential forces in the lives of girls. A 16-year-old sophomore, Stephanie, told us, "A girl can be anything . . . as long as she is thin and pretty." No matter how much has changed for girls, this attitude is part of the idealized folklore of modern femininity. "Pretty" is *the* standard by which girls are judged, and the media promote this tyranny of beauty.

The messages girls get from the media are destructive. They sell the idea that girls should be beautiful. In the past 30 years, the idealized woman has shrunk from Marilyn Monroe's size 12 to the insane size 0. Lisa, a mom who said she always thinks about her weight, got visibly angry when she said, "Size zero—just think about it—we are literally supposed to disappear! It's insane, and I'm not immune, which is why I'm so frustrated and mad!"

In the film *Miss Representation*, gender expert Jackson Katz explains this phenomenon of the shrinking ideal. He believes that as women have been challenging men's power in business, education, politics, and other areas of life, the images that have seeped into popular culture are of smaller women taking up less space. They are less threatening and highly sexualized, and Katz believes this is no coincidence. We see the image of physical power being taken away from women as they are challenging men in the larger world. The real danger of a narrow definition of beauty is how it erodes our daughters' confidence and contributes to eating disorders, putting our children in real danger (The Representation Project, 2014b).

The restrictive standards for how girls should look and act (thin, blond, tall, big breasts, long legs, straight hair, trendy clothes, tanned and smooth skin), are communicated through popular culture, other girls, and parents. As girls develop into young women, many of them struggle to attain a body type that nature never intended them to have. In 2010, the Girl Scout Research Institute in New York studied body image among 1,000 girls aged 8 to 17. While they found that about 63 percent of the girls surveyed think the models they see are too skinny and unrealistic, nearly half wish and strive to be as skinny as the models they critiqued. "The girls have a cognitive dissonance," explains Kimberlee Salmond, a senior research strategist at the Girl Scout Research Institute. "They know it's wrong for them and yet they continue to aspire to it" (Yadagaren, 2013). The problems associated with this cognitive dissonance and lack of self-esteem can lead to disordered thinking and destructive behaviors around body image, weight, and diet.

At the *Essence* Seventh Annual Black Women in Hollywood event, actress Lupita Nyong'o brilliantly articulated the power of seeing realistic images of yourself reflected in the media:

I remember a time when I too felt unbeautiful. I put on the TV and only saw pale skin. I got teased and taunted about my night-shaded skin. . . . And when I was a teenager my self-hate grew worse, as you can imagine happens with adolescence . . . then Alek Wek came on the international scene. A celebrated model, she was dark as night, she was on all of the runways and in every magazine and everyone was talking about how beautiful she was. . . . When I saw Alek I inadvertently saw a reflection of myself that I could not deny. Now, I had a spring in my step because I felt more seen, more appreciated by the faraway gatekeepers of beauty. But around me the preference for light skin prevailed. (*NewsOne*, 2014)

Because the predominant media images didn't reflect back her beauty, Nyong'o still felt unbeautiful. However, she found strength in the words of her mother, who said, "You can't eat beauty. It doesn't feed you," which Nyong'o heard as meaning beauty isn't enough to sustain you. She ended her talk with the hope that all teenagers can "feel the validation of your external beauty but also get to the deeper business of being beautiful inside. There is no shade to that beauty." Nyong'o's comments demonstrate that it's very hard to be satisfied with what you don't see.

Parents should ask themselves how they can protect their daughters from this onslaught of unrealistic body images and loss of self-esteem. What can you do to expand a girl's definition of beauty? There's nothing intrinsically wrong with girls trying to look the best they can. The problem is when girls damage their physical or psychological health in the pursuit of an unattainable marketed ideal of perfection.

Preoccupation with physical appearance is usually about fitting in. Teenage girls believe looking a certain way provides them access to the right clique and acceptance by boys. This preoccupation and dependence on external feedback is only a temporary fix; it doesn't sustain self-confidence. Nevertheless, the "appearance" of what good looks and an attractive body offers is so powerful for girls that it can undermine their individuality and competence.

The media's manipulated and perfected examples of beauty have created impossible standards. Even African American girls, who generally are more likely to be satisfied with their bodies, want to be thinner (Ross, 2014). This leaves millions of girls feeling inadequate, often causing eating disorders and other psychological challenges. Food is one of the few things they can control. Adrianne, a 15-year-old freshman, explained, "When I went into a new high school, I wanted desperately to be part of things. Everyone looked thin to me, so I thought if I had a better body, people would like and accept me."

When we sat at a kitchen table next to a male college student who was poring over his sister's latest issue of *Bazaar* magazine, the absurdity of an ideal appearance was obvious. Unprompted by us, he was stunned by the images he saw and told his sister,

> The women in this magazine look like they stepped off a doll assembly line. They are perfectly molded and sculptured pieces of art—not people. Art without the merit of creation or eye candy! Is this what women want to be? High heels—those can't be comfortable! Are they sexy? Yeah, but that's not what makes it for me. Why the overkill? These magazines create the illusion that this exaggeration [five-inch stiletto heels] is necessary. This is garbage. Your uniqueness is what is necessary. You need to set yourself apart, because you're never going to meet up to these standards.

What is so powerful about this unsolicited description is how surprised this young man was at the pressure girls feel to look a certain way—an impossible goal. It's no wonder generations of women seek irrational means (from starvation to surgery) to look a certain way. Trying to meet this ideal is impossible without Photoshop, airbrushing, and filters that make emaciated bodies look "better." The result leaves girls and women feeling bad about themselves, no matter how healthy, thin, disciplined, or fit they are.

Some environments, like gymnastics and ballet, are particularly punishing when it comes to body image. Barbara, the mother of 13-year-old Sydney, said,

> I really couldn't believe it when she came home from ballet and said, "Mom, Amy and I are the only girls who sweat, and my teacher told us to lose a little weight." This was horrifying to hear, especially because Sydney had always been pretty slender, and Amy was average size. I was outraged. I try hard to counter the images on TV and magazines by telling my daughter how unrealistic they are. And now her ballet teacher, who she really likes and wants to please, is undermining it all. My first impulse was to call the school and give them a

piece of my mind, but Sydney begged me not to call. I'm very torn. What about all the girls who don't tell their mothers when they are told to lose weight by teachers and coaches they respect? Do they then internalize the rigid ideals of these misguided mentors? The challenge of counteracting our culture is really more complicated than I thought.

Pretty Poison: Eating Disorders

American culture is preoccupied with body image and weight. Our advertisements are filled with images of beautiful young women used as backdrops and ornaments to sell cars, cake mixes, and cell phone service. In the United States, advertisers spent over $142 billion in 2010 (http://www.statisticbrain.com/ad-spending-statistics/). To understand the enormous size of this amount of money, imagine that 80 percent of the countries in the world have a gross national project lower than that (The Representation Project, 2014a).

An excessive struggle for perfection can result in a girl starving herself to attain a dangerous ideal, and just about every girl and mother we spoke with had stories to tell about eating disorders. As a consequence, some girls lead secretive and isolated lives, disconnected from family, friends, and themselves. Carly, diagnosed with bulimia, offers this blog post about her struggle:

It isn't easy to start being bulimic. It's gross and stupid and extreme ... but it's not easy. I remember with perfect clarity the first time I made myself throw up. I binged and binged so that I could get myself to the point where I didn't feel good, and then it took me about an hour to get it to come back up again. I don't write this out to be gross. I'm writing this out because there's a level of commitment to bulimia that is overlooked. It's not enough to just dismiss it as a behavior that can be discouraged with an after-school special. By the time you get to the point of actually crouching for an hour while you struggle with your gag reflex, you're beyond after-school specials. You need a solution. (Morgan, 2010)

The obsession with weight affects more girls than boys; as a result, girls struggle more with eating disorders. One former anorexic who now counsels teenage anorexics tells us that, in the 1990s, she worked with girls as young as 13, and now she's working with girls as young as 11. Obsession with weight is particularly painful for girls during puberty, when they tend to gain weight. Many girls don't understand that weight gained during puberty is not permanent. This is quite a stressful and emotional time, resulting in girls' being depressed twice as often as boys (The Representation Project, 2014a).

The diet of distorted images fed to girls is "disturbing and powerful" in the words of one focus-group teen. Seventeen-year-old Brook bent her head, looked up timidly, and said,

> I have to be honest, and I can't say that I haven't thought about how easy it would be to stick my fingers down my throat and get rid of the massive dinner that I had just eaten. But I can tell you for sure that I have never gone through with the temptation. I'll never forget being sick with the flu and vomiting in the bathroom. I must have been about 15, and while I was throwing up and my mother was holding my head over the toilet bowl, I told her that my teeth felt awful. My mother, who rarely misses any opportunity to pound some life lesson into my brain, regardless of her tactless timing, said, "I know, honey, this must be what they say a bulimic feels. They always say their teeth feel awful." The image is so gross and powerful that it is permanently burned into my brain.

Eating disorders are one subject where knowledge may not be a protective factor, because many anorexics hide their disordered eating and go underground. In the past, girls would exchange information about vomiting techniques in the school bathroom or at a sleepover; now they can find each other on the Internet, 24/7. Websites that surface under many names geared to girls who look for "thinspiration" include photographs of emaciated women that can entice a wavering anorexic back into a destructive eating pattern. Anorexics who would never have communicated with each other before can now find a community of like minds on the Internet. The *Daily Mail* quotes a teenager who states, "'I used to love trawling the pro-ana websites for tips and looking at pictures of the girls with their bones jutting out. I thought they were beautiful, and I started up my own blog, where I posted pictures of me, for other people to judge. They'd say I was too fat and I just wanted to please them by losing more weight" (*MailOnline*, 2013).

Anorexics view eating as weak and are proud of their willpower and control because they are able to endure starvation. The danger in this "outlaw" community is that the aberrant behavior is reinforced. The support girls give each other helps them deny that starvation is dangerous, a denial that ultimately can be deadly. Knowledge about the prevalence of eating disorders will not protect your daughters. However, by helping them to deemphasize the importance of physical appearance, you can mitigate the messages to be excessively thin.

Unlike with some issues, mothers and daughters must be in this struggle together. As one mother of a 17-year-old girl said, "I have been losing and gaining the same ten pounds since I was fifteen years old. Will I ever relax and just accept the size my body really wants to be?" Another mother said, "When I went to a dinner party with a new family, I couldn't stop looking at their fourteen-year-old daughter. Her face was so beautiful, but she was about twenty pounds overweight. I felt bad for her because her mother was so thin and small. I'm so obsessed with my own body size that I find myself ruminating over anybody else's weight." If we express this obsession about weight, our daughters will follow in our footsteps.

Nothing we are saying is news to most people who will read this book. However, you can make a difference in your daughter's acceptance of her body, and it has to begin with a mother's acceptance of herself. You must believe that you are "more than just a pretty face" and be intentional about what messages are sent to your daughters. In the film *Miss Representation*, Gloria Steinem says, "If every time you pass a mirror and downgrade your looks, remember a girl may be watching you, and that's what she is learning" (The Representation Project, 2014b).

In the midst of a teen climate of eating disorders, some teens do thrive. Seventeen-year-old Robyn said,

> My parents always made me feel beautiful. They loved the way I looked. I'm certainly not thin, but I'm not going to allow ten or fifteen pounds to stop me from feeling good about myself. I row crew for my high school, and in the boat, my strength and size really matters. Being on the crew team helps me believe that I am much more than my body shape, and if other people have a problem with it, it's their problem, not mine. Look at Lena Dunham—she's not thin, and she sure struts her stuff.

Although female film roles have become more varied, the images, as a whole, remain daunting. With the exception of Lena Dunham in *Girls*, most actors fit the thin body image mold. The actors playing the roles of police officers are strong and powerful but still beautiful and thin; actors playing the roles of lawyers are smart and articulate but still beautiful and thin; and doctors are skilled and compassionate but also beautiful and thin. We continue to give girls a mixed message; as Stephanie said earlier, "A girl can be anything . . . as long as she's thin and pretty." The power of the media is enormous, making too many of our daughters feel fat, invisible, or unacceptable. Media's impact is primary because it is ubiquitous, and children begin absorbing its imagery before they are toddlers.

Advertisements and Magazines: Shop Till You Drop

Absorbing all these idealized images contributes to many women's evaluation of their bodies. Amber, a 17-year-old, said,

> I remember looking at the underwear ads and comparing myself to the bodies in the advertisements. The camera angle gave the models a dramatic elongated look. I'm five feet four inches, and most of my

height is from my waist up. I think that I am really supposed to be five feet two inches. The models in the ads were stripped of their clothes, and their bodies were so sleek, even the men. Not like my legs. I wax, I shave, and I still have bumps. I used to look in the mirror and obsess over my short legs.

It's important for parents to be knowledgeable about what advertisers are trying to sell kids, how products are packaged, and how advertisers manipulate consumers by using idealized physiques. These Photoshop-enhanced images have a profound power that your children internalize, which can only be balanced by becoming media savvy.

Ashley, a 17-year-old, said, "It's a little crazy making; these teen magazines try to educate girls about things like birth control and healthy girlfriend-boyfriend relationships, and then they show us looking like tramps in stilettos. I wish they'd make up their minds: Are we adults or kids?" While some of the articles are informative, magazines depend on selling advertisements. One mother said, "If most girls felt good about themselves, if they didn't smoke, drink, or wear makeup, advertisers would really suffer." Therefore, most teen magazines have resorted to the same ads as women's magazines, featuring rail-thin models and articles about dieting. In "Trash Magazines with Training Wheels," Janelle Brown reports that the teenage market represents $158 billion in spending power, and girls spend 75 percent of this money on clothing. Magazines and online sites are perfect vehicles for getting a portion of the teens' or parents' wallet and heavily influence what teenage girls buy (2001).

Impact of Negative Body Image

Another reason why it is so important to be aware of the messages you give your daughter about her appearance and capabilities is that depression in girls is often connected to negative feelings about their physical features and abilities. One exasperated mother said, "The other day, my daughter, Caitlin, said to me, 'Mom, I'm having fits. I'm so fat.' And I didn't say anything. I didn't come back and say, 'Oh, no, you're not, honey.' I just said, 'Well, if you want, I'll go walking with you later this afternoon when you come home,' and Caitlin's response to me was, 'Well, thanks a lot for not being there.'" Lydia, the mother of 17-year-old Samantha, says,

> It was pure heartache when I took my daughter, Samantha, to get a prom dress for the junior prom. She cried and said that every dress made her look fat. After looking at the pile of crumpled gowns on the dressing room floor, I felt so disappointed, frustrated, and sad that her image was so distorted. I finally said to her, "Samantha, how could you look fat in a size eight?" I haven't been a size eight since I was in seventh grade. Get real—don't ruin a potentially wonderful time with an inaccurate self-perception!

A teenage girl's constant worry about how the outside world views her is distracting to her well-being. These worries drain a girl's energy, enthusiasm, and focus on other attributes, including competence. While much of the pressure to be thin comes from the media, the earliest and most influential messages regarding our bodies do come from family. Your unintended comments can demonstrate how daughters (and perhaps sons) can resist this pressure. The easiest way for you to encourage your daughter's healthier body image is to refrain from commenting about your own weight, being fat, or constantly judging your own looks and others'. It's perfectly normal, for example, for adolescent girls to have body fat. Most young girls put on weight before they enter puberty and grow; this is nature's way of getting women ready for reproductive development.

Beauty doesn't guarantee self-esteem. Physical appearance is only one element; it may get you in the door, but it doesn't keep you there. But even though we may say, "Beauty's only skin deep," few believe it! Sometimes we can learn these lessons from our daughters. Alison, an

18-year-old high school senior, told us about her mother's body fixation:

> Ever since I can remember, my mother warned me about getting fat. I was never fat, but could always stand to lose about 5 to 10 pounds. I know that this doesn't sound like much, but all of it sits on my hips and rear, and I can go down a whole pants size if I lose the weight. My closet has two pants sizes, chubby Alison and thin Alison. I am not as tortured by this as my mom. Even when I feel fine about myself, I sense her eyes settling on my rear. She offers me unwanted advice on how to dress defensively and looks pretty outraged when I don't try to mask my figure faults. When I ask her why she just won't give it up, she tells me that it's for my own good.

Alison continued, "Thank God for sports. It's been like an antidote to my mom's pressure for me to be thin. I think I have a healthier view of my body because I'm athletic and play varsity field hockey. These legs work fine. My hips and rear don't interfere with my performance on the field, and most guys don't seem to mind either."

Alison's story demonstrates how providing other spheres of interest can increase a positive self-concept and serve as a protective factor. Girls who are athletic present themselves with confidence for many reasons. They are fit, tend to have higher self-esteem, and are focused on their performance, not just their appearance. They also create deep bonds of friendship with teammates, giving them a solid framework of friends.

Slutty Dressing: Sexualized and Provocative Images

Today's fashions are more physically revealing than ever before, and parents are battling with their daughters about what is too sexual. Many girls want to fit in, and they confuse being "sexy" with being cool. One middle-school teacher said, "The issue of provocative dressing and body image is such a tough one. I can remember being sent home from school when my skirt was still covering my kneecap. Now girls show skin and underwear routinely. Underwear is now outerwear. I would've died if either my bra strap or slip showed when I was a girl." Furthermore, the practice of girls dressing more provocatively is happening at younger ages.

"Slutty" dressing can be viewed in two contradictory ways. On the one hand, you could see provocative dressing as a statement of independence and freedom. On the other, it is surrendering to the sexualized culture to gain attention. When we asked younger teenage boys what they thought about sexy dressing, they usually smiled and said, "What do you think? We're boys; we like it." But boys a few years older had very different reactions, especially to the younger, middle-school girls who dress like Miley Cyrus. Noah, an 18-year-old, said, "When girls begin dressing in a sexually stimulating way, at even younger ages, we pigeonhole them into sexual objects with less power than guys."

Parents are uncomfortable, too. The mother of 13-year-old Lucy said,

> I'm mortified to admit that last week I told Lucy she looked like a slut. I know that calling your child names is found in the "don't ever do that" section of any childrearing manual, but I finally lost it. She layers two tank tops with her bra straps hanging out. I wonder what corporate head decided to manufacture mini adult items like shoes with high platforms for tweens and dresses that fit like tube tops? Certainly one without a young daughter! I'm at a loss. All her friends, some of them really good students, dress incredibly provocatively, so I'm confused about how much to rein her in. I don't think she understands what message she is sending to boys and men. I'm worried that someone will take advantage of her.

When we talked with young men aged 22 to 30, we found that they, too, were uncomfortable with this in-your-face sexuality of young girls. Many were concerned because they could no longer distinguish between girls they should ask out and "jailbait."

Too often, parents are reluctant to step in by refusing to buy suggestive items or making their daughters change clothes, because they want to be liked and they want their daughters to "fit in." You need to make sure that your daughter, in the name of self-expression, is not projecting an unintended (or even intended) sexual message.

Makeup and the Dream of Beauty

In today's culture, makeup serves a variety of purposes for girls throughout their development. Young girls are first introduced to makeup through play. Many parents worry about their daughters' early interest in makeup and conclude that a girl's attraction to it forecasts obedience to popular culture; others see it differently. The mother of 14-year-old Annie shared her concerns:

> I'll tell you what I found out with these kids, with my own anyway. They loved makeup. They bought it a lot, not unlike boys collecting baseball cards or like when I collected stickers. My daughter, Annie, collected makeup and treated it as a cross between a grown-up product and a toy. For Annie and her friends, makeup helped them to straddle child and adult worlds.
>
> Now I view Annie's interest in makeup with a whole different mind set. I realize that the significance I attached to makeup is loaded, and that it may have a completely different meaning to many pre-adolescents. I worry that Annie's overly attached to the idea that she has to be a slave to beauty, but I may be overreacting.

Indeed, with some girls, it is helpful to steer them to an interest that isn't associated with society's mandate to be beautiful. Makeup, in and of itself, is another transitional object, one that can take on a greater or lesser importance. Whether or not you condone your teenage daughter's buying and wearing makeup clearly depends on what she is expressing.

The Sky Is Not Falling: Healthier Messages

A parent's best instrument to combat the bombardment of simplistic messages and marketing products is literacy. Look at your daughter's magazines and read them with her. Ask her whether it makes sense that they feature healthy eating while picturing waif-like anorexics selling products. Ask her if the article about college majors makes sense next to the ad showing the back of a half-naked woman sitting spread-eagle in a very suggestive position. Explain to your daughter that the photos of the beautiful models are not real, and remind her that those images are the result of the magic of enhanced imagery; with computer software, filters, and touch-ups, we would all look different.

In spite of all the changes in the last several decades, author and doctor Nancy Snyderman believes, girls still wrestle with the dichotomy between the old messages of femininity and the new messages of be all you want to be (2002). This conflict is confirmed by women's obsession with physical perfection. They still are driven by their desire to be appealing, especially to men. We have to teach our daughters that their bodies are not the "ultimate" or only expression of self, despite the countless seductive messages society concocts to sell products.

You should teach your children to be critical consumers by becoming aware of what teenage girls read, listen to, and see on every screen. Teenagers need to understand that advertisers target them to sell products by playing on their insecurities. Assist them to be cynical and insightful about consumerism, including what they read and see. Teens learn that by becoming knowledgeable, they can help themselves, and they can make a difference to others when they become more critical consumers.

Want to see how scary it is out there? Websites such as www .pro-thinspo.com and others offer "thinspiration" tips for limiting eating, along with advice on hiding an eating disorder. The content features a photo gallery of emaciated girls and women. It advocates for treacherous behavior, like the "50-day anorexic diet," eating

500 calories or less. (See Fact Sheet 4, "Warning Signs of an Eating Disorder," at the back of the book).

The Internet is no different from any marketplace where you can find good along with bad. Recently, the Dove Campaign for Real Beauty (Unilever, 2004) is broadening our view of women's beauty. And when Spain banned extremely thin models from fashion runways, Dove responded by producing a wonderful video showing one model before and after a makeup application. The video, which depicts the makeover of a real woman into a model, powerfully demonstrates how unrealistic perceptions of beauty are created (Unilever, 2006). Antidotes to the inundation of false images exist, many on the Internet, but we have to look for them. Unfortunately, they are less accessible than the enormous onslaught of perfection fed to both girls and boys. That's where parents must help. We can find them and be deliberate about searching and sharing them with our families. Positive changes come as a result of raising consumer consciousness and speaking out.

The best advice to parents is to seek out powerful and positive images for your daughter. The film *Real Women Have Curves* (2002) features America Ferrara advocating for her right to be respected for her larger body. In one of the most inspiring scenes, she undresses and instructs the women working with her to see themselves for the beauties they are, cellulite and all. Another film, *America the Beautiful* (2007), is about our nation's obsession with beauty. It's an account of a 12-year-old model growing up in the fashion industry, but it also touches on plastic surgery, celebrity worship, airbrushed advertising photographs, and human insecurities. *Beauty Mark* (2008) studies how our disquieting perceptions of beauty are shaped, shown through the eyes of a former triathlete and psychotherapist. We are encouraged by these examples that challenge the status quo and expand the notion of what is acceptable.

Since the 1972 education amendment, Title IX, which mandated equal funding to women's athletic programs, we have seen an explosion of strong, competent female athletes. Parents can use this attitude shift to reinforce the idea that being fit and healthy is beautiful.

"Self-Esteem and Young Women" reports that the African American and Latina influence on the broader culture helps to redefine the notion of beauty (Office of Juvenile Justice and Delinquency Prevention, n.d.). Mariela, an 18-year-old Latina in a focus group, said, "I don't need to see my ribs or feel my bones. In fact, when I'm thin, my face looks sick. Size twelve (on a good day) and size fourteen are fine for me. Hey, I'm just a big girl who likes to feel powerful." Mariela speaks for many "low-income Anglo and African American young women [who] did not experience the same pressure to conform to society's standards of femininity as middle and upper class Anglo young women."

Television is beginning to offer girls honest, intelligent, and highly capable role models. Pick almost any prime-time drama, and you now find women portrayed as competent professionals and equal to men. They now total close to 40 percent of prime-time characters (The Representation Project, 2014a). Women in these programs, while still pretty and thin, play confident and independent characters. They are no longer damsels in distress waiting for the hero to save them.

Be aware of healthy images in the media, and point them out to your daughter when you see them. Draw on these examples to build resiliency in your girls. If you teach your daughters to be critical observers and consumers, they will learn for themselves the differences between what feels right to them and what doesn't. They will develop more confidence in their own opinions, rather than allowing themselves to be overly influenced by what others may think.

Your efforts will enable them to have a broader sense of what is attractive and to put that more accurate vision into perspective. There also appear to be more choices for girls in terms of careers, skills, and relationships. We can use media as resources to get positive messages across. If you have certain values about what is important—achievement, kindness, self-sufficiency, "being sturdy"—you can fight alongside your daughters to resist the barrage of media messages claiming that there is only one standard of beauty.

Pumping Iron and Bigger Is Better

Dissatisfaction with bodies is no longer exclusively a girl thing. Like their sisters and their female cousins and friends, boys are paying more attention to their bodies and a new idealized version of the "buff" guy. Boys are influenced by media stereotypes of ideal six-pack physiques on movie stars and in videos and magazines. And while girls are more dissatisfied with their bodies than boys are, boys are not immune to this pressure. The defining difference between the genders is that boys don't want to get smaller; they want to gain size and bulk up.

Emily Fox-Kales, author of *Body Shots: Hollywood and the Culture of Eating Disorders* and clinical instructor in psychiatry at Harvard University, says, "Just what it means to be a real man in the world today is changing—and that's part of what's making muscles a growth industry in Hollywood" (Keegan, 2011). She sees this as the result of men losing economic power: "As men have lost more economic power, more social power, they've wanted to look more pumped up. . . . The recent recession . . . disproportionately hit male-dominated jobs like construction and manufacturing. Muscles have become an accessory, like pickup trucks." This thought was echoed in an article about body image in the *Harvard Gazette*: "Women now command spaceships and serve as CEOs of large corporations. . . . To compensate some Western men are fixating on muscularity as 'the last bastion of masculinity'" (Cromie, 2005).

Today boys and men are working harder and engaging in risky behavior to alleviate their dissatisfaction with their bodies. The parents of 14-year-old Nick told us their story:

> Nick is a pretty driven kid. When he gets his mind set on a goal, he dives in headfirst. So at first we were happy to see him focused on what he was eating and getting exercise. But that morphed into something more obsessive. He spends an hour and a half lifting weights in his bedroom and asked us to let him add creatine (to promote weight gain) to his diet. He is more focused on his body

than we anticipated, and the battles over protein shakes and food additives are endless. In response to our resistance to these additives, he shows us an article or infomercial online to get us to agree to something we're against.

The Internet has also influenced 16-year-old Justin, who is frustrated and tired of being the "chubby best friend" to all the girls he hangs out with. In his words, "I finally decided to stop hiding behind these extra pounds and, on a dare from my mom, cut out sugar, soda, and fried food. To my surprise, I lost fifteen pounds of stomach fat. I also use some YouTube videos to guide me through a conditioning routine." With America's ongoing obesity epidemic, media can be used to access valuable tools for encouraging a better relationship with food, resulting in healthier men and women. However, we always need to strike a balance between trying to be healthier and muscle dysmorphia, where one obsesses over muscularity and never feels muscular enough. When boys focus on losing body fat and building muscles at any cost, they risk having a disordered body image (Wilmore, 2012).

Unfortunately, taking risks means that more boys than ever are willing to experiment with illegal steroids or other dangerous supplements to achieve an idealized body. The *Journal of Pediatrics* recently reported that over 40 percent of boys in middle and high school exercised in order to increase the size of their muscles, 38 percent reported using protein supplements, and about 6 percent have used steroids (Quenqua, 2012). There is additional risk for middle-school boys, who are still growing and developing. Wise parents and pediatricians are starting to warn boys against hazardous methods that promise to achieve washboard abs. One father, who is a long-distance runner and was preparing for a marathon, recalled walking into a natural-food store for some carbohydrate powder. All he could find was protein, protein, and more protein. He noted that the marketing emphasis was focused on built-up or "cut" muscles. A mother in one of our groups joked that her childhood image of masculinity did not imagine muscles. "Now the body ideal my sons see is only possible by using dangerous supplements. They want to be lean and mean—all muscle, no body fat. I worry about them just I as do my daughter."

Now boys, too, must conform to a standard of beauty that exaggerates their sexual identity—in this case, maleness. To attain this aesthetic ideal, many are using drugs, dietary additives, and extreme forms of exercise. We find ourselves asking what happens to boys who, like their sisters, can't attain society's standard of body perfection. Nicholas, a high-school senior, shared his story:

> I was always chubby and didn't care about it until I hit middle school. Then I became the butt of name-calling and bullying. Boys called me lard-ass, and I pretended to not care. I did care and felt ashamed and sad. I loved to act but never tried out for a school play for fear I'd be jeered at. I was saved by a late growth spurt in eleventh grade, when I grew four inches and slimmed down. Thankfully, I can start over again in college. But I still see a fat boy in the mirror.

In an interview with the *Huffington Post*, Brian Cuban, the brother of Mark Cuban, said his body repulsed him every time he looked in the mirror. "Men can also be affected by the Internet-driven, hot bod image explosion that tells us we simply don't measure up to these perfect, airbrushed images." When he talks about his experience with a 30-year eating disorder, he says, "I had no idea the words bulimia or anorexia existed. They were simply behaviors I engaged in to survive day-to-day to take control of a body that repulsed me every time I looked in the mirror" (Cuban, 2014).

Boys, like girls, exhibit self-image disturbances. These include bulimia, "bigorexia" (the obsessive desire to bulk up), and steroid use. Donna, a high-school nurse for more than 20 years, observed a change in the students who came into her office to use the scale. She said, "At first, it was nearly all girls and only boy wrestlers who wanted to weigh less. Then about fifteen years ago, it quickly became mostly boys who wanted to bulk up. The pressure on girls to be thin has long been strong, but over the past fifteen years, boys have gained muscle mass and lost body fat."

The pressure on boys has been overt: supervised, encouraged, and according to many parents, required at times by their athletic coaches. One coach said as much:

> I see some boys who are under five feet, eight inches weighing over two hundred fifty pounds with less than 3 percent body fat. I don't think you can get that body without using supplements! Yet I know other coaches are putting pressure on their boys to start weight lifting earlier than some parents think is wise and the culture pressures the boys to bulk up any way possible. This doesn't surprise me. When I was a young wrestler, I would take laxatives for days before my weigh-in to qualify for a lower weight class. Now the pressure to be a certain size is widespread, involving more sports and affecting more boys than before.

Where else are our boys getting these ideas? Just like girls, boys are an important consumer group, and companies use male bodies to attract viewers and sell products. The pressure to become muscular begins earlier and earlier, as evidenced by the extreme bulking up of male action figures. GI Joe and other superheroes have become far more muscular. Even some Halloween costumes for young boys are padded to make youngsters look like they have six-packs. Everywhere our boys look, they are besieged by Photoshop-enhanced, airbrushed, pumped-up, idealized, and chiseled bodies, especially in athletics. Just as for girls, the images they see are not attainable naturally, but when they're young, boys don't have the knowledge to understand the difference (Poncelet, 2014).

The Internet complicates matters. In a *New York Times* article, Douglas Quenqua reports, "On Tumblr and Facebook, teenagers post images of ripped athletes under the headings 'fitspo' or 'fitspiraton,' which are short for 'fitness inspiration.' The tags are spin-offs of 'thinspo' and 'thinspiration' pictures and videos, which have been banned from many sites for promoting anorexia" (2012). Not unlike girls' "thinspiration" sites, where unhealthy information is blasted, there are bodybuilding forums for young boys, where they judge each other's body fat percentages. As these sites proliferate, boys are at risk when they turn to supplements or steroids to pump up. The goal for all teens should be fitness and health. If that includes being strong, great, but not at the expense of their health.

Man Up: The Strong, Silent Type

The media promote the ideal male as tough, confident, and without doubt, which often hides a much more vulnerable teen. Boys are required to hide their true selves behind a mask. This mask of toughness, so celebrated and promoted by the media, can lead to isolation. Rob, a high-school freshman, ran into that problem:

> This year was really hard. Not only am I a ninth-grader in my first year of high school, I'm young for my age. My old friends from middle school have become girl crazy and go to parties where there's smoking and drinking. They stopped calling after I made up so many lame excuses. It was too hard to tell them I felt scared and uncomfortable, because they were all having a great time. Yes, I'm lonely. I spend most of my weekends by myself in my bedroom playing Minecraft.

The most popular male characters on television, in film, and in sports are those with great physical strength who exhibit aggression and unequaled bravery; they include "gangsta" rap stars, action-movie heroes, wrestlers, and characters in video games. Violent behavior for men, including its rewards (money, power, and notoriety), is encoded into our consciousness through mainstream advertising that uses common themes such as "acting out exhibits bravery," "strength is power," and "attitude is everything." The message is that cool is defined as being tough and rebellious, traits seen as desirable.

In their *Boston Globe* article, "The National Conversation in the Wake of Littleton Is Missing the Mark," masculinity researchers Jackson Katz and Sut Jhally say, "The issue is not just violence in the media but the construction of violent masculinity as a cultural norm. From rock and rap music and videos, Hollywood action films, professional and college sports, the culture produces a stream of images of violent, abusive men and promotes characteristics such as dominance, power, and control as means of establishing or maintaining manhood" (1999).

If it's difficult for boys to acknowledge weakness to themselves, you can imagine how hard it is for them to admit they're overwhelmed or in trouble and to seek help. In general, they are encouraged to act like a man and suck it up. In this environment, it's hard for parents to detect when their son is struggling with body shame, fear, depression, and anger. After Columbine, William Pollack, the author of *Real Boys*, was often heard to say, "When boys can't cry tears, they cry bullets" (Pollack, 1998).

Teenage boys could benefit from seeing more media stories with emotionally complex themes, endearing human connections, and important feelings. New avenues for personal connection are on the Internet with apps and sites that promote communication—for example, Instagram, Snapchat, and Twitter. Websites like TellingSecrets.org invite anyone to post a shameful secret anonymously. Danny, 15 years-old recounted how this kind of site helped him:

> My piano tutor touched me when I was in eighth grade, and I've never told anyone about it. I begged my parents to quit piano, but they thought it was because I was too lazy to practice. I didn't want him near me and couldn't convince them to let me quit. I took lessons in his house and was too scared to push him away. One day, I read the postcard on Postsecret.com about a teen who was touched as a kid, too. It was the first time in two years I didn't feel alone. While I personally couldn't speak up, I showed this other boy's secret to my parents, and they finally asked enough questions and figured it out.

More than 658 million people have read PostSecret, an online community.

The way to keep our sons safe is through open communication, but we understand this is easier said than done. Stay informed about the realities of today's boys. That's the first step in starting meaningful conversations with our sons about the tough issues they face.

Words of Wisdom

One of the unintended results of dismantling gender stereotypes is that boys and girls have adopted some of each other's worst behaviors. In addition to the age-old challenges facing teens, both girls and boys binge drink, smoke earlier, use offensive language, and have indiscriminate sex.

Be up-to-date and savvy about your teens' world by learning from other parents. Don't dismiss your teens' concerns with their physical self-image by thinking they can separate themselves from all of the flawless and false images they see around them. It's unrealistic for girls to expect boys to have six-pack abs with sculpted muscles and for boys to expect girls to be supermodels, gorgeous and with legs that don't quit. Talk to your teens about the impact of media, and acknowledge how hard it is to develop a good self-image while being fed a diet of perfection and perfect muscle tone.

It's important for boys and girls to avoid the pervasive messages driven by commerce. Teenagers are an economic force and could be empowered to use their influence and dollars to benefit others. By the way, for all of your telling them what to do to be media literate, adolescents won't always give you the satisfaction of letting you know they've heard you. Be like the media. Be persistent and share personal stories with flash and drama (if you can). Finally, don't let media coerce *you* into being victim of their perfection myth or an unsophisticated consumer of their advertisers' products.

5

Screenagers

My Internet was down for 5 minutes so I went downstairs and spoke to my family. They seem like nice people.

—Twitter

Growing Up with Gadgets

Historically, children have hung out only on two playgrounds, one at school and one at home. Now they operate on a third playground, the digital universe, a playground that is infinite in size, difficult to regulate, ever-changing, and beyond our comprehension. Anyone, anywhere can post and read posts without accountability. Without military-quality encryption, there is no privacy.

Our children are digital natives with parents who are somewhat like first-generation digital immigrants. The cyber-universe has few meaningful boundaries or filters, making it difficult for parents to protect their children from the vast amount of information flowing into or out of their family rooms and bedrooms. The parents of today's generation of teenagers did not grow up with the Internet or use social media until the last 20 years. The ever-changing character of the digital world makes it challenging even for parents who first used the Internet in the early 1990s to keep up with what's out there. As a result, they are missing some of the experiences of their teens' world. A responsible parent must try to be as digital savvy as possible.

Not all teens use the Internet for the same reasons. Some spend their time socializing, texting, chatting, creating a network of friends, and interacting with those friends online. Some do most of their communicating using IM (instant messaging). They IM while watching TV, listening to music, doing their homework, and sometimes juggling several different friends at the same time. Some look for music, follow indie groups, read about different artists, download interesting music, and post on blogs. Others are passionate gamers, participating in communities built around shared expertise in games like Minecraft. Others watch media, movies, and old TV shows online, replacing the TV as their primary source of entertainment. And some use the Internet to participate in social action, express themselves anonymously, support a passion, and/or create a blog to talk about what they find interesting and important. Many teens share a big chunk of their lives online. The takeaway for parents is to be proactive and curious about what most interests their teens, how they use the digital world, what attracts them on the Internet, and why.

While much of the generation gap between parents and adult children has shrunk, the one place where it may still exist is in the digital divide. Although parents may believe they are digitally savvy and admit to being tied to their cell phones and tablets, they are no match for their teenage children. Providing the guidance teenagers need is difficult when parents are often two steps behind them, unaware of the hottest, most current sites and apps while their kids have already moved on to the next new site. Regardless of how techno-smart parents are, the world has changed, and there's no going back to rotary phones, typewriters, pen and paper, and newspapers. You need to get smart!

The Internet has an infinite memory. Much of what our children post leaves its trace. Anything put out on the Internet is indelible;

there are no real erasers, even after you hit Delete. There are no more Hansel and Gretel crumbs that birds can snatch and nibble without leaving a trace. Nothing can disappear, and our children's words are indelible footprints that can be recaptured even after they press Delete.

While technology has radically changed the landscape (the playground), the basics of teenage development and behavior remain the same. Teens still do what they've always done—socialize, check in, hang out, and seek acknowledgment. They are still driven to connect and engage with one another. The developmental goal of figuring out their identity and finding out where and how they fit in is the same; it is the environment that has changed dramatically.

In this chapter, we explore the digital world of teens. We discuss the impact of social media on the lives of teenagers. In addition, opinions on the impact of the technology explosion differ, and we provide a variety of experts' perspectives. Before parents can set appropriate boundaries, they must know more about the advantages and disadvantages of technology.

Totally Wired

Parents and teenagers have become psychologically dependent on cell phones, computers, and tablets. They wake up to the alarm set on their cell phone, carry the phone into the bathroom, and then play music while they get ready for school or work. During breakfast, they check for texts and peruse Facebook, Snapchat, and/or Instagram to see what their friends have posted since they checked in the night before. Teenagers are never far from their phone, keeping it in their purse, backpack, or pocket. There is incessant connection; the phone is really an extension of their body. Many kids feel incomplete without their cell phone, and it has quickly become the most important possession of a teen. In the words of 16-year-old Jenna, "It is literally a lifeline; without my phone, I'm anxious." Many teens say texting is the first and last thing they do every day (Li, 2012). For teenagers, social networking is not a distraction from their offline life; they use it to define their life.

Many people would rather leave their wallet at home than their cell phone. A father of two teens is a case in point:

> I can remember losing my wallet in college and feeling totally lost. I felt unanchored and naked without my ID and credit cards. Now I would feel awful if I lost or forgot to bring my cell phone. I'd feel disconnected from the outside world. It's a security blanket of connection. When I'm stuck in traffic, I can call ahead, and if I'm on line at the bank, I can look at Twitter. The cell phone is an indispensable part of me, an extension of my hand. My wallet is now just a wallet.

Our teens are experiencing the same attachment to their technology.

However, it's one thing to have a cell phone in your backpack and another to leave class or sneak a look while in class to check your e-mail or texts. The dad of 15-year-old Emma said, "I find it troubling that my daughter is so connected to her cell phone. It would be a crisis for her if she lost it. Her twin brother loses his all the time. He's even retrieved it from the toilet twice!" The allure of texting, e-mail, Instagram, and Twitter is the intermittent reinforcement teens feel they need when they check their phone for a new post. The randomness of the posts reinforces their dependence and need to check. If posts came every hour, they would know when to look, just as adults used to wait for regular traffic and weather updates on the radio. The addictive quality of digital media is a real concern. This worry is one that parents understand and fear, particularly because they struggle with a similar addiction.

One mother said, "In the words of my child's pediatrician at his last physical after I asked if my son were ADHD, 'Is *he* ADHD? I don't know. I think we're *all* ADHD. I refer to myself as an adult with *acquired* ADHD. The world is just moving so fast. The information is endless, and we are all compulsively checking our devices.'" Another parent added, "I just saw a cartoon of a mom, dad, and two kids with their heads buried in their various screens. The caption read, 'Where should we go to stare at our phones this summer?'"

The generation gap is apparent in the social language of the Internet. While most parents embrace technological tools and utilities like syncing family calendars and sending group e-mails, for them technology is just that—a tool. They use their phones, laptops, and tablets to make their lives more efficient. And many parents are not very fluent in the Internet's social language. Every generation of teenagers has used its own slang, and today's teens are fluent in the abbreviations and phrases known as *netspeak*. Their abbreviations are sprinkled in their texts, making them illegible to some parents. To stay an informed parent, you have to know what your kids are writing, and the Internet has sites such as the Internet Slang Dictionary and Translator (http://www.noslang.com) and NetLingo (http://www.netlingo.com/acronyms.php) that can be helpful in decoding the new slang or abbreviations for parents. Here are a few examples of netspeak:

GTG: got to go
NMU: not much, you?
OH: overheard
OMG: oh, my god
ORLY: oh, really
P911: parent emergency
PAW, PRW: parents are watching
PIR: parent in room
POS: parent over the shoulder
PRON: porn
QQ: crying (this means that the person typing is crying)
RUOK: are you okay?
S2R: send to receive
SWAK: sealed with a kiss
SWYP: so what's your problem?
TDTM: talk dirty to me

VSF: very sad face
LMIRL: let's meet in real life
GNOC: get naked on camera
ASL: age, sex, location

Teenagers today are extremely comfortable living their lives online, trying on new identities in public for their close friends as well as the friends of their friends and strangers. One mother told us that her son came out online on Facebook before he told his own brother. Another parent said, "My daughter, Jesse, was at a pool party at her friend's house. After she dove into the pool, her bikini top came off, and she freely posted the topless photo of herself emerging from the pool on Instagram. However, Jesse was terribly humiliated when a friend of hers shared it with her mother, who shared it with me." Teenagers have always hidden some of their behaviors from their parents. What has changed is, instead of sharing with one or two people, they now share their conduct with the potentially billions of people who use the digital universe.

Daily Use Is Significantly Up

A Pew Internet Project survey (Zickuhr, 2010) found that 75 percent of children aged 12 to 17 have cell phones, an increase from only 45 percent in 2004. The significance of this finding is that parents can no longer monitor their children's exploration on the Internet. It wasn't long ago that placing the computer in a public room like the kitchen would be enough to help you keep a watchful eye on your teen's Web surfing. One mother still laughs when she thinks about her son, now 29, innocently opening a photo his cousin had e-mailed him. As the photo slowly appeared—slowly because it was in the days of dial-up—first the head, then the naked breasts of a woman, her son turned beet red. If your children have a smartphone, they can access the Web from anywhere, so you will miss these moments and won't have the advantage of letting him know it's inappropriate.

Cell phones, laptops, and tablets also make the Internet omnipresent. The use of technology touches virtually all parents and teens. There's no way to shove the genie back into the bottle, so we need to understand the use of social media. In 2010 the Kaiser Family Foundation studied the use of technology and media by contemporary 8- to 18-year-old children (Kaiser Family Foundation, 2010). The results of the study are considered one of the largest and most complete sources of information about media use among American youth. One finding is startling: children spend more than an average of 7.5 hours a day engaged in non-school-related technology, a two-hour increase over prior findings. If true, this reporting shows how ingrained the Internet has become in our children's lives. Seven and a half hours of entertainment media use per day adds up to more than a full-time workweek! The study also suggests that children spend much of this time multitasking. It's hard to wrap one's mind around this.

Multitasking presents a serious challenge to developing concentration, focus, persistence, and imagination. Approximately 40 percent of high-school students report that they use more than one medium at a time—for example, listening to music while watching TV or using their computer at the same time (Kaiser, 2010). In fact, teens in grades 7 through 12 spend over 1.5 hours sending or getting texts a day. We all experience the impact this has on concentration and focus. Most of us can recognize when the other person on the phone is either searching the Net or texting while talking to us. You sense a noticeable lack of concentration, and you start wondering if you're talking to yourself.

Although parents are aware of the issues related to the digital universe, they appear reticent to do anything about it. As of 2010, less than 36 percent of children aged 8 to 18 reported that their parents have rules limiting their TV, video games, or computer consumption. If these findings are correct, there is really no other explanation for this increased use other than parental enabling. We are the ones who have to buy the devices and the ones who should set the rules for teens. In fact, teenagers spend more time on their smartphones for things other than using it as a telephone, which is quickly becoming passé. The good news is that teens in homes with some limits spend almost three hours less with media than do those children without rules (Kaiser, 2010).

The Kaiser study shows a huge difference in media use of children from different racial and ethnic groups. The study found that Black and Hispanic children spend far more time with media than White children do:

Black and Hispanic children consume nearly 4½ hours more media daily (13:00 hours total for Hispanics, 12:59 for Blacks, and 8:36 for Whites). Some of the largest differences are in TV viewing: Black children spend nearly 6 hours and Hispanics just under 5½ hours, compared to roughly 3½ hours a day for White youth. The only medium where there is no significant difference among these three groups is print. Differences by race/ethnicity remain, even after controlling for other factors such as age, parents' education, and single versus two-parent homes. The racial disparity in media use has grown substantially over the past five years: for example, the gap between White and Black youth was just over two hours (2:12) in 2004, and has grown to more than four hours today (4:23). (Kaiser, 2010)

However, if Black and Hispanic teens are more likely to own a smartphone, it is possible that the smartphone could be the tool that eliminates the digital divide.

A Pew Research report on teenagers and smartphones (Madden et al., 2013) found that while teenagers are sharing more online than in the past, they feel confident in their ability to manage their online identity and take steps to shape their reputation by editing and deleting data they want to keep private. In essence, they are curating the content that others will read about them to present a certain image. Teens report that they have online experiences that boost their self-esteem and also report being harassed and/or embarrassed by something posted about them online. In response to all this online sharing, some teens decide to limit the amount of information they receive.

A recent MTV survey of 13- to 18-year-olds (referred to as young millennials) found that this group of teenagers makes a conscious effort to disconnect to reduce stress and overstimulation (Baird, 2013). They engage in something referred to as "monotasking" by focusing on a singular activity like sewing or baking. In fact, approximately 80 percent of young millennials say they need to unplug periodically and focus on one thing at a time to de-stress. Almost 60 percent choose to make something with their hands when they unplug, and more than 50 percent of girls report that they like to bake because it reduces their anxiety.

These teens sandwich their technology between the activities they do with their hands. They first research a project, go offline to do the project, and then go back online to share the project. In tech lingo, this activity is now referred to as "bookending." Anna, a high-school sophomore, said, "When I'm overwhelmed, I go online and look for a recipe for cupcakes, prop my iPad on the kitchen counter, turn on my music, and follow the recipe. After I've decorated the cupcakes, I usually take a photo and post it on Instagram or Facebook. It feels good to focus on one thing, and I relax when I'm baking." Anna's friend Lauren also bookends, only she doesn't bake. Lauren goes on the website Ravelry and finds a free knitting pattern for a scarf or socks. After she finishes the project, she posts a photo of it online for her friends to see. These activities are today's teens' way of reducing stress and expressing their individuality. They enjoy lying back, concentrating on one thing with a singular focus, and unplugging. However, they still want to go back online to let their friends know what they've done. Teens have figured out how to use technology as a creative tool as well as a stress reducer.

Life outside teens' bedroom windows seems enormously stressful and challenging. They are accustomed to walking through metal detectors and planning for their uncertain futures. Teens live in an age of economic downturn, where they see their college graduate cousins and older siblings struggling with college loans, and many worry about how this will affect their future. They are bombarded with news stories about climate catastrophes, like Snowmaggedon, Hurricane Sandy, and a never-ending number of mass school shootings. Over one-third say they design escape plans when in public places, because of events like Sandy Hook (MTV, 2013). Although half are scared of violence at school, they seem to have adopted a practical "Keep calm and carry on" mentality. Adopting survival strategies is something they think about because so many tragic stories and images stream into their lives daily. Technology is a mixed bag. On the one hand, social media connect teenagers to a larger community, prevent isolation, and foster creativity. On the other hand, they shrink the world, burdening our teens with national and global tragedies as if they were happening next door.

The Positive, the Negative, and the Unknown

It's difficult to imagine a time when there were no computers, tablets, cell phones, televisions, printed books, or even everyday use of the written word. More than 2,000 years ago, Socrates warned about the danger of the written word. He was concerned that by relying on a written record of history, people would lose the skill of remembering and transmitting oral history. It is believed (the translated words of Socrates via the hand of Plato from the *Phaedrus*) that he said, "This discovery of yours will create forgetfulness in the learners' souls, because they will not use their memories" (Berry, 2004). This historical forewarning serves as a powerful reminder that both validates our fears about overreliance on technology and normalizes our worry that the sky is falling.

Most of us say we can't remember things as simple as family phone numbers or birthdays. One father said, "I feel like my brain is full, and I wish I could add some memory to it as easily as buying a memory stick for my laptop." Each innovation evokes fear of change and worry that old and valued habits will disappear. The concern expressed by Socrates about the future is not a revelation to anyone reading this, but we were surprised to read what he worried about almost two thousand years ago. His remarks offer perspective to anyone who is concerned that change only leads to loss of something precious.

There certainly is a lot of debate about the pros and cons of the impact of our 24/7 wired lives. We wish we could tell you that physicians and researchers agree about the effects of texting, social media, and video games on the developing mind, but the studies won't reap results for years. Scholars are hoping to determine whether the Internet and social media are providing a rich landscape for identity exploration or whether they will erode teens' ability to decipher face-to-face social cues. What we can agree on is that teenagers today represent the first generation growing up with the impact of the Internet from birth.

From these studies and current research, we can see that there are no clear indications of the impact of the Internet and social media over time. This question remains: How much unplugging should parents enforce? In the absence of clear data, knowledgeable, tech-savvy parents will make decisions that are in the best interests of their children. The following paragraphs provide some of the pros and cons of teens' social networking and Internet use for parents to consider.

Researchers agree that the explosion of technology use has a powerful effect on young people. Many are focused on the negative effects on children's developing brains. Michael Richtel, associate professor at Harvard Medical School and executive director of the Center on Media and Child Health in Boston, says that when our children search the Internet, their "brains are rewarded not for staying on task but for jumping to the next thing . . . and the effects could linger: The worry is we're raising a generation of kids in front of screens whose brains are going to be wired differently" (Richtel, 2010). Daniel Goleman, author of *Emotional Intelligence* (2013), discusses the importance of developing the social brain with face-to-face connections in real time.

While he acknowledges that digital technology and social media expand our universe, he believes that they can also create a false reality, sometimes, at the detriment of interpersonal relationships. He finds it is too easy to get lost in the digital world, drawing us in by expanding our ability to connect information easier and faster than ever before. Further, Goleman observes,

The social brain is in its natural habitat when we're talking with someone face-to-face in real time. It's picking up information that it wants in the moment. It's reading prosody in voice, emotions, and nonverbal cues. . . . The problem with communicating too much via email or text is that they have no channels for the social brain to attend to. You have nothing for the orbital frontal cortex, which is dying to get this information to latch onto, to inhibit impulse and tell you, "No don't do that, do this." Without more visual cues, we're essentially flying without clear vision. (2013)

It's hard to help our teens understand the pitfalls of texting when their impulsive nature means they may post comments before self-editing or even understanding the consequences of what they write. Many teens are learning the hard way, after the fact, after the backlash and possible public humiliation. The things your children write today have an endless shelf life. This makes it hard for our children to escape whatever impulsive irrational or thoughtless comment or photo they post. Online is public! Even a photo on Snapchat, an app that has the photo disappear in 24 hours, offers no protection. Sixteen-year-old Courtney said, "I took a picture of myself in a sexy bra and sent it to my friend Haley. Haley took a screenshot of the photo and texted it to Jeremy, who I have liked since seventh grade. He had a field day texting it to other boys. I was humiliated and haven't talked to Haley since the incident. I can't look at Jeremy without blushing! I thought it was safe because it's supposed to disappear." No one wants to be reminded of the stupid things he or she said or did as a teen, but what is posted online lasts forever.

Sherry Turkle, a psychologist and the author of *Alone Together*, is concerned that today's teenagers rarely focus their full attention on a single task (Moyers, 2013). Frequently, teens watch TV, listen to music, text, and study at the same time. Not only are they not giving their full attention, they understand that it's reciprocal because their friends aren't paying full attention to them either. This behavior extends to parents of teens, who are also multitasking constantly. Whether it's checking e-mail while watching their teens at a game or scanning their Twitter accounts while engaged in conversation, their attention is pulled among friends and family and the virtual world.

Turkle adds, "What concerns me as a developmental psychologist is watching children grow in this new world where being bored is something that never has to be tolerated for a moment" (Moyers, 2013). Boredom leaves necessary space for creativity and reflection. When teens are inundated with information, they miss the opportunity to explore the nuance and depth of a topic.

Jim Taylor, author of *Raising Generation Tech: Preparing Your Children for a Media-Fueled World* (2012), agrees that teens are dominated and shaped by popular culture and technology. The problem with popular culture is that everything from *Here Comes Honey Boo Boo* to *16 and Pregnant* is available to teens in an instant, regardless of how base or crude it is. No distinction is made between popular culture based on positive values and popular culture based on self-aggrandizement. Popular culture is no longer confined to television, which can be turned on and off at a parent's discretion. The characters, ideas, and themes pervade society through Twitter, Facebook, YouTube, marketing, and online streaming, landing in the palms of our kids holding their cell phones and iPads.

Technology's Grip and the Developing Self

Adolescence is a time of experimentation, and teens are both vulnerable and impressionable. To establish their individual identity, teenagers are consumed with answering the question "Who am I?" They play out this search for self-identity through interacting with friends. Their universe has exploded, a teen version of the Big Bang. Taylor (2012) tells us that this technology explosion may be interfering with teens' ability to develop their sense of self. Technology has driven teens to focus on what others think of them instead of defining themselves based on what they think and their values, feelings, and needs. Taylor sees Facebook, Instagram, and other technology as forms of disguise. Teens are carefully curating their personas based on how they will be viewed by others. They want to ensure that their friends will see them in a positive light. Taylor believes what may begin as self-awareness and self-expression can sometimes become an unhealthy preoccupation with what others think (2012). One mother's story illustrates this:

> My son decided to forgo a tuxedo for his prom and bought a bright orange suit. He loved it and I was fully supportive of his originality. But after he posted a photo on Instagram, he questioned his choice and had some real regrets. His friends mocked it, saying he looked like he thought he was an NBA first-round draft pick. He still wore the suit, but he felt much more self-conscious because of their responses.

While social media can be a force for healthy exploration, it can also be painful if friends are critical. A teenager's youthful exploration could end in public humiliation.

Now that we all have a camera in our hands at all times, many of us spend our lives looking through the lens of our cell phones instead of using our eyes and being present. Many teens post videos of singing with girlfriends in pajamas at sleepovers, others pose in their seats at sporting events, and every moment that is recorded can detach us from the event. Teenagers who are not part of an activity are reminded by a friend who posts the event, making them feel more excluded and exposed. Of course, teens have always felt excluded, but now it's broadcast to any teen at school who follows the online posts of the kids at the party.

Talking, posting, and texting engage teens while they are coping with their sexuality and changing bodies and are forming their personal truths. What was once a personal journey is now public because so much of their personal story is exposed online and through social media. Marc Prensky, author of *Brain Gain* who first coined the phrase Digital Natives, argues that technology creates a new way of thinking. Today, the capacity of our minds may not be enough to negotiate our complex world. We rely on technology to perform functions that aid us with the growing complexity, fast changes, and ambiguity of modern life (Price-Mitchell, 2012).

Larry Rosen, author of *Understanding the iGeneration and the Way They Learn*, views Twitter, Instagram, and other similar social media as a positive force in teenage development. He argues that teens use social networking to help them forge their identity in the world. For example, they can experiment with different personas, behaviors, and sexualities online. In this way, teens get to "wear" different identities without making a permanent commitment (Price-Mitchell, 2012). One mother said, "My 15 year-old daughter, Ellen, is a good writer but never shares her work with friends. She worries they will laugh and mock her and she will lose her desire to write. Ellen started submitting her stories to a website called Fanfiction and has received a lot of positive feedback. Being able to navigate the Internet anonymously gave her the confidence to share some stories with friends." Online, teenagers are confronted with endless opportunities to discover who they are and who they want to become.

Parents also curate their lives using social media. They select what photos to post and which parties to mention to create a public self for others to view. We mold the image we want the world to see, posting only the selfies we find attractive. Teens put what they choose online and wait for others to react. One father said, "My son posted a video of his band playing a song they wrote and was embarrassed when he hardly got any 'likes.' The embarrassment is not as bad as his loss of confidence. He's no longer as proud of the music." Teens are vulnerable, so when someone doesn't press *like* about what they've posted, they can spiral down. However, online interactions can work both ways for our kids. Negative experiences may inhibit teens, and positive ones may increase teens' self-confidence. Only by understanding the totality of your teens' digital experiences can you play an influential role in their digital lives.

Come One and All

One remarkable aspect of the Internet is its public availability to everyone, regardless of wealth or class. Yes, you need to have access to the Web, but schools and libraries have public computers, as do many local coffee shops. The World Wide Web is an open system.

Accessibility both frees our children from the confines of their community and can transport them into neighborhoods that are developmentally inappropriate. There is a community for everyone. Once you turn on your computer, you have easy access to *everything*. When 15-year-old Sara did an Internet search for the keyword *breast* to learn more about her mother's breast cancer, she found as many hits for X-rated porn sites as she did for breast cancer. When Joey did a search on the Holocaust, he had access to thousands of links, including first-person accounts, historical films, and original documents. The Internet can be dangerous and enlightening. There is no denying the wealth of information and its centrality to our lives. In fact, teens generally consider access to digital literacy as necessary for obtaining successful cultural knowledge and development.

Besides offering teens insight into other cultures, the Internet brings a community to those teens who may feel isolated. In this way, access to the Internet mitigates social isolation. Even shy, socially awkward teens report that they find using social media an easier way to communicate. It's less intimidating than talking face-to-face.

The Internet addresses another cause of isolation. In the past, teens had more mobility to wander and roam in the physical world. Today's parents are more protective from early childhood to adolescence, making teens less able to seek opportunities for connection by themselves. Danah Boyd, author of *It's Complicated: The Social Lives of Networked Teens*, argues, "Teenagers aren't doing much online that's very different from what kids did at the sock hop, the roller rink, or the mall. They do so much socializing online mostly because they have little choice. . . . Parents now generally consider it unsafe to let kids roam their neighborhoods unsupervised" (2013). They have much more mobility and freedom online than they do in their day-to-day lives because, until they drive, teens are dependent on the kindness of older teens or their parents to drive them places. Spending time online is the way teens hang out today.

Social networking has become an extension of our teens' friendships and helps them make their social plans. A mother of two teens recalled how this used to work:

> I can vividly remember trading phone calls with three to four girlfriends on Saturday afternoon to make the final plans for the evening. The calls started late afternoon, around four o'clock, and continued back and forth, between me and my friends until seven. Inevitably, my mother would finally intervene after she watched this play out with no clear decision whether we were going to a movie, shopping, or just to one of our homes. She was endlessly frustrated by the indecision. Now I watch my kids text back and forth, and because it transpires mostly under my radar via texting, it's not frustrating to me because the chaotic process of teens making plans is less obvious to me.

Today's teens continue to make their plans and hang out like they always have. The difference is that they now connect to more friends and at a faster pace.

The Internet also provides teens with a community with which to share their unique interests online. Teens with disabilities, chronic conditions, or other challenges can connect with other teens with similar difficulties. There is comfort in finding other teens struggling to overcome challenges; they no longer feel so isolated and can enjoy the support of their peers. In the past, if you were an LGBTQ teen in a rural area, there might have been no place to turn to find a community. According to the website of the Gay, Lesbian & Straight Education Network (GLSEN.org), the Internet helps LGBTQ teens handle negative experiences by offering important tools to help them cope. The site also gives them access to supportive friends and crucial information that they couldn't find elsewhere (GLSEN, 2013). For those teens keeping a secret like alcoholism, drug use, or sexual abuse, there are forums and sites where they can get anonymous support. In general, teenagers say they feel more connected to their friends and with a larger group of others who share common experiences.

Nancy Lublin, CEO of Do Something, the largest organization for teens for social causes and change (over 2.4 million young people who comprise the teen-oriented social impact organization www.dosomething.org), created a site called Crisis Text Line (http://www.crisistextline.org) in 2013. The site invites teenagers to text a problem, and the site will connect the teen with resources and counselors. Lublin's expectation is that teens love texting, and she hopes to encourage them to use this form of communication to save lives. In the first month after the site's inception, she said that teens texted things like, "The kids are mean, I don't want to go to school," with the most serious being, "He won't stop raping me, it's my dad. He told me not to tell anyone, are you there?" (Lublin, 2013). According to Lublin, "Success is measured by messages like, 'I don't know if you remember when I took some pills and went to hospital—I want to thank you guys, you saved my life.'"

In general, technology connects teens with an important community and can provide a precious safety net. Technology is also a stand-alone activity, however. While hundreds of "friends" are at our fingertips, sometimes it feels like we're all just "bowling alone." Thus, one feature of technology is how many of us, parents and teens alike, spend time together alone. A dad of a high-school freshman commented about this concern:

> It's not uncommon for my wife, my son, and me to be together in the den with a device on each of our laps and our eyes looking down. And I know this scene plays out in millions of other homes. I've tried to institute no-tech Saturday, but we haven't been successful. I'm as tethered to my BlackBerry as my son is to his iPod, and I worry that I'm not interacting face-to-face enough with him.

Similarly, the mother of three girls said, "Yesterday my oldest daughter said she wanted to spend some time with me. So we got in the car to drive to the mall, and she immediately took out her phone to text a friend. I got the sense that even though she had her face down in a screen, she had the sense that we were together." It's as if parallel play, the developmental stage when two-year-old children play sitting side-by-side but not with each other has extended into adulthood. This is precisely why Sherry Turkle titled her book about our relationship with technology *Alone Together*. However, while the proximity of another person is a comfort, even if you're both doing something different, what we miss today is having someone's full attention.

What's a Parent to Do?

How do we sort through the pros and cons of technology, using the benefits to our advantage while not ignoring the negatives? The answer is simple yet extraordinarily complex: Parents need to find a comfortable balance between monitoring technology use and teaching values that will mitigate misuse. Parents also need to find a balance between being punitive and abdicating responsibility. Going overboard in either direction will be detrimental to your children. Most kids view taking away their phones as the worst possible punishment they could receive. Use this information wisely!

We don't have enough information to know definitively how this new digital world will affect our children's lives over the long term. No one knows how the new methods of accessing and retrieving information will affect our relationships, our means of communicating, and the developing brains of our children. The jury is still out. However, while still debating these issues, parents have to make the best and most informed decisions for their teens.

Keeping teens safe is the priority. Parents justifiably worry when their teens wander through the unsupervised terrain of the Internet. They worry about bullies, posting or receiving a sexually provocative text or photo, as well as the cumulative effect of all the hours their children spend online. While most children who use the Internet do not interact with predators or experience cyber-bullying, parents can best protect their children by teaching them to be "cyber-street-smart."

You need to discuss these topics with your children and teens. Teach them that a text or post that was supposed to be private may end up in public. Help them understand that sending anything over the Web is like taking out an ad in the newspaper. It's just that public. Talk to them about sexting and how embarrassing it is to see their indiscretions shared online. When something private becomes public, it's usually embarrassing. Otherwise, it wouldn't have been private!

There is no way to retrieve mistakes after pressing *Send*. Parents need to impress on their kids the permanence of posts, even those that are sent on Snapchat, the app that erases a post in 24 hours. Josh, the father of a 13-year-old, told how he did this:

> I told my son, Nate, the Delete function works only *before* you click *send*. If you're counting on what you send on Snapchat to disappear, think again. I want you to imagine Grandma Sarah seeing everything you send. Nothing disappears on the Net! Twenty-four hours is plenty of time for someone to take a screenshot and forward it to

someone else. Remember, think of Grandma reading and seeing everything you post!

Teenagers don't foresee consequences, so parents have to be their teens' frontal lobe and help them see the unforeseen damage that provocative photos, bullying, and sexting can create. Just as Nate's father did, ask them how they would feel if their teachers or grandparents saw what they text. Help them protect themselves.

Also help them become information literate, knowing how to decipher fact from opinion. Stephanie, mother of a high-school freshman, gave this example:

> Andrew had an assignment to write his first paper with references and was shocked to learn that Wikipedia was not a credible source to cite. I had to convince him that just because he reads something online, doesn't make it fact. I was able to help him understand that primary sources are vetted and Wikipedia is opinion written by random people, which is very different from verifiable fact. I even read online that a college professor gave a student who cited incorrect information from Wikipedia an F. Telling Andrew about the F was enough to convince him to broaden his research.

These are the years when our teenagers are forming their own ethics and values, which are highly influenced by their parents as well as their friends. They are in the process of individuating, often in conflict with parents, and need skills and information to keep them safe on the Internet. Even with the normal conflict with teens, staying engaged with them is essential to support and help them to navigate the vastness of the World Wide Web.

Every family is different. Some parents may require their children to "friend" them on Facebook so they can monitor their exposure, while others may rely on parental controls and software to limit their children's access. In each family, parents need to find a way to monitor their children that is consistent with their parenting style and the individual needs of the children. Some choose to limit the amount of time teens spend online, and others do more minimal monitoring. Unless the entire family lives off the grid, a parent is not likely to try to prevent a child from accessing and participating in the e-universe. Indeed, denying access may assure their children's social isolation at school. Regardless of what limitations you choose, you must educate yourself about digital media and have conversations with your teens about their online use.

Parents should model and encourage a healthy and balanced relationship with technology by assisting teenagers to use social media as a positive force in their lives. Remember, your children learn from your behavior. Think of this when you find yourself too engrossed to take your eyes off your screen. Everything is better in moderation, including technology.

In her blog on the *Huffington Post*, Lisa Belkin questions whether her love of technology is having a negative impact on her children. She sums up her philosophy with the following thought:

Every generation is a social experiment with no control group, resulting in young adults who are products of their times and who then go on to raise children who, in turn, are products of different times. As parents we can only learn what we can, then do our best, with no do-overs and no way of knowing what would have happened if we'd done differently. (2012)

We may not know what is the *right* way, but we can educate ourselves, communicate values, and help our children learn to use the new technology to their advantage. Be diligent in staying current, and understand the ramifications of the digital world. Help teens to think a step ahead of what comes naturally to them. Be an anthropologist in your teenagers' world. Be genuine and curious; study the digital world as if you were a visitor to a new and interesting country. When teenagers know their parents understand this part of their lives, they are more likely to include them in their online world. There is no going back.

Your Daughters and Sons at School

Talent comes and goes, but it's your ability to dig deep when times are hard and make things happen for yourself that's the difference between just an average life and success. . . . It's also about things like grit. It's about determination, resilience, about the ability to overcome adversity.

—Michelle Obama (2013)

Students who succeed in school have several characteristics and values in common. Successful students are self-motivated, self-directed, persistent, conscientious, and resourceful. Successful students take responsibility for their learning and behavior both at home and at school. Successful students understand the value and purpose of homework and don't have to be monitored as frequently. Successful students understand that their performance in school affects their future. As Michelle Obama tells us, academic performance—indeed, lifelong success—is directly tied to perseverance and grit.

We believe, and the data show, that parents are the first and possibly the most effective teachers of these characteristics and values (Tough, 2012). According to researcher Dr. Sarah Mattson with the Tennessee Comptroller of the Treasury's Offices of Research and

Educational Accountability, for children to be successful at school, they do have to have a strong relationship with their parents (Mattson, 2010). Teenage rebelliousness notwithstanding, our children need and want our guidance. Just don't expect them to tell you so! In Mattson's survey of secondary school students, 54 percent said they wished to spend more time with their parents; however, only 30 percent of these children said their parents know what they worry about. It's not surprising that the teens getting grades of D and F are far less likely to communicate about grades than students who perform better at school.

While parents start off involved in their children's preschool and elementary experiences, many tend to back off in the secondary years, even though their children still need support. Although parents may attend back-to-school nights or sporting events, many choose to stay in the background rather than being partners in their child's academic efforts. In contrast, those years of sitting side-by-side and doing homework with your elementary school children model high expectations for learning. Although what you do to express high expectations and model interest in learning is different as your children get older, these efforts are just as important. James, a teenager said, "My parents expect me to get my work done; slacking off isn't an option for me." Yet, Anna, another teen explains, "When my parents stand over me and constantly ask me when I'm going to finish my homework, it makes me want to do the opposite." While engagement is essential in your teen's education, it can be difficult to figure out how much to be involved and how best to present guidance.

Being involved with your children's education is not just about what you can do, but also about what you can do in partnership with schools and other parents. The effort begins with a clear understanding of your expectations for your child's learning environment and the learning itself. The mother of a 15-year-old boy gave this example:

> When Tony was in eighth grade, I was diagnosed with breast cancer. I worried about the stress my chemo and surgery would have on him. My husband and I called a meeting with his teachers and guidance counselor to let them know exactly what our family was going

through. Tony is a sensitive kid, and I was afraid he'd just zone out under the stress. We were so glad we were proactive. While Tony would never have sought out help, every week or so his guidance counselor would let him know she was there.

Tony's parents did exactly the right thing. Their expectations began with the requirement that the school provide Tony with a physically and emotionally safe learning environment. Parents should also expect an intellectually rigorous curriculum. Only when these goals are met can teens learn to the best of their abilities. These goals are more likely to be met when the partnership between home and school is genuine.

Parent engagement plays a central role in teens' educational experience. Anne Henderson, an expert on the relationship between families and schools, and the coauthor of *Beyond the Bake Sale*, defines family engagement as "Everything that parents do to make sure their children succeed" (personal communication, July 8, 2014)—for example, attending parent meetings and conferences, supporting learning at home, and volunteering at school. Parental engagement demonstrates the value parents put on education and gives them essential information about academic achievement, extracurricular activities, assisting teens who don't fit in, and dealing with sexual harassment. In this chapter, we explore these dynamics that shape (or skew) teens' self-image and, therefore, success. We discuss friendship and the influence of peer groups and bullying in Chapter 7.

It's Not Personal, It's Adolescence

For girls and boys, adolescence is filled with powerful physical, cognitive, social, and emotional changes. Adolescents are going through puberty, which for girls can begin as early as 8 years old and for boys can start two or so years later. At the very same time, our educational system requires teens to master more challenging academic demands and navigate the complexities associated with multiple classes and teachers. Cognitively, between the ages of 11 and 14, adolescents begin to develop the ability to think about multiple options and possibilities; logical thought processes ("what if?"); abstract thinking skills; and the ability to process what they are thinking, how they feel about it, and how others perceive them. There is so much growth and this time is so confusing that one educator joked, "We should close middle schools and send the kids to the country or to a ranch while they deal with all the raging hormones and additional angst and stress."

The changes teens undergo translate into behavior we all recognize. These behaviors include high levels of physical and emotional energy, difficulty keeping on task, curiosity, risk taking and adventurous behaviors, failure to realize and recognize limits, and intense concern about how their peers see them and about what are seemingly less important adult opinions Their contradictory expectations include seeking independence while wanting protection and parental nurturing, demanding privileges, and avoiding responsibility.

Teens begin to challenge adult explanations and prefer to learn new things rather than review or improve previous work, making it hard for them to hone skills. They begin to exhibit a justice orientation, see things in black and white, and have difficulty accepting moderation or seeing shades of gray. They may respond to your advice with comments like "You'll never understand "or "My life is ruined." Most difficult for parents is the fact that teens tend to believe that no one else has ever experienced feelings and emotions similar to theirs. Their sense of justice leads teens to become cause oriented. One father said, "After reading a book about cruelty to animals, overnight my son became a vegetarian." Another dad reported, "All it took was one visit to the baby animals in the San Diego Zoo to make my daughter stop eating meat!"

Creating safe and equitable schools depends greatly on adults' effectively transmitting and modeling the emotional support, caring, and consistent expectations so critical to teens' development. In addition, teens themselves must have the opportunity to develop self-esteem, learn about and be respectful toward others, and be held accountable for their behavior.

The Power of Family Engagement

We believe you are your children's first and most important teacher, despite competition from other powerful influences. Schools place children in contact with their peers, who have great influence on social perceptions, values, and conduct. Social media, television, and music offer our children front-row seats to popular culture's manipulative view of cultural values, delivering powerful messages day and night into every family's living room. Despite the fact that more parents are psychologically and media savvy, most adults are just as clueless about their children's "second family"—that is, their school, peer groups, and adolescent pop culture (Taffel, 2005). It's you against Lady Gaga.

Family engagement is defined as a shared responsibility among schools, families, and communities throughout children's lives and carried out everywhere that children learn (Weiss et al., 2010). When family engagement is meaningful and linked to learning, the benefits for students can be extraordinary. They include higher grades and test scores, better attendance and homework completion, increased English-language acquisition, lower dropout rates, more positive attitudes and improved behavior at home and at school, higher graduation rates and greater enrollment in college, and improved parent-child and home-school relationships. Decades of research show that not only does family engagement ensure a greater likelihood of students' success in school; it also has a positive impact on the rest of their lives. When families are involved at home and at school, children do better in school, and schools get better. (Bryk, A. et al., 2010; Mapp, K. L., & Kuttner, P. J., 2013).

As parents, you can make a significant contribution to your children's education. Here are some things you can do:

* Support your children's learning at home by providing an environment that promotes and reinforces what is taught in school.
* Demonstrate skills and teach knowledge that enriches the instructional program.
* Provide experiences that enable your child to develop an appreciation for learning and the benefits that are derived from persistent efforts to achieve.
* Advocate for your child and other children, and require the system to be more responsive to all families.
* Work collaboratively with teachers, administrators, community members, and other parents to improve schools and increase academic achievement.

With shared decision making and two-way communication, you can become full partners in educating your children, helping them reach the highest possible personal and academic achievement. It all begins at home. Children do not raise themselves once they start middle school, even though parents sometimes are treated that way at school. Staying engaged is critical; schools cannot do it alone.

The Everyday Experiences of School Life for Boys and Girls

Sixteen-year-old Jessica offers this description of the high school experience:

> For school we have to have an open mind, get good grades, and participate in class and activities; we've got to have an attitude, a certain perspective. You have to suck up sometimes, you have to be

quiet, you have to know certain people, you have to try to be yourself, you have to be attentive, on task, and you have to study a lot. And to be accepted, you have to wear the right clothes, you have to have the attitude, you have to be willing to bully people, you also have to suck up to like your friends or whatever, you have to be outgoing, daring, you have to know certain people, and sometimes you have to be mean.

It's a minefield out there.

At school, girls and boys alike face social judgments that discourage them from achieving to the best of their abilities. This pressure can come from many sources: counselors, teachers, friends, and parents. A dad shared this story about a middle-school counselor:

My son had some learning disabilities and was slow to learn to read. We made sure he had the right kind of support to do well in school and held high expectations for his academic achievement. We were working with Adam on his high school courses and had a discussion with his counselor. She said very clearly that we shouldn't push Adam so hard and we should accept the fact that he would be a mediocre (C average) student. In fact, she said we have to accept, and be satisfied, with the "fact" that he would only go to vocational school and wouldn't be a candidate for a university. My wife and I were furious that she would decide my son's fate as a 13-year-old. Adam worked hard in high school and did get into the University of Florida, where he excelled as a student. My message is, don't let anyone tell you what your kid can or can't do. You know your child better than anyone!

School life also is somewhat different for girls and boys. For girls, the stereotypical concept of femininity may interfere with their taking on leadership roles in class and school. (Yes, girls are still accused of being "bossy.") They also may have to work hard to overcome the social judgment that goes with pursuing challenging fields of study that remain predominantly male (math, science, technology). Boys in school may resist facing shortcomings in their performance and working to improve. Boys of color also must combat the negative stereotype that being African American or Latino and masculine does not match up with being academically smart and successful in school (Fergus et al., 2014).

School becomes the laboratory where kids practice their life outside their home. As parents and teachers, we have to acknowledge our teens' emotional state during this time while continuing to have high expectations. Teachers and parents must work together to communicate to teens that effort is the key to success in school and in life, and that intelligence and mastery can improve through effort, persistence, and hard work.

Classroom Climate

Boys and girls are bombarded with overt and covert messages about what they can be and do, based on their gender. Although this has changed somewhat in the last four decades, there is still work to be done. Because the messages concerning appropriate roles for females and males have become more subtle (the hidden curriculum), many teachers and students have difficulty recognizing gender bias.

In the classroom, bias and discrimination still exist. First, girls are still too often cut out of the process. For example, teachers still call on boys more often than they do on girls, and girls often continue to be rewarded for being compliant and quiet. Positive classroom interaction builds students' abilities to think and reason, but boys demand and receive more attention from teachers and counselors for both positive and negative behaviors (Pellegrini, 2011). A teacher offers an explanation:

> Part of my tendency to respond to the boys first was a behavior management concern. While the girls were sitting respectfully, raising their hands, the boys were having difficulty controlling their behavior; they were wildly raising their hands, spilling their

solutions, and knocking over their test tubes. So calling on them first helped them to stay focused and keep their experiment intact.

By giving these boys more attention, the teacher sent a message to the girls: their classroom contributions are less important. It is the teachers' responsibility to keep their students engaged, and it is the parents' responsibility to ensure that their teens' teachers reward constructive and collaborative learning.

The traditional classroom is not a great fit for boys. The elementary school environment is not structured for a young boy's mental or motor skill development. Boys are physically more restless and impulsive. When they enter school at the age of five or six, their motor skills—such as the ability to hold a pencil—are usually less developed than those of girls. Girls, by comparison, learn to read more quickly and are better able to focus (Thompson, 2007).

The culture of school can undermine the best efforts of parents and their sons. Early on, reading is a critical challenge for boys, making school difficult and discouraging for them. Adolescent boys are, on average, 18 months behind their female peers in reading and writing. According to the U.S. Department of Education's National Center for Education Statistics (2013a; 2013b), girls dominate in national reading scores and math scores. As one elementary school teacher observed, "Girls have a realistic expectation of what school is like and are more likely than boys to be ready to sit still and listen." Young boys tend to be more active than girls, and in the school environment, this is considered bad behavior. The result is that young boys begin to experience frustration with their academic abilities and self-esteem early on (Kantrowitz & Kalb, 2012). These gender-based issues are more complex when race and ethnicity are introduced into the equation. African American and Latino boys raised in expressive cultures may have the most difficulty with the more traditionally passive and quiet European American models common in most U.S. schools (Fergus et al., 2014).

Gender stereotyping becomes a predominant concern by the time children enter middle school. We asked boys in our focus groups, "Do you think people treat you differently in school because you are a boy?" The majority responded with a resounding yes. Teachers and administrators expect certain behaviors from boys, such as aggressiveness and social immaturity. Teachers too often expect disruptive and antisocial behavior from boys of color, but they expect girls to be compliant, good students. These expectations can result in teachers overlooking students' need for assistance. Stereotyping contributes to a self-fulfilling prophecy, where boys and girls behave in a way that is expected of them, rather than behaving authentically.

Students notice the consequences of stereotypes. For example, boys tend to receive harsher punishment than girls for similar infractions. In one of our focus groups, Julia, 16, explained that she is consistently late to one class but is simply given a verbal reminder to be on time. In contrast, she has noticed that the teacher removes boys from the classroom for being late. Ashley, 15, told of a similar experience. She has noticed at her school that girls often get away with walking freely down the hall during class when it's obvious they don't have a hall pass. In contrast, Ashley has seen boys stopped and questioned even when they openly display their hall passes.

Scenes like this one play out daily in schools across America: Two seniors, Kyle and Michelle, arrive at their high school English class 15 minutes late. The teacher stares at them as they enter the room. "Kyle, do you need a special invitation? Is it too much to ask that you get here on time? Never mind. Sit down and see me after class. [Pause; voice softens.] And, Michelle, I'm disappointed in you." Brittany, a high school sophomore, said, "Shawn would eat in math class or talk to his friends, and Ms. Smith would always kick him out. She had no patience for the boys in the class. However, me and my friends would sit eating and giggling, and nothing would happen to us." An observer in a seventh grade history class told the following story:

> Joe, a particularly active boy, continuously disrupted class. Mrs. Bell's energy and attention were spent trying to keep Joe in line. He continued talking, and Mrs. Bell sent him to the vice principal's

office. During the same class period, Emily, a loud, talkative girl, was disruptive as well. Despite Mrs. Bell's warnings, Emily continued to talk to the girl behind her. Mrs. Bell asked Emily to stay after class, at which time she received a mild reprimand.

Our focus group students reported that Latino and African American males are the most likely to be reprimanded severely or bullied by teachers in or out of class. The focus group students' experiences of disparate treatment of boys and girls in school are consistent with classroom research. Studies show that boys, particularly boys of color, experience discipline suspensions, and expulsions substantially more than girls do. Boys account for 71 percent of students suspended (Center for Civil Rights Remedies, 2013).

Girls face some different hurdles. Teachers react negatively to girls who are outspoken and challenge them. Informal surveys of teachers and counselors have found that they view girls who push back or question as aggressive and emotional, while casting the same behavior by boys as evidence of assertiveness and leadership. Amanda, a 17-year-old girl in our focus groups, confirmed the survey findings, telling us that one of her teachers makes girls feel uncomfortable about being "too outspoken." She told us that this teacher, who also coaches the baseball team, jokes around with the boys for half of the class period. He then becomes hostile or sarcastic whenever one of the girls asks a question or raises a concern.

This type of intimidation can affect girls' ability or willingness to demonstrate their knowledge of the material. Fourteen-year-old Kayla told the following story:

> Paralyzed by anxiety, I sat motionless at my desk. I tried to ignore the sounds of classmates arguing over math formulas. Finally, the teacher arrived, intimidating as ever. With a twisted smile, he handed out the tests. The paper shook in my hands. I did the first problem as a warm-up. I got it! The next problem seemed difficult, so I turned the page. Glancing over the paper, I froze. All the

problems were about baseball and batting averages. I knew very little about baseball, let alone how to compute a batting average. As the lump in the back of my throat formed, I found it hard to swallow. I pushed back the tears and tried to do other parts of the test; however, every problem looked foreign. A boy in my class yelled out, "Hey, Mr. T, these problems are really cool!" I closed my eyes, my cheeks burning with frustration and disappointment. There was no hope. The math I knew was useless. I was not smart enough and did not belong. How could I apply formulas I did not understand?

This was Kayla's experience in advanced mathematics when the content (sports) left her out of the learning. Similarly, while it is important that we enroll students in science, technology, engineering, and math (STEM), IB (International Baccalaureate), and AP (advanced placement) programs, we must also ensure that their diverse learning styles are met. Supporting teens in advanced courses may require parents to intervene when the classroom climate is ineffective or counterproductive.

Outside the Classroom

Extracurricular activities in a school can reinforce gender stereotypes. Our culture places a high value on sports as the place where teenage boys can participate in a group and show their emerging manhood. Parents of boys, particularly boys of color, must provide other opportunities to develop skills, knowledge, and self-expression, thereby encouraging them to seek a broader range of learning experiences.

When gender drives participation in school activities, it becomes an "inflexible code." Girls and boys tend to participate in different types of extracurricular activities, representing traditional areas of gender stereotyping. When asked what clubs or activities they participate in, the boys overwhelmingly listed various team sports. Very few of the boys listed other clubs, such as ethnic-affiliation clubs. When asked why they didn't participate in a greater variety of activities, the boys indicated that sports were a societal priority they were expected to pursue. Sixteen-year-old Ethan talked about how his teachers rewarded his participation on a varsity sports team: "Some teachers are more lenient with male athletes; they let them get away with more." Several mothers of boys in one of our focus groups said that boys will participate in an activity outside of this "inflexible code," like the film or chess club, only under unusual circumstances, such as in a nontraditional, more intimate school environment.

Girls are one and a half times more likely than boys to participate in nonathletic school activities, including student government, academic honor society, and yearbook or newspaper. Females are also more active than males in community service. It is interesting to note that, even when community service is required, girls select activities that build relationships, like working at a senior citizens' home. Boys are more prone to clean hiking trails in the forest and parks or to work on building projects (Domangue & Solmon, 2009). In our focus groups, girls cited a wide range of activities in which they participate, including but not dominated by team sports. Unlike boys, girls don't feel constrained by social expectations when selecting activities. They believe they have unlimited options to explore. One girl explained that she consciously chooses to participate in activities to establish her individuality among her friends. Another girl reminded us, "There is a bunch of different groups of girls, and they are accepted. But with the guys, there is one cool group—athletic."

For boys, "cool" may also be defined as being completely uninvolved in or aloof from school. One assistant principal told us how tenth-grade girls hold all of the leadership positions and take part in a variety of school activities, while boys who are considered cool occupy their time by throwing each other into lockers and tossing pinballs down the hallways. It is interesting to note that this participation for girls reflects their investment in relationships. They are joiners, and this holds true throughout their lives.

Both athletic and non-athletic extracurricular activities have substantial developmental benefits for teens. Parents can enhance their teen's development by supporting choices that depart from gender stereotypes. Parents should join with teachers to provide girls and boys with an equitable learning environment, so all students can participate in activities based on interests and skills and achieve to the best of their abilities.

The first step toward changing the negative consequences of gender patterns in school is raising awareness. Parents should join with teachers to provide girls and boys with an equitable learning environment, so all students can achieve to the best of their abilities.

Academic Achievement and Social Acceptance

Teens often experience a powerful tension between academic achievement and social acceptance. Beginning in middle school, some regrettably sacrifice academics. These teens allow their peers to define them. For boys, especially boys of color, there is a disconnect between being cool or swag and being smart. The result is that as students move through school, they become increasingly alienated from academics to be accepted. In addition, our schools and culture discourage Latino and African American boys from academic or intellectual self-expression (Holcomb-McCoy, 2011; White House, 2014). We wish teens could acknowledge their success without thinking they have to choose between friends and performing well. Parents have to help their teens navigate this tension so they can choose to succeed in all areas.

These are the years when being popular and fitting in too frequently take precedence over being assertive and competent and taking academic risks. Boys are very concerned about being perceived as not having things under control. This concern can manifest itself in masking the need for assistance, avoiding challenging courses, or putting on a bravado persona. According to gender expert Jackson Katz, this guise of masculinity leads to devastating consequences (2013). For example, eighth-grade boys are 50 percent more likely than girls to be held back a grade. Boys are also more likely to drop out of high school than girls and are three times more likely to be victims of violence. Boys also commit the majority of adolescent crimes (Pellegrini, 2011).

Girls are very concerned about friends or potential partners perceiving them as undesirable. Girls may not want to stand out and may avoid the spotlight. One focus group mother told us this about her daughter, Amber, currently a ninth grader:

> My daughter was told by her music teacher that she was a fabulous singer. Amber responded with, "Not really, not fabulous. When I was in fifth or sixth grade, I had a lot of nerve. See, I didn't care what people thought of me then. But when I was in the sixth grade, I sang Carly Rae Jepsen's song 'Call Me Maybe' in front of the whole school. And if I had any way of changing it, I would dial back time and delete the entire performance." I asked Amber if it was because of the song she chose. Amber answered, "I was really uninhibited and belted out the song. I stood out, and people think it's weird, that I'm asking for attention. The boys think so. . . . I think I'd rather have friends and things than be that good."

Kaitlyn, a high school senior, remembered how others reacted to her: "Saying what I really thought got me into trouble with teachers and with my friends. I was always on the verge of some disaster. I was a bitch if I spoke out, especially if I was willing to argue with boys, and my teachers always presented me as 'challenging' to my parents at back-to-school nights."

This concern also can manifest itself in dropping traditionally masculine subjects such as math, science, and technology courses despite having succeeded in and enjoyed these subjects in elementary school. Although eighth-grade girls and boys perform equally well on math assessments, many teen girls still feel uncomfortable pursuing STEM courses and careers. Samantha told us, "I don't want to be the only girl in a group or class." This reticence in middle and high school results in fewer young women pursing STEM in higher education and choosing STEM as a career (STEMConnector & My College Options, 2013; National Women's Law Center, 2012). Even when girls are successful in STEM courses in middle school (in particular) and high school, they may attribute their good grades to luck rather than skill.

Parents have to work with schools to get children what they need and not make assumptions about their needs based on gender. At the same time, parents have to encourage and support their teens to make choices that are best for them rather than responding to social pressure. We must teach our teens the skills and values that enable them to manage social pressure successfully while achieving in school and maintaining positive relationships.

Girls: Great Expectations?

Over the past quarter century, the United States has witnessed dramatic and positive progress in the lives of women and girls. We can clearly measure their increased participation and achievements in school and society. There have been specific advances in education, including increased enrollment and better performance in mathematics, science and technology, athletics, postsecondary education, and professional fields such as law and medicine (White House Council on Women and Girls, 2011). Girls are benefiting from innovations in educational environments and the classroom climate, more equitable teacher expectations and student-teacher interactions, and culturally responsive practices. This progress is the result of hard-won laws and policies, including Title IX of the Education Amendments of 1972 and others.

Forty years of social transformation have greatly expanded educational and career opportunities for young women. For example, data show that beginning in 1971 and continuing through every year of assessment, females aged 9, 13, and 17 have tested higher than their male peers in reading assessments (U.S. Department of Education, 2013). Girls have also increased the kinds and numbers of courses they take in high school (Niederle & Vesterlund, 2010; White House

Council on Women and Girls, 2011). Girls are choosing more classes based on their interests and skills rather than on traditionally presumed or identified gender roles; they are more likely to enroll in college immediately following high school; and universities are enrolling more women than men. For 350 years, men outnumbered women on college campuses. Now, in every state, in every income bracket, in every racial and ethnic group, women on average earn 57 percent of all bachelor's degrees and 58 percent of all master's degrees in the United States alone. If this trend continues, demographers say, by 2020 there will be 156 women per every 100 men earning degrees (U.S. Department of Education, 2012).

There is no question that Title IX has opened some doors previously closed to women and girls. However, barriers still exist and must be addressed in collaboration between parents and school staff. For parents, the question becomes how to get their daughter ready to take advantage of these opportunities. This is where family support and grit and persistence become so important for girls to pursue what they really love and not be intimidated by social pressure.

When it comes to girls' achievement and taking risks for the sake of doing what they really love to do, dads have a particularly important role. When women who have achieved in nontraditional careers look back on their childhoods, they point to their father's expectations and encouragement as a key factor in their success. Brenda, who has one daughter, remembered the power of her father's unwavering belief:

> In college, I was accepted into the school of engineering. I enrolled and began what I thought was an extraordinary journey. Looking at the students in my first survey course, I counted 305 guys and 4 girls, me included. Only two of us got our degrees in engineering, and two dropped out. Sometimes I look back and wonder how I got through it. But in my heart, I know that I did it because my father believed I could. He never saw failure in anything I tried, and he continuously encouraged me to try anything and everything. It was my dad who recognized my math and science ability and ignored

my college counselor's advice that I major in liberal arts. My dad helped me believe I could do it when less than 2 percent of my classmates were girls.

Carol, a 48-year-old mother of one daughter and two sons, reminisced:

> I was an only child, and my father took me along to political demonstrations, chess club meetings, and his office. The only times I was permitted to stay up late were to watch television with my dad, usually something like the Discovery or History channel because he thought these programs were intellectual. My dad always assumed that I would finish college and suggested that I think about becoming a professional.
>
> At about 12 years old, I learned that many people had a different idea about the importance of education for a girl. When I was asked what I wanted to be when I grew up, my answers—a doctor, a scientist—always generated a chuckle or two. I remember a great feeling of indignation coming over me. How dare they ignore my dreams and pigeonhole me? My dad never did that. He stood in stark contrast to the discouraging messages that I received from other people. When the world around me said, "Carol, don't get ahead of yourself; keep your dreams simple," my dad showed me the way to stay in touch with greater possibilities. I eventually became a microbiologist and followed my dreams.

Fathers should take great satisfaction in the importance of their support for their daughters' ambitions and dreams.

A significant strategy to help your teenage girl achieve is for you to learn what she's interested in and use this knowledge to encourage and motivate her. Recognize her talents and provide her with opportunities to strengthen them. If she shows an interest in using computer software to create a movie for school, teach her how to edit and use the software skillfully, rather than doing it for her.

Critical factors for sustaining and improving self-esteem and academic success include having both parents hold high expectations for achievement, nurture interests and passions, and hold teens accountable for their own learning. At the same time, parents need to supplement this support with guidance and understanding of their teens' social life, which becomes more complex as they get older.

Boys: Great Expectations?

A dated assumption about boys would have us believe that boys "have it easy," and success comes to them effortlessly. In fact, this assumption has perpetuated the rigid models for raising and connecting with boys and has had a profound impact. Rachel, the mother of 13-year-old Brandon, said, "My 13-year-old son wears his heart on his sleeve. I see him trying on different roles, especially the 'tough guy' role, which is so out of character for him. I think about what boys go through at different stages, struggling to fit in and do well in school."

In the late 1990s, books began to appear that highlighted concerns about boys' social and emotional development and school performance. When academic expectations for boys are low, these youngsters are more likely to be identified for special education programs. Boys are more prone than girls to fail a course or repeat a grade level, especially students of color. In addition, boys score much lower than girls on reading and writing skills tests (U.S. Department of Education, 2013). For educators and parents, these findings raise a fundamental question about expectations for boys' academic performance: Is their poor performance a question of maturity that "boys will be boys" and then they'll catch up later? Or do boys genuinely underperform, so that we should rethink how they are raised and educated? Or perhaps the spectrum of academic achievement for males is wider. Some will rise swiftly to the top and become prize-winning journalists, while other males' futures are limited by their minimal reading and writing skills.

Challenges that boys face are often the result of how gender and cultural stereotypes truncate their academic achievement. The missing pieces include the differences in expectations for academic achievement between entitled boys and boys of color; the challenge of schools and families to promote the relevance of education, particularly for boys of color; and the disproportionate number of boys who are disciplined and identified for special education. Analysis by the Office for Civil Rights found that special education is largely a boys' club, with 1.9 million girls (34 percent) and 3.8 million boys (67 percent) nationwide classified as special-education students (2013). A large percentage of our schools serving low-income students and students of color have ineffective educational programs that result in low student performance (Boykin & Noguera, 2011). One reason may be gender and racial stereotyping. Boys are five times more likely than girls to be labeled hyperactive (Kadaba, 2014). The fact that boys are often labeled "hyperactive," "aggressive," or "in need of special control" may explain why so many of them are placed in special education programs even though they may not necessarily have a learning disability (Bloom et al., 2013).

Although we have presented the research that documents different expectations for boys and girls, we must remember that there is considerable diversity within each gender. These differences are especially evident in the way children learn. Parents shouldn't make assumptions and impose expectations about what boys and girls can and cannot do based exclusively on their "nature." As a parent, your job is to nurture individual potential and talents.

Of course, dads have a big role. Engaged fathers and other significant role models have a major impact on boys. Data show that when fathers are involved in school, boys are more likely to maintain a higher grade point average, have greater motivation to succeed, have higher self-esteem, have more confidence, have fewer health and emotional problems, are less likely to use drugs, and are less likely to become teen parents (Rosenberg & Wilcox, 2006). Dads are essential to the success of both boys and girls.

Missed-Fits: The Outsiders

Your son or daughter may be an individual, one who marches to his or her own drum, as one parent described: "To Shana, the world looks real different, and the way other kids respond to her is very different." Not fitting into the culture of middle and high school can be a difficult and painful experience that we call a "missed-fit." We coined the term *missed-fit*, rather than misfit, because misfit is a projection of someone else's standards and carries a negative connotation. The experience doesn't have to be all bad, but being on the outside does present challenges. The biggest challenge for teens is the message they receive that they aren't acceptable the way they are. These teens can look different, have different interests, or have a different sexual orientation. Teenage boys and girls also can look like and act like other teens (dress, hairstyles, mannerisms) but feel different from most of those around them.

Megan, 14, said, "When I'm with certain people I'm not that comfortable with and try to make conversation, I'm like really fake because I'm trying to be like them. I don't have much in common with them, and I have to think of things to say. I can usually come up with something to say, but I don't like the way I feel when I have to pretend." Parents may not remember that these feelings are a part of teens' normal life. We often underestimate what kids are really feeling when they act this way. The good news is that focus group teens said their parents' stories help to normalize these feelings.

Many boys feel intense pressure to fit a mold. Michael, 17, said, "I've never been interested in following football or basketball. Trust me, life would be easier if I did. Sometimes I get tired of being clueless, so I watch a game just so I can participate in conversations at school. But I often say something that gives my ignorance away, like thinking Tom Brady is the quarterback of the Steelers. My mistakes immediately make me look like a poser, which, unfortunately, I am." Boys also hit on girls and/or act tough when it's really not in their character to act out so brazenly. Tim said, "Sometimes I act all cool and say something to a girl just to look like I'm tough and don't give a damn.

Yesterday, a girl in one of my classes asked me to help her after school, and I laughed in her face. If I was alone and not surrounded by my friends, I would have been much nicer."

Teens who don't fit in suffer. Peer groups can torment girls through indirect aggression and exclusion and can exclude boys from social groups and make them feel they aren't cool enough. You can't protect your teens fully from this cruelty and rejection; however, you can help to create opportunities for them to develop success in other spheres. Ask yourself whether your teen is really different or playing an outsider role for protection.

Even if your daughter looks and acts the part of a girl who fits in, sometimes you have to look deeper, because she may not feel that she fits in. This is where a parent's awareness can make a difference for a daughter and, ultimately, how she defines herself. Stacey, a 52-year-old mother, said, "I never thought of myself as not fitting in. I was a cheerleader in high school, was popular and got good grades, but some things bored me that other girls enjoyed. I had more interest in carpentry than cooking and have always noted that if you knit, sew, and build but don't cook, other women always comment on your lack of skills."

Sixteen-year-old Nicole, dressed in black from head to toe with shoe-polish hair, combat boots, and blood-red lipstick, said, "I'm not one of those petite, squeaky clean, kiss-ass girlie girls. This is who I am, like it or leave it." Her mother said,

> Really, who is Nicole? Is she Goth because she doesn't fit it, or doesn't she fit in because she's Goth? I'm not clear, and I worry that Nicole has created this persona in her own defense.
>
> Nicole's way of rebelling forces her to the opposite side of the spectrum. I just want her to know who she is, because being Goth gives her the false illusion of choosing whether she is in the popular group or not. Nicole's defense is that she thinks she has rejected the popular kids, and I'm not sure she really believes that. She has chosen an extreme persona, and really, Nicole just wants to feel like she's the one in control.

Psychologist Susan Mikesell says, "If you can pass as a successful girl, your feelings of being an outsider might be hidden, even from yourself" (personal communication, April 15, 2004). Nicole's mom continued, "Because I have had so little interest in traditional women's tasks, I've labeled myself as 'lazy,' a tag I've carried for a very long time. Only recently have I learned that I wasn't lazy, I was just different. Now I appreciate my skills in a nonpejorative way."

Seventeen-year-old Lucy shared another perspective on the issue:

> I wish my mother could have helped me to appreciate my own talents, but how could she? Imagine! She could play golf like a pro and build furniture, but her lack of ability in the kitchen, including storing the napkins in the oven, was the subject of many family jokes. With my own daughter, I feel I have an opportunity not only to give her permission to stretch out of the boundaries of what "traditional" women have an interest in and are supposed to be good at, but also not to judge herself negatively if she doesn't choose to excel in traditional women's roles and work.

As parents, we have to help our kids to choose what is right for them. Most important, we must support their decisions so they don't feel embarrassed or ashamed. We must try to be very sensitive when choosing words to describe differences and must avoid harmful judgment.

When kids feel they are a missed-fit, the school can sometimes be helpful. The parents are really in a better position to help their child, but it is the school's responsibility to make sure your teens are not harassed or bullied at school because of their difference. Addressing teens' sense of difference has two parts: helping teens find a place for themselves and helping them feel good about themselves. Many teens become frustrated and angry when their parents, peers, school, or society do not support them because of their difference. Ali, now 15, was happy with who she was until her friends started to exclude her in middle school. When she would go to the mall with a friend, Ali could tell that her friend was ashamed to be seen with her, because her friend had joined the "girlie" pack. The friend would tell Ali to pretend she didn't know her if they ran into other girls from school.

At 13, Ali was feeling so ostracized that she couldn't stomach the image of Barbie. Barbie represented all that she was not; weight was an issue for Ali, along with looking a certain way so she would fit in. One day she set her Barbie doll on fire on the front lawn of her house. Ali called attention to herself by doing extreme things. She saw herself as the "weird girl" and acted out the role well over the top. Her relationship with her parents was strained. Although they were supportive of her individual traits and strengths, in their effort to tell her to try to fit in and "act normal," they gave her a strong message that she was not normal, not OK, and a disappointment to them. This only reinforced her extreme behavior and her belief that she was odd. Their expectations created a self-fulfilling prophecy.

As a result, Ali doesn't have a secure sense of self, which causes her to establish new relationships too quickly with people who ultimately tire and disappoint her. Her identity is built around calling attention to herself by saying things such as, "You remember me: I'm the weirdo, the one who threw herself on the gym floor at the school dance." The label "weirdo" has given her an identity and entitles her to act out. Unfortunately, as a result of this behavior, she feels alienated rather than empowered.

Ali has pulled away from her parents and is doing poorly in school. Her parents went to the school counselor, who recommended a summer wilderness program for her to gain confidence. At the camp, Ali lost weight, found a place for herself, and gained confidence. Her parents are pleased and tell her how good she looks. So why isn't this a slam-dunk success story?

Losing weight and changing one's appearance create a dilemma. Ali's mom is proud of her daughter's changes and tells Ali that she looks good. Ali is getting the message that people enjoy and accept her more. The dilemma is that she feels better and looks good, but only because she now fits into the mold she fought so hard to reject. Ali's parents are so relieved to see their daughter fit in better that they neglect to appreciate her need to develop an identity as someone other than the weird girl who lost weight. They could help her grow by understanding why many of her feelings make sense and by validating them. With appropriate help, Ali can use her parents' support to build an inner core and present herself in an authentic way, rather than in opposition to other girls (because she doesn't fit in), which results in her being the odd or weird kid. Ali needs to value and continue to work on her real qualities and to verbalize her hurt.

This anecdote is an example of how much more difficult the passage to adulthood is when parents, in spite of their commitment to their children and desire to see them be happy, don't give them the validation they need the most. In many instances, parents may not have the skills needed to help their teens. If you find yourself struggling with the problems that interfere with your teen's happiness and ability to belong, you should seek professional guidance for added support. This guidance may be as simple as going to the school counselor, seeking parenting education information, or talking with friends you think have wisdom to share. The school was able to help Ali's parents find a camp where she was able to lose weight comfortably and fit in better, but that was just half of the solution. Her parents then had to work with Ali to help her to feel good about herself, totally apart from the weight issue.

Your job is to teach your teens the value of who they are and to highlight what is special about them. Teens who learn to like themselves because of who they are have a much better chance of attracting friends who also appreciate them for who they are. Having a few soul mates is all any of us needs. Every teen has talents and unique qualities; if you recognize these traits in your teens, you can help them feel good about themselves. Much of teenage conduct is really a search for self. Even if teens struggle in their peer group, they can get through this period with appropriate parental and other adult support.

One very traditional mother, who still matches her shoes and purse, shared the story of her son, who was a very edgy teenager. Their differences created a potentially toxic combination. Jordan dyed his hair purple and had multiple piercings and "thought" tattoos. At first she thought she wouldn't survive this period, because her son seemed so strange. But with help from friends and a therapist, she learned to appreciate her son's numerous talents. He was a good writer, did community service, and was respectful and kind. Once Jordan's parents gained this insight and recognized his assets rather than being put off by his rebellion, they could grow as parents. They were able to give him authentic validation, which in turn allowed Jordan to use his independence in a positive way. The mother survived, and Jordan thrived.

His mother said, "I look at Jordan with awe. After he dropped out of college freshman year, we made him pay for the credits he missed. Jordan moved back home to make enough money to get an apartment. Once he had a steady job, he moved out and went back to college part-time. Jordan just graduated college at 25. I have no doubts that he can succeed, and by the way, his hair is back to its original color." This story demonstrates that when you support your teens, regardless of how different they are from you, they can develop into competent and self-confident adults. As always, looks are very deceiving.

Flirting with Danger: Sexual Harassment at School

Sexual harassment affects all students (Hill & Kearl, 2011). It often starts in elementary school with teasing or other inappropriate remarks regarding another's body as well as bullying and playground roughhousing. Gendered harassment is any unwanted behavior that reinforces traditional heterosexual gender norms and includes taunts related to gender stereotypes, homosexuality, and gender nonconformity. Lesbian, gay, bisexual, transgender, and queer (LGBTQ) students experience more sexual harassment and bullying than do heterosexual students (79 percent versus 50 percent) (Poteat et al., 2012). Often perceived as "normal" adolescent behavior, sexual harassment persists as a social problem. Such behavior may even set the stage for date or acquaintance rape or physical and emotional abuse—all of which center around the power of one person over another. Parents and school officials cannot afford to ignore signals of distress or deny these issues altogether, and complaints must be pursued with vigilance.

The American Association of University Women's 2011 study of sexual harassment in schools, "Crossing the Line" (Hill and Kearl, 2011), revealed that sexual harassment is part of everyday life in middle and high school. Nearly half (48 percent) of the students surveyed said they had experienced some form of sexual harassment, and the majority of them (86 percent) said it had a negative effect on them. Girls were more likely to be targets of harassment (56 percent of girls versus 40 percent of boys), and the harassment they experienced was more physical and invasive. As a result of the harassment, 22 percent of girls and 14 percent of boys had trouble sleeping, 37 percent of girls and 25 percent of boys didn't want to go to school, and 10 percent of girls and 6 percent of boys wanted to change the way they went to or from school.

Not only is it problematic in the long run to enable behavior that routinely involves disrespect for other people's bodies and words, but the real and tangible negative effects are ignored and minimized. It's common for kids who have experienced sexual harassment—call it whatever you want—to hear, "It's not a big deal," and to be told that they shouldn't be "so sensitive." This minimizes what they are experiencing, denies their reality, and teaches them that what they think and feel doesn't matter.

Though schools have policies against it, sexual harassment remains an all-too-common problem. While students say they are aware of school policies dealing with sexual harassment, increased awareness has not translated into school practice. Kara, a middle-school girl, said, "Policies just don't stick." Policies don't stick because they are often implemented inequitably, unfairly, or not at all. Parents and educators need to do a better job of educating students about what is and isn't appropriate school behavior. Schools have to do a better job of establishing and implementing practices and procedures that are accessible for students, parents, and staff. For these policies to stick, training of staff and students has to be ongoing, and parents need to be engaged in this process.

In simplest terms, sexual harassment is deliberate and/or repeated sexual or sex-based behavior that is not welcome and is not asked for. It may take any of the following forms:

* Physical, such as unwelcome touching or interference with movement
* Verbal, such as epithets, derogatory comments or slurs, sexual gossip, pressure for dates, and/or sexual activity
* Visual, such as displaying derogatory cartoons, drawings, posters, or media messages

A hostile environment usually involves a series of incidents that poison the environment by creating an offensive, intimidating climate that interferes with work performance and academic achievement. Consider the following examples.

Victoria, a seventh-grader, went to the counselor's office in tears. She said Anthony, an eighth-grader, would wait for her in the cafeteria each day. He persisted in standing behind her, patting her backside, and asking her personal questions. Anthony would ask, "Are you still a virgin?" and, "How would you like to do it with me for your first time?" Some of Victoria's friends thought she should be flattered by the attention. After all, Anthony was good-looking, bright, and popular. In spite of what her friends said, Victoria was intimidated by his attention.

In a suburban middle school, during the time when students are moving from one class to another, several male students seem to make a point of brushing up against female students and making physical contact. Occasionally, an angry female student will report the incident. When this happens, male students criticize their accuser for being a poor sport or say she's making a big deal out of it.

During lunch at another school, female students walk down the hallway to their lockers. Male students frequently congregate along the hallway and make comments about the girls' appearance as they pass. They rate the girls on a scale of 1 to 10.

A teacher shared the following story that took place in her high school U.S. history class:

> I called on one of the female students to answer a question. Just as she began to speak, she slammed her hand down on her desk, turned around to face the male student sitting behind her, and shouted, "Stop that! Don't say things right behind my head so I can't think and can't answer the question!" He said, "I didn't say anything." She answered, "You always say terrible things just behind my head so the teacher can't tell that you're doing it."
>
> I moved the male student to the one vacant seat in the front of the room for the rest of the period and talked with him after class. I began to pay more attention to spacing out the desks just before the start of class and watched to see whether this behavior could be occurring in other classes. I did notice and stop other instances of distracting or harassing a student who is trying to formulate an answer to a question. The students seemed shocked that I noticed, and the harassers were so surprised that they couldn't even come up with words to deny that they were doing anything wrong. Until the one brave female student made me aware of this type of harassment, I had not been aware that it was taking place!

Girls also can be harassers. One parent shared the following incident involving her son:

> Luis recently transferred to a new high school. He passed through the art corridor, a favorite hangout of the older girls. Brooke and her friends, Leticia and Maria, ranked Luis as he passed by. Luis overheard Brooke say, "Can't wait to undress you," while Leticia patted Luis's butt and commented, "Nice butt. Can I photograph you for my project?" Maria laughed the whole time, and other students who were nearby, both male and female, started coming closer to see and hear what was going on. Luis mumbled something under his breath and quickly continued down the hall. He was mortified and avoided that area whenever possible.

At first, I told Luis that this was just part of high school life and not to take it personally. But after repeated incidents, I went to the counselor. Luis didn't want to get the kids in trouble. As a new kid in school, he knew that would be the end of him. The counselor helped Luis practice various responses to the harassment. After a while, it worked, but I'm sure the girls went on to torment other victims.

Boys harass other boys as well. A friend's son played the trombone, and other boys at the back of the school bus harassed him for having such a big instrument. The mom ended up driving him to school, which didn't take any action against the other kids. Another mother observed, "My son likes to express himself in his clothes. He's very flamboyant and has to put up with a lot of negative reactions and horrible teasing whenever he veers from the standard boy fare." Fifteen-year-old Jack said, "I work hard in school. I come prepared and like to participate in class. But lately I've stopped raising my hand so much because other boys call me Mr. Suck-up." As a result, Jack isn't participating in his classes and is feeling insecure about how he should be behave to be more accepted by his peers.

If your teens are courageous enough to tell you about incidents that cause them intense pain or embarrassment, you should not dismiss the behavior as "boys will be boys" or "girls will be girls." If you trivialize such incidents—or actually condone them—girls and boys learn to mistrust adults and the environments that should protect them.

Date Rape: Out-of-School Harassment

If date rape is difficult for adults to define, then it is even harder for young people, who are just beginning to understand the complexities of sexual relationships. According to a study released in 2013, one in three youths aged 14–20 has been the victim of dating violence, and almost one in three admits he or she has committed an act of sexual violence (American Psychological Association, 2013). The most instructive finding, however, was that children who engage in these behaviors feel no sense of responsibility for their actions. This makes sense, since one of the defining characteristics of people who abuse other people is a sense of entitlement. In a society with media messages saturated with violence and sexuality, predominantly against women, we fail to cultivate empathy and accountability in boys.

Although schools cannot control what happens to students outside of school, these institutions and the courts are grappling with schools' responsibility for off-campus but school-related activities. Parents and educators can help boys and girls understand that date rape is a form of violence against girls and women, rather than minimizing the violence or making excuses for the perpetrator. Educators should promote a school climate based on respect and dignity, and parents must model that behavior for their children and expect them to behave accordingly.

At a minimum, schools must inform parents and students about the school district's sexual harassment policy and codes for student conduct. They should also indicate the proper person(s) in the school with whom to talk if parents suspect their children are being harassed. It is important to acknowledge that, in many cases, harassers engage in behaviors that they never learned were inappropriate. Stereotypical images of men and women perpetuate interactions that normalize conflict with the other sex and as within the same sex, particularly if the boy or girl "doesn't fit in" or doesn't meet traditional stereotypes.

By the time children have reached the teen years, sexist attitudes are well embedded. Societal myths tell teenage boys what is expected of them: to be macho, in control, dominant, and aggressive. Too often, males think that females want constant sexual attention and that conquering a female is necessary to build the male ego. Females are considered to be sex objects (if you have any doubts about that, check out the teenage pornographic websites that creep into your computers) and are encouraged to believe that males can't help themselves and their libidos are out of control. Or girls who are not wanted—romantically or sexually—by boys don't feel good about themselves. These sexist attitudes encourage sexual harassment.

It is in everyone's best interests to help our children develop healthy attitudes about personal boundaries and sexuality, and to intervene when we see inappropriate behavior at home and school. When children are little, they have to learn to respect other people's boundaries and listen to their words. The younger the better, because the consequences get more serious as children get older. All children need to learn what unwanted touching is, how not to do it, and to trust their instincts when they are the targets of it. That starts with habits at home and is reinforced by practices in schools.

By intervening, we can support both the perpetrator(s) and the victim(s). Parents and schools have to work together to eliminate sexual harassment. Talking to children about bodily integrity, autonomy, consent, and other people's rights cannot happen in schools in a vacuum. And conversations like these aren't happening enough in homes. The harm caused by sexual harassment and abuse doesn't end with high school graduation. Young women and men take their experiences to college campuses and the workplace, where the detrimental effects of sexual harassment continue to take a toll. On college campuses and in the workplace, sexual harassment litigation costs millions of dollars each year. Unless we stop such harassment in our schools and create a consensus early on that this behavior is wrong, our children will pay for this conduct as they grow up. Unless we talk to our children about these issues, you can be sure of one thing: if we do *not* talk to children about their bodies, their boundaries, and their rights, sexual harassment will continue to be pervasive.

Creating a Positive and Powerful Learning Environment

A supportive learning environment is fair, with high expectations for both behavioral and academic success. All children should feel safe to learn in school, and they should be able to achieve according to their potential. Teachers who are evenhanded and consistent in classroom management are preparing students for educational accomplishments. When teachers are not fair, students will know it, feel it, and challenge it. Students may react with thoughts like "You never call on her" and "You're always hassling him." Teachers must make sure that curriculum and instructional practices are free from bias, parents must encourage their teens and be involved in their education, and schools and parents have a responsibility to make this happen. They must intervene when they see disruptive and/or destructive behavior. However, when parents and educators do step in, they must be tuned in to teenage social dynamics, and parents must grasp the reality of their teens' fears and emotions.

Children respond positively to high expectations and challenges. Some children work better in certain learning environments, whether a highly structured program or a single-sex classroom or school. For middle school girls and boys, the safe environment of single-sex classes can be critical to their identity development. The downside of single-sex education is the lack of a comprehensive social education.

New reports on single-sex education indicate that a "good" education fosters student achievement regardless of whether girls and boys learn separately or together. A "good" education includes small classes and schools, a focused and rigorous academic curriculum, controlled and disciplined environments, and gender-affirming instruction. Teacher training and positive classroom climates are keys to eliminating sex role stereotyping in both single-sex and coeducational programs. Although all-girl or all-boy classes are being studied within coeducational learning environments, school districts are cautioned against setting up separate classes or programs for girls and boys, because they may face almost immediate government scrutiny or legal challenges (Bohm, 2012).

Single-sex education is evidence of the fact that public schools, which more than 90 percent of our children attend, are unable to establish and maintain effective coeducational, bias-free environments. While single-sex education may address the academic concerns of some teens, we don't assume that they would resolve the greater social issues. They can send a message that some teens need special attention, which can undermine rather than be empowering. In addition, according to Galen Sherwin, a senior staff attorney with the ACLU Women's Rights Project, "There is no solid evidence supporting the assertions about supposed differences between boys' and girls' brains that underlie these programs, and there is absolutely no evidence that teaching boys and girls differently leads to any educational improvements" (Sherwin, 2014).

A study published in the American Psychological Association's journal *Psychological Bulletin* looked at the effectiveness of single-sex education on a global level. According to the APA's analysis of 184 studies and more than 1.6 million students worldwide, single-sex education is unlikely to offer an advantage over co-ed schools (Pahlke, et al., 2014). Janet Shibley Hyde of the University of Wisconsin–Madison presented her findings in a February 3, 2013, APA press release. "Proponents of single-sex schools argue that separating boys and girls increases students' achievement and academic interest," Hyde says. "Our comprehensive analysis of the data shows that these advantages are trivial and, in many cases, nonexistent" American Psychological Association, 2014).

The real issue is what should go on in the classroom. If it works in single-sex classes, why not use it in mixed classes? Charter schools, magnet school programs, and International Baccalaureate (IB) programs offer other options. Teens and their parents are happy they have choices.

Sports and other team experiences (science and other academic competitions) provide great experiences for developing the confidence of boys and girls. The skills that teens develop as a result of participating in team activities are undeniable. Sons and daughters, teachers, coaches, and parents see teens who participate in these activities as becoming more goal-oriented, increasing teamwork, being unafraid of competition, feeling courageous, developing persistence, having integrity as a result of learning to make a commitment and keep it, and becoming resilient. These are all character traits that we want our children to have and that encourage academic achievement.

Culturally responsive schools value and respect all cultures, thus strengthening our communities. This involves culturally responsive professional development, discussions about race and culture, male role models and mentors, and strong partnerships with parents. Building a culturally sensitive school provides a better opportunity for teens to gain the necessary coping strategies and academic skills to invest in school and their future.

Parents should make it clear that they expect dedication and maximum effort from their teens in all endeavors. At the same time, they should avoid putting unnecessary pressure on their children by keeping in mind that effort and accomplishment go hand-in-hand. Of course, for a child with special needs or learning disabilities, definitions of effort and accomplishment are somewhat different. For all students, we have to be mindful of acknowledging the quality of effort as well as the outcome.

In a piece discussing the importance of the SATs for getting into college, Jay Matthews, education reporter for the *Washington Post*, reminds us, "At big-name colleges, extracurricular activities (no more than two great ones, not a lot of little ones), teacher recommendations and essays make the difference, in descending order of importance" (Matthews, 2014). He goes on to recommend that students take the most challenging high school courses they can handle, get deeply involved in one or two activities, and get to know one or two teachers very well. "Students who pay attention in class and do their homework will get into fine colleges," he says. "They will discover that success in life, as the research shows, has little to do with the SAT average of one's alma mater. It's what you learn and how hard you work, not what you score that counts." A student's selection of colleges and performance in school require another shift in parenting. It is the time for them to take personal responsibility for their emerging adult lives.

"The Good, the Bad, and the Ugly" of Teenage Friendships

And for the crowd you have to wear the right clothes; you have to have the "attitude"; you have to be willing to bully people; you have to suck up to like your friends or whatever; you have to be outgoing, daring; you have to know certain people; and sometimes you have to be mean.

—Jenna, 15

The need to belong. Many teens feel that they don't belong anywhere or with anyone, so they begin to act insensibly and thus run into trouble. Many kids will do anything so they can be "cool" and belong to a group. For example, some may try drugs so their "friends" will like them.

—Jaden, 16

Parents Are Their Child's Primary Role Models, Their Obi-Wan Kenobi

Obi-Wan Kenobi, a character in the 1977 film *Star Wars*, understood the importance of parenting. Research has found warm and responsive parenting to be the factor most consistently associated with children's development of skills that enable them to form good friendships and positive social relationships and to avoid negative relationships (Ginsburg, 2011). Beginning in the home, children learn the value of relationships and friendships. From birth, and through high school and well beyond, parents influence healthy social development. As teens observe interactions among parents, family, friends, and even colleagues, they see models of the way people should treat each other. These interactions, when healthy, help teens develop social competency, commonly referred to as social skills. These skills include empathy, compassion, self-control, and resiliency. Children without these skills are more likely to have psychological, delinquency, and bullying problems (Tough, 2012).

Parental support takes more than telling your teens that they're fabulous and deserve awards and recognition for everything they do. For supportive parenting to work, it has to involve sincere, caring, and honest discussions about the issues teens face and good modeling of friendships and other relationships. Thoughtful sharing of personal experience makes parents more believable and authentic and normalizes teen experience. Danielle, a junior in high school told us how her parents do this:

> I'm close to my parents. It's nice the way my mom shares her stories and normalizes my experiences. She and my dad validate my feelings and help me to get through the times when I am not invited to parties. I know I can get through it. They also make it all right to be upset about it. Parents can give you perspective. My dad will tell me, "Get over it; this stinks, but you will feel OK." He reminds me that one of his college friends had a wedding in Hawaii and was left at the altar. He'll say, "So, tell me again your problem." It's still OK to feel upset; I can feel it and move on.

But this isn't easy. To parent effectively, we often must run a gauntlet of challenges imposed by the realities of teens' emotional development. From personal experience, we all know the importance of friendships during the intense teen years. Yet when we try to guide our teens through difficulties with these relationships, we often feel confused and helpless as our teens push back when we act like their teachers. We get stymied with our teens' half-stories, anxiety, drama, and resentments. And often, after we try to help, they move on and may forget to tell us if and when their problem with a friend has been resolved. Despite all this, we must be calmly tenacious, supportive but not controlling, open to discussion but not pedantic, and always conscious of the impact of modeling relationships. But no pressure!

Social media notwithstanding, we learned from our focus groups that the nature and dynamics of friendships haven't changed all that much for this generation of teenagers. Today's teens deal with the drama of teenage life: how to cope with the "cool group," dependency on their friends, and a strong need to belong. Teens confirmed that they appreciate hearing about how their parents handled the social pressures of middle and high school. It should reassure parents to know that sharing their adolescent experiences will have more of an impact than they might think. Sharing these experiences is an effective way for parents to stay engaged and plugged into their teenagers' lives.

In this chapter, we describe the landscape of teen friendships from middle through high school. We discuss the skills teens require to develop and maintain good friendships. While each child's sense of self, social relationships, methods of expression, and interactions can vary, we find that teens share a common need for friendship. We have separated the discussion by gender to give insights into the similarities and differences that boys and girls experience in their quest for friends. Unlike in previous generations, one significant pattern is the importance of boy-girl friendships that are not romantic.

We also discuss cliques and bullying, the "dark side" of the teen relationships, which the use of social media is making more pervasive and complicated. Cliques and bullying are all too common in the teen landscape. In their social universe, teens struggle to hold their place, achieve self-confidence, and overcome insecurity. All teens wrestle with this struggle, regardless of how they present themselves. As part of this struggle, virtually all teens must decide whether to join cliques, exclude or include others, bully or support bullying, and/or cope with exclusion or bullying directed at them.

The Changing Landscape: Stuck in the Middle

In middle school, the wide variation in emotional and physical growth exacerbates what is already a complex process of development. This is a time of constant emotional upheaval when long-standing friendships can blow up in an instant. Middle school is also the time when kids begin making new friends based on common interests, worrying about fitting in, stressing about being teased, and feeling self-conscious about how they look. These are additional sources of change and adjustment. Jennifer described how this time affected her:

> When I was in seventh grade, I looked like I was ten years old. I was straight all over and could practically fit a bracelet on my thigh! My best friend, Courtney, acted like a girl in high school and had the body of a woman. We made a funny pair. For a year or so, I stayed away from Courtney and her new friends. They were very social and went to parties that sometimes had drinking. I was too scared to go. We had few interests in common, and I felt left out of her new group. It was lonely and tough, but I wasn't yet interested in hanging out and flirting with boys. I was barely finished watching Nickelodeon. Eventually, I, too, grew, but the friendship was different. I found other friends in the meantime, but it wasn't easy, and I really missed Courtney.

Girls develop physically and emotionally at such different rates that, as one mother described her daughter's friends, "One friend of Sarah's still looks like a little girl, and another looks like she could be birthing babies." The hormones kick in, and when they do, some girls are more socially sophisticated than others, become boy crazy sooner, and are less interested in their friends who are not primping and grooming and hanging out at the mall. Jennifer's and Sarah's experiences are universal because the range of development in 12- to 14-year-old girls is so diverse and so visible. These differences complicate friendships for girls because what they once shared as children no longer exists; they are literally at different life stages. For example, the mother of 13-year-old Erica, said,

> Some of the girls are ready for girl-boy parties. For my daughter, she is only ready to play with flirting by instant-messaging boys. If girls aren't ready for boy-girl parties, they usually aren't in the popular group. Erica wasn't being called for sleepovers anymore because she wasn't ready for boys and her former friends "didn't want a baby around."

For most teens, middle school is the period of transition between the solid friendships of elementary school and the social pandemonium of early adolescence. During this period, teenagers become aware that friendships are a fragile commodity that must be earned and nurtured. Navigating this transition is one of the greatest teen challenges for children and their parents. For this reason, many parents approach the middle-school years with trepidation. The mother of 14-year-old Katie shared this story:

> For my daughter, middle school was a series of losses. She lost friends because she wasn't as precocious as some of her elementary-school friends. They wouldn't speak to her and actually told her she wasn't welcome in their group any longer. Katie lost confidence in herself and spent a lot of time alone watching TV and reading. It was incredibly painful for me to watch. Although it was painful for Katie, I'm not sure she didn't survive it better than I did. Once she got to high school, there were so many more choices of activities where she could meet new kids.

The father of 13-year-old Tim told us a boy's version of this challenge: "My son has experienced more pressure and conflict with his peers than he did in elementary school. He just doesn't have the social skills that would help him to get along better with his friends. Tim is also slow to mature, and he gets teased by his more developed classmates. It's just hard." Many boys may not enter puberty until the end of middle school, while others will have attained almost full growth by that time. This allows for a huge variation in the size and appearance among boys of the same age; some may look like older elementary-school-age children, while others will clearly appear to be nearly adult men! Nicholas, 15 years old, said:

> Middle school was the worst three years, so awkward. I could have skipped it and lived my whole life without missing it! It's weird, maturing while others don't. Starting in the spring, lots of kids sat out on the field for lunch; all I saw were people sitting in groups, in defined pods. Everyone turned around when you walked out, and if you couldn't see to join your friends, you would go back inside and eat alone. High school is so much better.

The Still Changing Landscape: High School

Friendships do change during the high school years. There are more options and greater opportunities for autonomy and interest-based relationships. This is true for both boys and girls. The teens in our focus groups agreed that as long as they have a stable group of friends, they are comfortable in high school. All of them seemed to agree that they are so happy to be through with middle school. Rebecca, a 14-year-old high school freshman, said, "It's OK to be in a loser clique in high school; it's harder in middle school because you're more noticeable."

In today's culture new avenues have opened up for teens to acquire social capital and a sense of belonging. It's no longer only designer labels, beauty, and athletic abilities. Skills, talents, and unique forms of expression open up new paths to acquire friends and social status. Teens have diverse interests, a wider variety of extracurricular activities, and the opportunity to form friendships based on these interests. Examples include the teens who create an app for fantasy football, organize other students to march for gun control, post artistic photos on Instagram, or post skateboarding videos on YouTube.

This is good news, along with the fact that groups are now more fluid, which means that some teenagers can move more freely between various groups without fear of exclusion. One mother said, "Joey would have been considered a loner in the past, and was in middle school, but now that he posts his songs on SoundCloud, he gets a lot of positive attention because other kids like his music. This attention has helped him to make new friends and come out of his shell and blossom." Another mother said, "Carly designs fashions for teens and created a website where she posts her designs. She now has a few hundred kids who follow her posts. This positive attention has been like an inoculation against insecurity and a booster shot of self-esteem."

Hierarchal and exclusionary behaviors are common and part of teen and adult life. Alexandra Robbins, author of *The Geeks Shall Inherit the Earth*, says it's a natural part of cognitive development for students to cluster into groups.

> They begin to form their identity based not by their family but by their friends," she says. "Forming boundaries, judging people by external characteristics, and labeling them is all a part of students' learning to structure the world around them" (Long, 2013).

The title of Robbins's book does affirm that the "geeks" and others who may not fit the cool stereotype will be successful in life!

The bottom line is that it is unlikely that parents and their children, or even a group of parents, can make major changes in the social dynamics of a school. However, parents can help their teens cope with specific incidents and provide opportunities to excel at one of their passions. In high school, parents can't butt in and do it for their teens.

Getting overly involved can backfire and ostracize your teens. Parents in our focus group shared stories of other parents who, as one mother described, "support the pecking order." The mother explained, "They are happy if their kids have many cool friends and are invited to all of the parties. It's almost as if they [the parents] are cool if their kids are in a cool group."

So how can we as parents guide our children through the high school social scene? There are more groups to choose from, and teens need some close friends, not a pack. Parents also must remind their children that exclusion and bullying are unacceptable, and they should talk with their children about feelings regarding rejection. Almost everyone can agree that the power of cliques should change, but without an intentional effort by parents and other adult role models, this behavior will persist.

Encourage your children to find their uniqueness. Help your teens to develop skills and follow their passions. Your children can draw tremendous strength from knowing they are competent. Sara said, "When I'm feeling really down, I go to my room and play my guitar. Many nights, I write lyrics instead of writing in a journal, and put them to music. I'm not sure how I'd cope without my music." Dancing, playing a sport, being a member of a band or a theater group, social activism, painting, blogging, cooking—we could go on and on—are all antidotes to the inevitable social rejection teens feel at some point. "Do unto others as you would have them do unto you" is still a good model for behavior. Being friendly and treating others with respect can provide some insurance against being excluded. It is helpful to have friends when walking down those hallowed hallways.

The Good: The Strength of Teen Friendships

While sitting with focus groups of teenage girls, we were struck by the "buzz" that constantly surrounds them. They exert so much energy, sometimes like the flutter of butterflies, other times like a gaggle of geese discussing and laughing about every aspect of their experience. When watching a group of boys interact, we saw them slouching comfortably side-by-side, talking and laughing, but not with the same volume. Both boys and girls talk and maintain relationships through texting and IMing. The reliance on this new form of communication may not be the face-to-face we're used to, but they seem to interact, nevertheless. Though experiences are expressed differently, friendship seems to offer both teen girls and boys a tremendous opportunity to experience invaluable companionship and support.

Psychologist Jennifer Watling Neal's recent study looks at how girls' and boys' relationships develop over time. While girls tend to get together in more intimate groups than boys, these differences disappear by eighth grade. Neal said, "Although we tend to think that girls' and boys' peer groups are structured differently, these differences disappear as children get older," according to Neal. "Younger boys and girls tend to play in same-sex peer groups, . . . But every parent can relate to that moment when their son or daughter suddenly takes an interest, whether social or romantic, in the opposite sex. While the size of boys' peer groups remained relatively stable, girls' peer groups became progressively larger in later grades" (Michigan State University, 2010).

By adolescence, the characteristics of positive friendship are what all teens have in common. A positive teen friendship incorporates loyalty, trust, and collaboration. These same characteristics of friendship sustain us as adults. Many of us can trace friendships back to elementary school. We can move cross-country and not talk to each other for months or years. But when we meet again, perhaps through Facebook, it's as if we just saw each other.

Positive friendships offer priceless lessons in relationships. They teach boys and girls about empathy, support, nurturing, love, and loss. We saw our focus-group teens crave and experience these kinds of friendships and experiences. One group of ninth graders had been meeting together in a mother-daughter book group since they were in second grade. Another group of seniors had been playing soccer together since they were in kindergarten. Although some teens from each group now attended different high schools, their connection, respect, trust, and reliance on emotional support were strong. Michelle, 16, said,

> I count on my friends for everything. I have one friend whose parents recently split up, and I was talking to her about how she felt. She said her parents wanted her to go and see a therapist, and she told them, "If I can't say these things to my friends, then how can I say them to a therapist?" That made me think about the depth of friendships at this age.

A parent of a high school junior described her son's group as "a very welcoming and dependable posse. Their friendships don't conform to the nasty things we read about. I feel the boys watch each other's backs." One mother said,

> My father died on Kristi's sixteenth birthday, and instead of celebrating with her, I flew to Chicago to plan the funeral. It was gut-wrenching on many levels, and I worried about leaving her to deal with her shock and grief without me. But she was not alone. Her friends, both her boy- and girlfriends, surrounded her with comfort and warmth. Her friends had so much emotional wisdom, which they generously shared. It was such a relief to know she had the support of such a solid group of friends.

Fifteen-year-old Madison said, "I know there are girls who are mean to each other. They say they're friends, and they act like they're friends when they're with each other, but they always talk behind each other's backs. My friends are over that now. We support and comfort each other; we are really just there for our friends." Madison's mother confirms this observation: "I tell Madison how important it is to be straight with your friends, but more significantly, I try to model how to be a good friend." Positive connections and friendships get us through life.

Jonathan, 16, said he understood friendship differently after going to Africa for a community service project:

> I couldn't bring my phone; you weren't allowed to. I actually talked to people. Developing a relationship in person is so different. People don't know how to do it anymore. In the hallway at school, I would pretend to be on the phone so I didn't have to make eye contact. Now I try to put my phone away and actually talk to people. Sometimes they are shocked!

So how can parents help their children to understand and facilitate positive teen friendships? Make sure your children participate in formal and informal activities that foster positive adolescent values, strengths, social skills, and contributions to others. Parents also should model how to be a good friend, acting with empathy and compassion and valuing others. This includes knowing how to disagree and fight fairly. And last, parents must enable their children to accept that intense emotions, powerful as they are, are fleeting and impermanent. Emotions at this age are often fluid.

The critical skill in friendship is communication, and today's teens do a lot of it—not by talking face-to-face, but by texting, posting, and sharing photos. As parents, you must teach your teens about the risks with friends and the consequences to them from careless use of social media. You can teach them that texting is never private; it is short and lacks nuance, and messages are easily misunderstood or misused. They should expect that anything they text and any photo they transmit will be distributed to everyone they know, people they don't know, and people whom they don't want to see what they send—for all time.

Regardless of how well we guide and teach them, our teens will make mistakes. Mistakes present opportunities to learn about the consequences of their behavior and the importance of appropriate boundaries and respect. These lessons will help them navigate the emotional turbulence of teenage life. When teens live fully in the present, such as when they send provocative photos to their most current crush, they may have difficulty accepting that the relationship may not last forever. As parents, you can present the longer view, a perspective that inherently challenges teens.

To be clear, your efforts to guide—maybe a better word is *coach*—your teen will fail if you present your thoughts as lectures, moral strictures, and judgments. Certainly, conversations about behavioral consequences are part of your parenting tools. However, we believe that teaching the lessons we are addressing here—self-worth, empathy, respect, integrity, and being a valued friend—are best presented by sharing stories, examples, and experiences. Even decades later, your tales will guide your teens through difficult patches.

Boys and Girls as Friends

Friendships between boys and girls provide a special opportunity for openness and a safe place for them to explore and learn about relationships. Matt, 17, said,

> Girls have an easier time being friends to boys because they are satisfied with being friends without the sexual component. I think we aren't as critical as girls, and we see things from a different point of view. My best "girl" friend, Stephanie, usually calls me to see if she is overreacting to something her boyfriend, Justin, said or did. Social stuff is not as dramatic for us, and we can be helpful by offering a different perspective.

Hannah, a high school junior, said,

> Thank God for Sam. I asked him to so many dances; he's my default date. We're just friends, but I count on his friendship and unconditional support. When he's standing with a group of guys, I never have to feel uncomfortable about joining them. When I walk up to the group, Sam puts his arm around me and welcomes me with the sweetest hello. I've cried on his shoulder and listened to fears that he tells no one else.

Boys connect when they are comfortable and safe. But when threatened, they often use language shields or become silent, sullen, or angry. Boys are often more comfortable being friends with girls and sharing their feelings. Ben said, "You better believe when it's late at night, if I'm texting, it's to one of my girl friends. For some reason, I'd never text a guy late at night. But my friend Kori is so easy to talk to. We share things, and I trust her. It's nice knowing I can reach out to her before I go to bed."

The girls with whom we spoke also told us that boys do transcend their reluctance to talk in a personal way. The girls told us that in their one-on-one friendships with boys, they are able to communicate openly. One girl reported, "I have a really, really good guy friend. I tell him maybe more than I tell my girlfriends. And he shares everything with me, even emotions. I also find that I can do anything in front of him, and I feel comfortable around him." Friendships between girls and boys represent important connections for getting through these years intact.

Parents can encourage these rich relationships and should not assume all boy-girl friendships have to be romantic. Let them talk (usually text) and get comfort at a time in their lives when real friendships matter. For boys, who usually aren't taught the language of feelings, having a girl as a friend can allow them to express what they really feel and learn how to do it from those who do it often—girls. For girls, it's a safe place where they don't feel judged. Besides offering trust and intimacy without judgment, such relationships give boys and girls insight into how members of the opposite sex approach the world.

The Bad: Cliques

Friendships are a key to how girls and boys feel about themselves, yet they can have a dark side, called cliques, during these years. In every school or among social groups, there are people who radiate power, confidence, and influence. They can make people feel included or excluded. Peers of these young people are likely to see these cliques as cool. The cool factor perpetuates itself because other teens are drawn to them, which maintains their popularity and status.

When teens who radiate power, confidence, and influence include or exclude others, their group becomes a clique. Ask any teens, and they can describe in detail who belongs to the "in" clique, although they may not be able to verbalize precisely what makes those individuals cool. All teens go through the revolving door of social acceptance. Cliques are groups that make it clear to others just who is considered *in* and who is considered *out*. They usually focus on popularity and status, giving outsiders the impression that members of the clique think they're better than those outside.

The difference between a clique and a group of friends is the lack of freedom and movement that clique members have outside the clique. Members feel pressure to do *everything* with their friends in the clique. Julia offered an inside perspective:

> I was in a clique my freshman and sophomore years in high school. We sat together every day during lunch. There were times I wanted to sit with other friends from my soccer team but knew I'd be ridiculed as a traitor if I did. We walked around like we owned the school, but I felt so stuck. I worried about saying the right thing and got tired of feeling so insecure. For two years I was such a follower! It was very stressful and not at all what I had thought it would be like.

Julia's experience is not unusual; members of a clique are well aware that other members often resort to flattery and humiliation or rumors to manipulate the others and maintain the clique's tight hold on each other. Fourteen-year-old Rachel said, "My friends are my life." Alexis, a high school senior, said, "Nothing is worse than a friend's betrayal." Another girl reported, "My worst fear is being alone." One mother said,

> Alyssa is reserved and anxious to please. She wants to be liked more than anything else. She is so self-effacing that she doesn't take credit

for what she does and is much more comfortable in the background. I know this because I watch her stepping back and waiting to hear how her friends think before she speaks. Sometimes I overhear her agreeing with her friends about something that we've talked about, and I know she really has a different opinion.

Even when you're in a group, you may realize that you are considered dispensable. In general, teenage girls are continually being pulled in two directions, wanting to be different and accepted at the same time. Remember, you want teens to learn to behave in ways that are consistent with their own values, not just follow a clique. While the criteria and rules for cliques are often very specific, they differ from school to school. What is cool in downtown Denver may not be cool in the suburbs of Los Angeles, and what is cool in New York City is not the same as in Seattle. However, regardless of where you live, no one feels really secure in a clique.

Parents and teens alike often struggle to figure out why certain kids are more popular than others. Brianna said, "The worst part of cool is that I am always comparing myself to them and always find myself wanting, no matter what. Once me and my friends start comparing ourselves to the cool group, even if we don't really like them and they usually don't like each other, we always feel bad about ourselves." Students who try to figure out who they are by comparing themselves with others rather than getting to know themselves are too often going to feel that they don't measure up. One mother relayed the following conversation she had with her teenage twins:

> I kept saying to Alex and Ryan, "What is it about this group that I keep hearing about? Are they smarter? Do they get better grades? Are they richer? Do they have bigger houses? What is it that identifies them?" Alex kept saying, "No, it's not that. It's not that." Ryan finally said, "I think it's just that they assume that they are popular and they're entitled to belong to this group, and the rest of us will go our merry way and make our friends elsewhere. One of the girls

in the group is very nice to me when I see her in history, but when I see her with her posse at parties, she's absolutely obnoxious. They think they're in this golden bubble."

They are not easily defined, but everyone knows who "they" are, even parents and teachers. Drew, a college sophomore, says, "I was so obsessed with chasing coolness, which was such a pointless and intangible thing. It kept slipping through my fingers when I tried to catch it. I'm finally happy, but I never got a chance to actually get comfortable in high school."

Complicated Girls

Books about mean and troubled girls have painted a dismal picture of teenage female culture. We often hear about and see images of the tall, shapely blonde at the center of the social hub who uses her good looks and popularity to attract or marginalize other, "ordinary" females. These are the cool cutthroat girls who value their social omnipotence over friendship, solidarity, and compassion. Then there are the girls who will follow any given formula to gain the good graces of the cool girls. There is still another group of girls we don't hear much about. These are the more average-looking, studious, kind, compassionate, and free-spirited girls who feel comfortable in their own skin and don't feel it's necessary to put someone else down to enhance their social stature. These girls may be so busy reading or spending time with family members or with special-interest and/or faith-based groups that they don't get caught up in the need to be (or appear to be) socially savvy.

By following a self-designed path on the outskirts of the group, these girls develop insight and maturity beyond that typically found among their more group-dependent peers. Their experience with groups is more fluid; they have the ability to move in and out of groups at their own initiative. Unlike the popular girls, who seem to have the greatest pressure to grow up quickly, these girls often have the self-confidence and self-respect that allows them to escape the peer group pressure to experiment with drugs and early sexual activity.

Some girls choose not to get caught up in what can be a vicious cycle of instant inclusion and exclusion. These girls may share three or four best friends and treat everyone else, as one girl described, as "an associate." Not depending on a particular social group allows girls to explore interests, develop skills, and avoid being boxed in by a particular set of norms and standards. The mother of 16-year-old Jasmine described her daughter this way:

> Jasmine keeps it simple. She doesn't aspire to be in any group, but you can always find her with one of her four best friends. I have taught her that only she is important to her development and state of mind. I want her to be who she is, not what others want her to be. Other than me, Jasmine knows that nobody can take better care of her than she can. She has to learn to take care of herself, not at the expense of others, but to learn to trust herself.

Girls who are always trying to be popular often do not get the opportunity to think independently. Even for those girls who always "dress the right way," the challenge to maintain this status can be limiting. Parents who have chosen not to push or fixate on their children's popularity can take comfort in knowing that there are benefits to not belonging to the cool group.

For all the power residing with those in the cool clique, the social terrain of middle and high school can be rough for even the most popular girl. Understanding the landscape and how it works is paramount for effective parenting. Backstabbing, gossiping, bullying, nitpicking, and ostracism have long been elements of teen girl culture. With the advent of the Internet and smartphones, these elements are now a 24/7 nightmare. Adolescent girls live in a world where best friends can become enemies overnight, where one look from another girl can mean the difference between isolation and belonging. It's a world where no one tells you why you can no longer sit at the lunch table with your friends, where secrets are traded like currency and gossip is devoured like candy. Rejection and isolation are common, public, and difficult to defend against. Parents must try to prepare their daughters and support them in managing the culture of teenage girl life.

Earlier in this chapter, we discussed coaching teens to enhance their self-awareness, values, and social skills to build and maintain positive friendships. All of those lessons apply equally when learning to cope with a "mean girl." But the terrain is a bit different, and application of these lessons more specialized. We have observed that girls experience social exclusion as devastating because they define themselves in relation to their peer group. The mother of 13-year-old Heather told the following story:

> My daughter was invited to a sleepover. She had swim practice the next day, and I didn't want her to be tired. She is usually OK about coming home at a reasonable time on Friday evenings, but this time she went ballistic on me. At first, I couldn't get her to tell me why it was so important to sleep at Julia's house. But Heather's reaction didn't match the content, so I knew something else was going on. Finally, she told me that a group of friends were spending the night, and if she wasn't there, she could be their next victim. Heather actually said, "Mom, they'll kill me off if I'm not there to protect myself."
>
> I really didn't know what to do. I knew that if she spent the night, Heather might as well forget about swim team practice, but she seemed so vulnerable that I didn't want to put her "in harm's way." I let Heather make the choice. She decided to spend the night but wanted to be picked up early enough to go to swim practice. I agreed to take her. Heather was so appreciative of my not forcing her to go to practice and letting her make the decision. This incident gave us a good opportunity to talk about the meaning of friendship while at the same time learning how to watch your back. All I know is, I wouldn't want to be 13 again!

In one of our focus groups, another mother said, "The horrible treatment some girls inflict on others creates scars that can't be seen."

The pressure to fit in, to achieve in school, to be nonthreatening to boys and other girls can chip away at a girl's self-image. Consumed with being liked by others, they don't get around to liking themselves. Often there is a "mean girl" or a clique of "mean girls," who add to this diminished self-image. Even a couple of decades later, mothers can recall the girls who had social power when they were in school and how those girls made them feel. The mother of 15-year-old Laura said, "When my daughter is sad, it is so painful to watch. I know I bring my own baggage to the situation. No one that I know would ever want to go back to being a 14- or 15-year-old girl." Unfortunately, a lot of this exclusionary and hurtful behavior stays under the radar of many teachers and parents. For several mothers, the memory of the powerful, mean girls who decided who would go to which parties and who would be allowed to sit with them during lunch still stings. Olivia, 16 years old, said,

> On Monday, I had five girlfriends who ate lunch with me every day at the same table in the cafeteria. On Tuesday, I felt an icy chill when I put my tray of food down at the table. Natalie looked up from her sandwich and snarled, "Olivia, there's really no room here for you!" I was totally clueless about what was going on, and I practically had to get on my knees to find out why Natalie was mad. I apologized for something I don't even think I did, but it was the easiest way to avoid her anger. I was scared that she'd get my other friends to treat me like a leper. What really gets me is that I never call her on how petty she is. I'm too chicken to shake the boat, so I suck it up and hold it in.

In this instance, Olivia, like so many other girls, chose to be silent and hide her real opinions to avoid conflict. She learned that hiding part of herself is a way to maintain her place in the groups.

Girls' friendships in adolescence are filled with pitfalls because their social life involves negotiating cliques, gossip, and power plays.

Gossip is the background noise that girls accept within their peer groups and that allows them to express unsafe feelings, such as anger and aggression. Texting and social media have made this a minefield. We can remind our daughters that girls often behave this way because they are also afraid of being left out, so they go along. In one of our focus groups, Kelly told us she had left the cool group for another group of friends because she was tired of mean girl behavior. Trying to keep up is challenging for even the meanest of girls. It's exhausting! Finding another group of friends, where the pressure is less and acceptance is more the norm, is the best antidote to this ordeal.

Complicated Boys

Boys' friendships with one another don't seem to have the complexities that girls' friendships do. One boy said, "You hang out with boys you are comfortable with based upon sports, video games, music, and other common interests. You don't question why or whether or not you are good enough to be someone's friend. It just happens or it doesn't." The main criterion for boys is comfort; there isn't any subplot. They don't judge each other to the same degree as girls do about physical appearance or what kind of clothes they wear. If they do, it may be a minute or two of sarcasm or teasing, and then they're done. They are less concerned about whom you were texting last night. There is less pressure to fit in, because there are fewer criteria. There is no spoken analysis. They don't easily feel rejected, and they have a strong sense of loyalty. John said, "We don't say whether or not Jim is good enough to hang out with. You just do or you don't."

They do get comfort in just being together. In middle school, boys play video games on various platforms and sports. It's not that they don't worry about their hair, acne, or other aspects of their appearance. They see it, deal with it as best they can, and don't dwell on it. They do share more with each other as younger adolescents, but as they grow older, they become much more cautious about sharing feelings. Boys want to avoid being labeled soft, weak, or gay. Discussion, if any, usually takes the form of a smart-ass comment and grunts. It isn't that they don't have or need emotional connection; it's just that they do it with less drama and far fewer words.

Does that sound simple and appealing? It's not quite. The consequence of "boys will be boys" is that teenage boys are continually trying to prove their manhood. Boys are not necessarily antigay as much as they buy into the importance of guys "acting like guys" (Way et al., 2013). Niobe Way, author of *Deep Secrets: Boys' Friendships and the Crisis of Connection*, draws some conclusions from her research with boys over the past two decades:

The popular stereotype is that boys are emotionally illiterate and shallow, they don't want intimate relationships or close friendships. I have discovered that not only are these stereotypes false, they are actively hurting boys and leading them to engage in self-destructive behaviors. The African American, Latino, Asian American and white teenage boys in my studies indicate that what they want and need most are close relationships—friendships, in particular—in which they can share their "deep secrets." These friendships, they tell us, are critical for their mental health. But, according to the boys, they live in a culture that considers such intimacy "girly" and thus they are discouraged from having the very relationships that are critical for their wellbeing. (Way, 2013)

A narrow definition of masculinity forces boys to carry a shield of armor that limits their emotional and relational development. Such behaviors have a profound effect on how boys form friendships. It's not surprising that, in high schools across the country, athletes who play major sports attain the highest status. In healthy psychological development, a teen would typically acquire new skills and qualities in a progressive fashion; as each one is acquired, the teen makes it a part of his or her maturing self. In contrast, traditional male socialization, as described by psychotherapist Terrance Real, reflects a process of disconnection marked by successive "disavowing" and loss of qualities for themselves and in relationships with others, all essential to boys' emotional and psychological well-being (1997). Some of these qualities include sadness, vulnerability, pain, and empathy. This lack of emotional connection is often combined with a sense of privilege, power, and entitlement that also stems from traditional masculine ideals. It isn't surprising that these factors influence boys to behave in disrespectful and antisocial ways toward their parents, teachers, and peers.

The protective shield of boys leads them to be careful about not only whom they talk to, but also how and what they say in specific groups. When we asked boys to talk about themselves in our focus groups, they frequently did two things. First, they defined themselves by stating not what they were, but rather how they were different from others (usually girls) in the group. For example, they would make statements beginning "Boys aren't" rather than "Boys are." Second, boys often referred to themselves in either the second person ("you") or the first person plural ("we"). Rarely did boys use the first person singular ("I"). These patterns of speech may suggest reluctance on their part to talk in a personal, intimate way.

Even though boys may find occasional safe outlets for their emotions and behaviors, their shield is the primary image they show to the outside world. This manufactured self-confidence and bravado may be masking a more damaging self-concept.

The Ugly: Bullying

Bullying involves aggression and a systematic use of power. The problem may begin at home with family interactions and as early as elementary school. It includes physical aggression, such as hitting, and verbal aggression, such as name-calling, making threats, or spreading rumors. Jaden told the following story:

> My friend Vanessa was in geometry class. She sat in the first row, and
> I sat behind her. Whenever the boys would call her names, I would

tell them, "Mind your own business." She was in tears after they called her "horse face" and told her, "You put the *u* in ugly." I said to Vanessa, "Let's go to the cafeteria and have lunch; no one will bother you."

But today because of social media, there is really no safe space. (Olweus, 2005)

According to a recent report by the American Educational Research Association (AERA), "Bullying presents one of the greatest health risks to children, youth and young adults in U.S. society. . . . Its effects on victims, perpetrators, and even bystanders are both immediate and long term and can affect the development and functioning of individuals across generations" (2013). The following list of statistics may seem overwhelming, but we provide it so you will understand how pervasive bullying is and that in a given year every teen is vulnerable to bullying:

* One of every four students is bullied.
* One of five students admits to having bullied others.
* Every day, 160,000 students miss school to avoid being bullied.
* Each year, 100,000 students carry a gun to school to protect themselves from bullies (Sheridan, 2010).
* Forty-two percent of kids have been cyberbullied.
* Nine of 10 teens have had their feelings hurt online.

All of these statistics are from Nobullying.com (2014), except where another source is cited.

Bullying is endemic to school culture, and as adults, we know it is endemic to life, at home and in the workplace. It is practiced across every gender, race, ethnicity, and socioeconomic status. However, students who do not conform to traditional gender norms are more likely than their peers to report being bullied at school (56 percent versus 33 percent; Gay, Lesbian & Straight Education Network [GLSEN] & Harris Interactive, 2012). In 2012, approximately 30 percent of U.S.

teens and preteens aged 12–18 reported being involved in bullying as victims, perpetrators, or both (Robers et al., 2012). Another high percentage of teens report being bystanders, making it likely that most students are affected by bullying during a typical school year (Wang et al., 2009).

The consequences to teens who are bullied by either cyberbullying or in-your-face bullying are substantial and long lasting. They include higher rates of anxiety, depression, problems with physical health and social adjustment, and poor academic performance (U.S. Department of Health and Human Services [HHS], 2014a). In addition, students who bully are at a higher risk of delinquency, criminal behavior, and social maladjustment in adulthood (Bender & Lösel, 2011; Farrington et al., 2011). The bottom line is that bullying is pervasive, has many causes, takes multiple forms, and has severe consequences. As parents, we have to take bullying seriously. It isn't just "kids will be kids."

Bullying plays out differently for boys and girls. While boys tend to get physical, girls more often bully other girls with verbal assaults that result in excluding another girl or spreading false rumors and gossip about her. Females are victims of electronic bullying (for example, social networking sites, instant messaging, text messaging) twice as often as males (Sheridan, 2010). Same-sex bullying is far too common and includes accusing others of being fags, gays, or lesbians. In fact, a large percentage of bullying among students involves homophobic teasing and slurs (HHS, 2014b; Poteat et al., 2012; Robinson & Espelage, 2011). Some LGBTQ teens report greater depression, anxiety, suicidal behaviors, and truancy than do their heterosexual peers (Kosciw et al., 2012). A middle-school counselor told us,

> The thing that is most offensive about homophobia in pro sports is the type of behavioral conduct that's not even questioned as tolerable among teammates. Rape, vehicular homicide, spousal abuse, vicious assault—a guy can be accused of or have actually committed one of those crimes (and those are off the top of my head), and not

one story will be written about how his teammates will accept him. It is more socially acceptable for men to tolerate and condone those types of criminal acts than it is for them to be understanding of or tolerant toward male homosexuals. Gay men are judged more harshly than violent criminals in America. This is what the Michael Sam story in which this gay football player publicly acknowledged his sexual orientation should lead us into talking about.

Bullying can have a profound impact on how teens feel at school. After repeated gossip about her sexuality appeared on the bathroom walls of her school, one high school girl told us, "The experience was awful. I didn't want to go to school. I felt rattled all the time, I felt insecure and vulnerable. School was no longer a safe place for me."

Students with disabilities also are often targets (HHS, 2014c). A parent recalled, "I knew a boy who was visually impaired who was punched mercilessly. A group of boys would come up to him from behind and punch him between his shoulder blades. Life is hard enough for kids who look different without these attacks." The sense of isolation and difference that some kids demonstrate and feel at school increases their vulnerability to being bullied by their more powerful peers.

The teachers with whom we spoke expressed the belief that those who bully are responding to the power differences they see in society, in the media, or at home. They may be also compensating for inadequacies, real or imagined. The teachers see these students copying these behaviors at school, where they use their power to intimidate others. One middle-school English teacher said, "When students do not have something in their lives that makes them feel good, they turn to negative behaviors. If they can't get positive attention, they will turn to negative attention rather than feeling powerless and invisible." As an antidote to this behavior, teachers suggested that schools foster a sense of community where the school encourages a sense of caring for one another, and for this strategy to work, teachers have to model this behavior. Research supports this strategy for collaborations that may allow bullies and victims to see themselves and their peers in a new way (National School Climate Council, 2010).

Alexis, 15 years old, recalled an example in which she asked for and received support at school:

> When I walked into French class, I saw a paper on my desk, and on it was written in bold letters, "DYKE." I quickly turned the paper over, slid into my chair, and unsuccessfully tried to hold back my tears. The truth is, I don't know if I'm gay, so I immediately felt exposed, humiliated, and frightened. After school, I told my parents about it, and they suggested that I ignore it. Ignoring it didn't make it stop.
>
> So I confided in my French teacher after class, and she suggested that I go to the counselor. I resisted at first, because it just seemed like an invitation for more abuse if anyone else found out about it. The teacher assured me that I could trust the counselor, and she took my situation seriously. She told me that the school had an antibullying policy, and there was a procedure for complaints. She was right. After talking to the counselor, I felt less ashamed.

If you want to help your teens, tell them they haven't done anything wrong, seek help when needed, and support them as they question issues of sexuality.

Boys report increases in how frequently they are called gay epithets as they progress through high school (Poteat et al., 2012). Logan shared the following story: "I was bullied from middle school through high school. I was ostracized and restricted to only certain bathroom stalls to avoid 'contaminating' the others, slurred and degraded in hallway graffiti, and pushed or shoved on my way to school because I was gay." Logan said the bullying was constant and unrelenting. He thought about killing himself and about how to harm his tormentors. Logan tried to talk to school officials but was afraid that if he made a big deal about it, his situation would get worse and not better. When he was a junior in high school, Logan finally found other students, and they started an antibullying campaign with the help of the student advocates. Logan said, "I began to stand up for myself and for other students, and I gained more confidence in myself, and it was only then that the bullying stopped. I couldn't have gotten through this without my new group of friends and my parents."

Because males' identity is so wrapped up in their physicality, boys who are slow to move through puberty or who might be on the smaller size of the height spectrum are also vulnerable to bullying. Said one mother, "My son, Eric, was five feet tall at fifteen. He learned never to stand in front of an open locker door because boys would shove him inside, calling him Fairy Mary. He would be banging from the inside, and the custodian would come to break it open."

We must allow boys to be boys in the most human sense of the word, nurture their natural emotional and social capacities, and encourage their close friendships. We need to make relationship and emotional literacy an inherent part of being human, rather than only a "girl thing" or a "gay thing." What makes us human is our ability to connect deeply with each other. We must figure out how to help boys and young men strengthen rather than lose these critical life skills. Only then we will be able to address the psychological and sociological roots of this crisis of connection and the negative consequences associated with it.

If you find that your child is the bully, you should be truly concerned. You should explain the seriousness of treating people disrespectfully and have swift consequences for continuing the behavior. You should also support the school's actions against the bullying behavior. Excusing or ignoring the behavior encourages it to continue. Bullies often don't really understand how their behavior affects others, because their feelings of empathy may be limited.

Teens who are targets tend to be more anxious and insecure and will continue to be bullied if they don't know how to stand up for themselves. They may not have the social skills to be able to defend themselves, however. With the indirect way that many girls bully other girls, it happens so fast and insidiously that it's often difficult to track the behavior quickly enough to make it stop. With boys, we need to help them handle their anger in a way that doesn't turn to physical aggression. If you learn of any incidents, the best way to stop the viciousness is to teach your teens how to defend themselves and what to say to the bullies. Please consider the age of your child when teaching them the following tips:

* Don't get angry; get funny. Respond with a joke.
* Ignore the bullying, which sends a message that you're not afraid.
* Tell the bullies that you don't like what they're doing; sometimes they may be unaware of their behavior.
* Tell them to stop and leave you alone. Ask your friends to go with you if you don't want to talk to the bully alone.
* Tell an adult what's happening. It is the adult's responsibility to help stop the bullying.
* Avoid being alone with the bully.
* Antibullying and antiharassment regulations exist to provide for student safety. Review your school's code of conduct and instructions on how to file a grievance (ask to see the Title IX policy at your school or school district office).

Schools can assist by having clear rules and consequences, rather than turning away from bullying incidents and treating the behavior as normal adolescent angst. Parents should demand that schools protect students from a hostile environment. Students should see schools as welcoming and safe. Schools that condone bullying, teasing, and cliques leave some students out in the cold. Teasing, name-calling, and bullying have been synonymous with adolescence, but a schoolwide culture of casual cruelty can leave many students feeling angry, afraid, and isolated. Students must be taught the difference between friendly teasing and bullying, between flirting and harassment. We must work with our schools to create a positive school environment where students feel welcomed and not alienated, where they are learning to behave appropriately and to decrease the rage they may be experiencing.

Making our schools safe places where all students feel valued and have the opportunity to achieve is the primary antidote to incidents of bullying, harassment, and violence.

Nothing can protect our children from rejection, exclusion, or worry about fitting in. Being left out—or worse, bullied—can affect a teen's sense of self-worth and academic achievement. You can help your children by making sure they understand how being targeted by a bully feels, how bystanders can make the big difference, and by praising them for more appropriate behavior.

Friendships: The Hearts of Teenagers

Making friends and keeping them is a primary activity among school-age children. For both boys and girls, these early friendships help define who they are and who they become. But while friendships between girls are often extremely fluid, those between boys generally endure. For example, Ethan said this about his friend Luke: "I want to invite Luke to my birthday party every year for as long as I know him." This loyalty makes young boys' friendships especially influential—and paying attention to them so very critical for parents.

What's tricky, of course, is that as our teens begin school, we no longer have as much control over the friends to whom they are exposed. How you talk to your teens at home, and how you choose to support their friendships, will help them make smart decisions when it comes to forming friendships when they aren't under your direct watch. Friendships enrich the quality of our lives, but enduring and authentic friendships take work. From the friendships that are worth the investment (not all of them are), teens can learn the value of staying in a good relationship. Many of the teens we spoke with said it was important to have a best friend, one who stood out from the rest. "In reality, you are truly blessed to have one true friend to the backbone," Travis, 14, said. "All the others are basically your acquaintances." That's what Rich, 17, meant when he described a person's friends as being "like a pyramid" with one at the peak and others in supporting roles.

Remember that quality is better than quantity. It's easy for parents to worry if it seems that their teens aren't making "enough" friends. Most teens average five close friends, but it's important to remember that there's a wide range of normal. Some teens prefer one-on-one interactions, others, a small circle of friends. Still others may call their entire class their "best friend." What's key is to ask your teens whether their friendships keep them interested and safe and make them feel happy.

We want our teens to become authentic adults; this process begins when they are children. Authentic friends give you permission to be yourself. They allow for disagreements and differences and avoid feelings of shame when a person has complicated and confusing thoughts. To protect themselves, teens must be self-confident enough to step back from the drama and create, maintain, and communicate their personal boundaries. By sharing their own experiences, parents can help teens see that moments of drama will pass and that the teens are and will be OK.

When teens know who they are and accept themselves, they can avoid making risky decisions because of social pressure. They can also make and keep friends who will stay connected to them even in the face of disagreements and disappointments. Parents can model for their teens how to build and sustain positive friendships. As a parent, having your childhood friends still present in your life is part of that modeling.

Show your kids that friendship requires a give-and-take and is defined by loyalty, dedication, and above all, respect. In the end, it's up to you to show them that one of the most important choices they can make is the company they keep. One of the best strategies for parents of teenagers is to become friends with the parents of your children's friends. This tells your children that you care about what they do and are interested in who their friends are. Parents should also support friendships between boys and girls and not assume there is a sexual component. Parents can validate for their teens the qualities that bring out the best and create friendships. Helping your teens to develop a strong sense of self is crucial for them to have positive teenage friendships. When they have confidence in themselves, can take personal responsibility for their own behavior, and can empathize with others, they have the characteristics necessary to be a good friend and to be protected from people who might harm them.

8

The Parenting Road Map to Communication and Connection

One good parent is worth 1,000 schoolmasters.

—Chinese proverb

The questions to ask during these formative years are, how do I want my child to be at the age of 20? And what will he or she need to get there? Communication and connection facilitate the growth and maturity of a healthy child. Your role as parents is to stay connected with your teens through effective communication. Connection and communication are not the same. Communication is the method you use to connect. Connection is the commitment to, and engagement with, your teens to build and sustain relationships. All of this is predicated on unconditional love.

Parents often underestimate the importance of their role during the teenage years. It's easy to assume that your teens are no longer interested in the same connection that began when they were little children. Part of being a teenager is beginning the separation toward independence. In addition, teenagers are struggling with how to gain autonomy—typically expressed as, "All right already! Get out of my business and leave me alone." To separate, it is normal for children to be critical and assertive. So when teens push back, parents often pull away. In fact, they should do the opposite, with care. Communication must persist for the connection to remain strong and for teens to have the safe harbor to make mistakes and learn to be independent. The truth is, you're still their most significant support system and their first and most important teacher. We can't say this enough!

Although teens beg for their own space and disappear into their bedroom cocoons to chat with their friends, they need more, not less, adult support and guidance. Survey after survey confirms the need for parental engagement during the teen years (*Join Together*, 2014; Students Against Destructive Decisions [SADD], 2000). Teens benefit greatly from information and strategies to cope with issues such as friendships, school, social media, relationships, drinking, drugs, and sexuality. Some of the questions that teens need help with are common ones: How can I say no when I don't want to go out with someone and still have that person as a friend? What can I say to my friend who talks behind my back? What do I do when I'm being bullied? How do I know whether it's time for sex? How do I tell someone I'm not ready? These questions may not be asked clearly, so you'd best have your mental Google Translate and/or Google Maps turned on at all times.

To be effective, you must present your guidance in a supportive, nonjudgmental way. Teens' issues are loaded for both kids and parents, and conversations can easily turn into conflict. The conflict can take different forms, but the intended result is the same. Girls' relationships with their parents are generally fraught with so much conflict that moms and dads tend to withdraw out of frustration and weariness. Boys give their parents one-word answers, and their residual silence makes togetherness tough. It is the parents' job to unpack the discussion for everyone's benefit. Try not to become discouraged and disconnect; all you'll get in return are eye rolls, anger, tears, defiance, and back talk. And you'll be understandably unsure of how to comfort and talk to teenagers without starting the adversarial cycle all over again. Jenna, a high school senior, recounted the challenge in her home:

> Dinner at my house usually began with polite conversation and civility. A few minutes into the meal, my parents would inevitably ask a question that felt like prying, and I would answer them with attitude. Then they would give me a look of displeasure, and I would respond with loathing and disgust. Many nights followed this pattern. My parents would ask me questions such as "Who are you going to see tonight?" and I would answer, "My friends." Then they would ask, "Which friends?" and on and on and on, until I would finally leave the house angry. They were never happy with the information I offered. It was never enough to satisfy their needs.

There is a delicate balance here. On the one hand, teens do need parents as they are growing from childhood through adolescence to adulthood. They need coaching and guidance, and they need enough room to find their own way. Parents are admonished for being helicopter parents and attacked for being absent. It's no wonder parents dread this difficult time.

By comparison, child rearing in the early years is, and often means, a walk in the park. It seems simple to protect younger children. It's easy to make them happy when we can just take them to McDonald's and buy them a Happy Meal. But time passes. One father later lamented, "I just want to wrap Melanie in cellophane until she reaches 25." Another parent wistfully recalled, "I'm no longer under the illusion that I have ultimate control. I lost it as my daughter got older; she beat it out of me." Yet another said, "I'd like to sleep for a few years and wake up when adolescence is over. The thought of my son driving and drinking fills me with terror."

Communication with Intention

Communicate early and often to establish a foundation for the years when your children are less likely to be forthcoming. All of our advice about connecting and talking with kids has only one requirement: talk with them when they're little. You can't build a house starting with the second story; you have to do a lot of groundwork first. Parents have to establish a line of communication early and work hard to keep it open. This is not a job for the faint of heart.

Communication with boys and girls is different, but their needs are the same. One father remarked, "There is more communication with daughters, so that I feel like even if I say something 'wrong' on Tuesday, we'll be chattering enough during the week so that we can fix it. With boys, you basically have to do it in three sentences or less, and at the most, that will be twice a week. There is no recovery opportunity. Rather than talking, I find myself trying to figure out the right thing to say." Parents of teenage boys feel pressure to say the *right* three sentences, so it's not surprising that parents so often don't know what to say. To improve our communication with our sons, we must first understand that, when boys don't talk, it's a way of protecting and preserving their egos. You should not interpret this as a lack of interest or a lack of need for emotional connection.

The typical pattern is that boys tend not to talk much with their parents, while teenage girls provide an almost excessive amount of information about their daily lives. One mother told us, "It seems that boys feel if they are too close, or give up too much information, they're giving up power." The boys in our focus groups confirmed this observation when some revealed that they were conscious of keeping their parents at a distance, in part by offering little information about their lives. A girl said it best: "Telling your parents things helps them to see that you're growing up. Boys shut parents out to tell them that they're growing up." Parents of a teenage daughter and son captured it clearly: "When our son, David, has a problem, we have to pry the details out of him with a crowbar, but every issue with our daughter, Amy, becomes a four-act melodrama that goes on and on." A teacher told a story of working with boys in her photography class: "When the lights go out, then they start to talk." It seems commonplace that our boys determine when they will talk and when they won't. Girls may happily share the minute details of their lives without revealing any important information. But whether your children are boys or girls, and whether or not they fit the pattern, your objectives are the same. You just have to speak their language, so they can hear and take in what you have to say.

You have to be ready to seize the moment when your teens come to you, because as one parent said, "It may not happen again for days." It's in these individual moments that you and your children build on earlier communication strategies and further develop a process for maintaining connection. The earlier you develop effective communication processes, the better. However, it's never too late, although it may be harder. This process of connection is nurtured by listening rather than preaching, openness, candor, respect, reasonable consistency, and clarity.

Power of Connection

How we define connection has changed because of social media, particularly because it's through these media that adolescents relate. If you're driving a car with two teens or more, it is reminiscent of parallel play when they were two years old. They text each other while sitting together in the car or standing together at a street corner. Similarly, parents must now use social media to connect with teens. Sometimes it's a good warm-up to text or e-mail something challenging before talking face-to-face.

Regardless of all the new ways to connect or disconnect through social media, some needs don't change and remain necessary for all children. Connecting with intention and understanding the world our children live in can create a secure attachment for our teens. A secure attachment is beneficial to developing satisfying relationships.

We can model the how-to and importance of relationships and friendships. One mother told of her experience with her women friends at the bridal shower of a friend's daughter. Judy said,

> For decades, our close-knit sisterhood-of-mothers has been a busy hive of love and community for our children. The phone lines light up with our crosstown chats. We trade worries and console each other with endless optimism. Unflagging support is a constant, even when it feels like we are failing miserably at our most important job—being a good mother. As fledgling nurturers, we asked, "Do you think she's talking too late? What happens if he *never* gets potty trained?" We shared names of the best pediatricians, helpful tutors, and savvy college advisors. And we're always on call to dispense down-home prescriptions for all manner of medical ills. We are women who are as different as snowflakes yet astonishingly identical, in one sacred way. Our kids are priority number one.

We also have found that the way adolescent boys connect with others is different from the way girls connect. Connection for an adolescent boy may not be based on a deep, emotional exchange with another. In fact, connection with an adolescent boy may be difficult even to recognize at first because of its subtlety and possible contradiction of what we acknowledge as connection. One mother said, "At eleven o'clock on a school night, my son Jake burst into our bedroom to share a scene from reality TV. His dad's first reaction was to tell him to go to bed. But I figured if he cared enough to share this with us, we should watch. We ended up having a good discussion about how reality fakes conflict for ratings. It was the perfect way to connect." In our focus groups, we learned that connection between parents and sons could take the form of a brief moment of agreement about an issue, an incident that reaffirms trust, or even an extended period of comfortable silence.

Another mother related a simple verbal exchange with her son after he missed a meeting with his teacher. At the time, her son did not respond to her advice. However, later, on the way to soccer practice, he told her that he knew she was always looking out for his best interests. Still another mother talked to us about taking an eight-hour car ride with her son in complete silence. She recognized that there was no need to force conversation. She recalled her own childhood and how comforting it had been to spend hours sitting next to her own father in total silence while they were fishing. She had followed her instincts, which told her that, for her family, silence was OK. The quiet fishing was a bonding experience and a moment for connection. Her intuition was affirmed when her son said he had a great time and enjoyed the ride.

Connection with girls is a question of negotiating too much chatter, which often conveys the same lack of information as a nonverbal boy does. With girls, you have to be careful not to misread the drama that often comes with being a teenager. You need to ask the hard questions: "Are you upset at me, or are you upset about something that happened with your friends?" "Are you going to Julie's tonight, or are you going to the party I heard about?" "Will there be drinking there?"

All parents need to help their teens better understand the reasons why they ask the questions they do and request information from them. Adults ask the same information of each other. We can say to our kids, "I know this question annoys you, but if you notice, Mom and I give each other this information all the time." Good communication, sharing information, isn't about control and lack of trust. It's more about mutual respect and looking out for each other. One mother, Maria, offered the following exit strategy she has with her girls:

> My girls and I have an understanding about how to get out of a bad or uncomfortable situation. I have told my girls that I'm their excuse when they're in a situation and don't know how to save face. They text me with an agreed-upon code. I text them back that I'm glad they got in touch with me because I will come and pick them up. They have permission to blame me or lie. We take care of each other, and they know this because I'm willing to give them tools to save face, because they still want to be liked. They know it doesn't matter

where they are; I would rather hear from them than from a third party. They also know if they lie, they're in trouble. So, if I hear, "Hey, Mom, I screwed up!" I am way more likely to forgive them when they take responsibility.

Objective (unemotional) and transparent coaching and critical questions are essential to get to the bottom of an issue. This is your chance to share your values, fears, and rules. For example, teens' relationships with their friends are important learning experiences and offer the opportunity for them to test your coaching and values.

Boys and girls also have much to learn from their connections with one another. Boys can learn how to be relational, how to be connected in a way that provides them with the nurturing that connection traditionally provides for girls and women. From boys, girls can learn to speak out, to say what's on their minds without equivocation, to demand to be heard, and to avoid a tailspin after a disagreement or an insult. Girls can learn how to move on and put everyday aggravations into perspective. You can help to foster the best qualities in both boys and girls.

Connection Is Hardwired

A child's development is strongly influenced by the expectations and behaviors of the child's parents and other adult role models. It's important for these adults to behave in ways that have the most positive effect on their children's development. To be a parent rather than a friend, you have to establish appropriate boundaries while maintaining connection. This objective and transparent engagement enables you to provide the impartial coaching that teenagers need during this period of development. Objective and transparent engagement requires taking a deep breath, stepping back, and thinking about what your own values are, what's important, what you're willing to do battle over, and what you wisely will let go. This process also requires you to filter out your personal problems before you act. Self-knowledge and self-reflection are critical parts of parenting, and self-discovery is a lifelong process.

In making decisions, you have to remember that your children have only been on earth for 13 or so years, so they only have that much knowledge; no matter how high tech and sophisticated they are or how much of the world they've seen, that's all they have the capacity to know. You have 40-odd years (or more) of life experience, so you're expected to reflect and guide your children in a positive direction.

When you address specific issues concerning your teens, understand that everything is interrelated: biology, culture, history, socialization, media, and technology. The more knowledge and self-awareness you have, the better you will guide your teens to adulthood. Because the world feels more threatening, we are more reluctant as parents to let our children go, and there are more factors to consider with every decision and every act. It's not that we don't want them to have experiences; we just have to work harder at teaching them to use good judgment more often.

Understanding your teens and keeping them safe is challenging. What you can do to help keep your children remain safe is to remind them about consequences and show them that you're always there to support them. At a recent funeral service for a dearly loved parent, her son told a story that resonates with us. He said that when he was in middle school, his parents said, "You can always come to us for any questions or help. If we don't know the answer, we'll find it or find someone who does." Unconditional love provides a sense of security and consistency. Even though teens can often be hard to approach, you and other adults in their lives have to initiate difficult conversations to keep the lines of communication open.

In a sense, human beings are hard wired to connect. With few exceptions (mental illness, narcissism, and other personality disorders), certain qualities can help parents to overcome barriers. If a parent is empathetic, responsive, and respects boundaries, close relationships are possible. Therefore, you should recognize that you have the ability to create an environment for your children that can increase their well-being substantially. George Will writes in the *Washington Post* that the developing brain of a child can protect him or her from vulnerabilities by promoting opportunities for connection, which creates resiliency. The "family is the most basic authoritative community . . . the most crucial [for developing social connectedness]. A child's relational context, which is just another way of saying connection, is what sustains and protects them" (Will, 2003).

The role of family as the source for connection is described well in *Tuesdays with Morrie*. When facing his death, Morrie Schwartz tells his former student, Mitch Albom, the most important lesson he has learned in his life. Morrie says, "Invest in the human family. Invest in people. Build a little community of those you love and who love you. In the beginning of life, when we are infants, we need others to survive, right? But here's the secret; in between, we need others as well" (Albom, 1997).

When you do this with your children, the prize is a lasting relationship with your children, who have self-respect and love and respect you. Connection is what fuels a parent's life. Relationships sustain us, and with a strong foundation, the parent-teen relationship can become a loving and nurturing parent-adult relationship.

13 Strategies for Being a Perfectly Imperfect Parent

Relationships require communication and connection. This chapter has led you from communication to connecting, deepening your relationships with your teens. This isn't simple. In our meetings with teens and parents during the course of writing this book, we were reminded continuously of the joy, complexity, and energy that teens bring to a family. We were also reminded that, without exception, no parents wanted to do their teenage years over. As parents of adult children, we also agree. Next to being a teenager, parenting teenagers is one of the most difficult life experiences.

Although strategies are interspersed throughout this book, we have summarized them here for easy reference. These strategies are all grounded in the analyses of what goes on in the lives of adolescents, as discussed in this book. We have formulated these strategies from our focus groups, from conclusions we have drawn from our experience as mothers, and from working with teens in a professional capacity. We believe that you can use these strategies to smooth—although never eliminate—the inevitable bumps in the road.

Children are very resilient and can accept imperfections in their parents. Nobody is perfect. Therefore, our strategies are based on the parenting style we believe to be most achievable and balanced—what we are calling "perfectly imperfect parents." If you acknowledge that no parent is perfect, you're a model who helps your teens navigate the complexities of life. Your role is to help your teens adjust, cope, and persevere. Parents shouldn't try for perfection, because perfection creates an impossible ideal, one that no teen can either emulate or live up to.

To understand the strategies in this section, first think about what it means to be the perfectly imperfect parent of a teen. When children are babies, perfectly imperfect parents provide for their wants and needs, but as children grow, these parents don't want to shield them from challenges and adversities. Rather, they want their teens to develop the confidence to take care of themselves. Perfectly imperfect parents give their teens the message that they want their children to be moral and responsible, to have the strength to make their own choices, and to appreciate their own abilities and talents. Perfectly imperfect parents don't see their teens' struggles or frustrations as proof that they aren't good parents. Instead, these parents see these behaviors as appropriate individuation. They understand that their teens may make very different choices in life from the ones they made, and they don't interpret this as a rejection or as a failure of parenting. Lily, a new mother, looked back on how her parents did that:

> Sometimes my parents were not the parents that I would have wanted them to be, but I think on the whole, they were exactly what I needed. I used to feel frustrated when they seemed preoccupied with their own lives and didn't make as big a fuss about birthdays

and holidays as my friends' parents did. They would say, "Lily, those are TV sitcom parents, and we will never fit that mold." Most parents I know try to provide their kids with an ideal childhood, and many of them try to become the perfect parent. I'm lucky to have my parents as role models; their example makes me sane when my stress level goes haywire. They don't preach to me; they let me vent and really listen.

Perfectly imperfect parents respect boundaries and demonstrate empathy toward their teens, facilitating a close relationship but not necessarily a friendship. A close friendship between parents and teens is a modern phenomenon brought about by a smaller generation gap and a more informal and open culture. The transition from parent to friend is clumsy and may create conflict because boundaries are less well defined.

Strategies: A Baker's Dozen

Keep in mind this introduction to perfectly imperfect parents as you read our 13 strategies for developing a gratifying relationship with your teen:

1. **Accept being a perfectly imperfect parent.**
   * Know yourself first, and forgive your imperfections. If you forgive yourself for not being an ideal parent, you become a much more powerful role model for your teens.
   * Don't view your teens' struggles or frustrations as proof that you aren't a good parent. As Stephen Colbert says, "Don't get me wrong. Being a parent is no picnic . . . it's a thankless job, like sheriff or Pope" (2007).
   * Give your teens the message that you want and expect them to be moral and responsible people, to have the strength to make their own choices, and to appreciate their own abilities and talents.
   * Understand that your teens may make very different choices in life (albeit sometimes reluctantly and with great

disappointment), and don't interpret this as a rejection of yourselves or evidence of bad parenting.

* Value your teens' feelings and see them as an opportunity for intimacy. Work at tolerating your teens' anger and frustrations, and don't give them verbal and nonverbal messages that you're uncomfortable with these feelings.
* Remember, you only have to listen; you don't have to fix it.

2. **Use the nuts and bolts of parenting teens.**
   * Be available.
   * Tell the truth.
   * Practice active listening.
   * Share your personal experiences and stories to normalize your teens' experiences.
   * Take advantage of teachable moments.
   * Focus on effort rather than on intelligence. Effort is the key to success in school and in life (Dweck, 2007). An overemphasis on intellect or talent—and the implication that such traits are innate and fixed—leaves teens vulnerable to failure, fearful of challenges, and unmotivated to learn.
   * Use humor, one of the best antidotes for tension. Laughing at yourself and even gently teasing your teens, at the right time, can alleviate tensions and put mistakes and failure into perspective. Teens who can take themselves a little less seriously are more likely to bounce back from losses.
   * Empathize rather than overly identify with your teen. Empathy is the foundation for mature relationships; it promotes connection by inviting intimacy. We define empathy as an awareness of the impact of one's behavior on others and a sense of responsibility for this. Empathy is also associated with sympathy, warmth, and compassion. Parents can accept inconsiderate behavior more easily if their children demonstrate empathy.
   * Don't dictate how your children should look or feel: "You're wearing *that*?!"

* Maintain appropriate boundaries—where to draw the line and when to step in. If you don't step back, it's easy to lose perspective.
* Don't jump in to save your children from making mistakes. Mistakes allow them to experience the natural consequences of their decisions.
* Create rituals as a family. Rituals provide wonderful memories and meaningful family time that all family members can participate in.

3. **Stay involved with your child's school from preschool through high school.**
    * Educators may be experts in how to teach, but you are experts about your own children. The school should involve you in decisions about their future. This means having a say in what your children are learning, knowing early what courses your children need for college, and understanding what happens if your teens are struggling.
    * Maintain high expectations for your teens' performance in school. When parents set high expectations for their children's school performance, teens are more likely to meet those expectations.
    * Encourage your teens to take personal responsibility for their own learning. There is no greater motivator than success, and success builds self-confidence and a lifelong learner.
    * Recognize your teens' academic accomplishments. Don't assume that because your teens are maturing, they don't want or need attention from you. Sometimes, teens' peers pressure them to *not* excel or to just get by. You can offset negative expectations with positive recognition.
    * Be especially supportive of your teens during transitional times—for example, when they first enter middle school or high school or move to a new school district. Meet with teachers and visit the school. Talk with school administrators

about school policies regarding discipline, homework, behavior, academic programs, and extracurricular activities.

* Keep the school informed of any significant changes in your family, such as separation or divorce, serious illness, or a death in the family.

* Provide a supportive home environment that encourages learning and good behavior in school. Monitor your teens' academic performance regularly, and work with teachers to address any performance concerns.

* Know the classes your teens are taking and how they contribute to your kids' preparation for the future. Assist your teens to plan for college or career opportunities. If your teens are reticent about taking more challenging classes, find out if you can address that reticence with support. If this is the case, talk to the school counselor and see whether tutoring would help your teens feel more comfortable taking a specific class.

* Get involved at school! Engagement includes ensuring that your teens attend school and are ready to learn every day. Your engagement gives you an opportunity to see your children in a different setting and whether they model what you value as important in the home. In addition, getting to know teachers and other adult role models (for example, coaches) helps to ensure that your children's needs are met when you're not present. Remember, it's as important for parents to stay involved in middle and high school as it was in elementary school. Achievement is very much tied to parental engagement.

* When families are involved appropriately in their children's education, teachers value them more, and children learn more.

* Affirm girls' intelligence, courage, imagination, self-confidence, and skills. Encourage your daughters to stretch themselves. Girls need to learn to take risks and to be willing to be criticized. Make sure that counselors are giving them the same message and that their teachers are supporting them.

* Advocate for ways in which your sons learn best. To express what they know, boys need to be exposed to a variety of learning strategies, such as hands-on activities, technology, artistic expressions, and oral presentations. Talk to teachers about what you think your sons need to reinforce their success.

* Be an advocate for your children. Talk with the teachers about your children's progress. If your teens are not in the right program, you can ask for a change. Check your children's grades and test scores. Ask for help if your teens are behind. Find out about the school's standards for what all students should learn, and ask how many students are meeting the standards and what progress the school is making. Start this process early in your children's education. If they aren't taking the best courses, they won't be ready for more challenging curricula as they move through the school system.

4. **Facilitate transitions to middle school, an intriguing new stage of development filled with physical, cognitive, social, and emotional changes.**

   * Set and enforce consistent rules.

   * Try to control your reactions when your adolescents make mistakes.

   * Talk to your children about the physical changes that take place during adolescence.

   * Talk to your children about sex, and discuss ways to promote a healthy and responsible attitude toward it. Provide accurate information, and respond to questions in a simple, straightforward way.

   * Make sure that your children have access to resources and appropriate teachers and other adults to talk about changes and feelings. The increase in academic demands and the complexity of middle school make the task of academic success more difficult than in elementary school.

   * Set aside an area, room, or space at home as your children's

study area. Check for and neutralize distractions in the home—noise, temperature, lighting, social media—as much as you can. Equip the study area with supplies and equipment, and work with your children to create a system for organizing the schoolwork they bring home. These study habits will help your children as they move through school and to college.

* Answer questions related to how to communicate effectively with teachers, peers, and other adults during the transition process to and while attending middle school. Explain the value of new opportunities as your children transition from one stage or grade to another.

* Offer opportunities to examine options and express feelings.

5. **Allow your teens to express a full range of emotions.**
    * Help your teens label their emotions. Foster and teach emotional intelligence. Help your children understand what they're feeling by reflecting what you see. Make statements like these: "That must have been really frustrating"; "I imagine you must be so angry"; "You look pretty disappointed. Something must have happened"; "You sound upset; you look really down,"; "I'm guessing you're feeling really sad about that"; "You're looking a bit worried"; "I think you must be feeling . . ."; "That must have hurt." Help your teens to connect the dots between being upset and understanding a more nuanced description of how they feel. And remember, much of your teens' communication is nonverbal. You might say, "You're pacing the kitchen. Are you feeling nervous or anxious?" or, "I can see from the way you are clenching your jaw that you're feeling irritated."
    * Be an active listener. Your goal is to listen to help your teens find their own solutions to build their confidence so that they can problem solve. Listen empathetically and validate your teens' feelings. This listening and coaching affirms to them that you support them when they are grappling with a tough issue. As

children get older, you want them to be able to trust their own feelings.

* Become an emotional coach. To communicate that you understand what your teens are saying, let them know why you believe what they are saying makes sense. Show you are engaged by asking questions such as "Do you want to talk about it?" and "How did that make you feel?" Ask whether they have more to say. When you just listen without rushing in with advice, your teens have the space to think, reflect, and come up with their own solutions. After they say they're finished, ask if they have any ideas about how to fix the problem. You'll be pleasantly surprised by their ideas. This process slows down emotions and allows teens to get in touch with feelings they may not have been able to express. Your patience with the process gives teens the space to think and cuts down on both of your reactions. You also give them the opportunity to become confident problem solvers.

* Refrain from fixing your children's pain. Concentrate instead on expressing empathy with expressions such as "I know how difficult this must be."

* Discuss issues openly and stay engaged even when things get tough. Anticipate that there will be disagreements, but this doesn't mean that either of you should stop talking or listening to each other, even when you might want to. Communication that builds trust is a two-way street and takes persistence.

* Give teens the opportunity to identify and manage their own emotions and respond appropriately to the emotions of others. Normalize the notion that we all have uncomfortable feelings, and help teens find their own means of relieving the situation.

* Help your teens understand that there are concrete things they can do to calm themselves when they're feeling overwhelmed. For example, listening to or playing music, writing in a

journal, reading a book, using meditation exercises, running, shooting basketballs, knitting, or building something will help them learn to self-soothe.

6. **Develop grit, perseverance, determination, and motivation.**
   * Communicate to your children that no matter what life brings them, when they stumble and when they soar, they'll be acceptable not just to you, but to themselves.
   * Let them know that no one is asking for perfection. There are no perfect children or perfect parents in our world—just the old college try, the gentleman's C, the good-enough striving. Help your teens set realistic goals and handle stress.
   * To set the stage for perseverance, show your teens that you care about them by demonstrating respect.
   * Teach them to overcome the fear of failure.
   * Keep your focus on the process rather than the outcome.
   * Teach your teens positive self-talk. Suggest that when they're feeling frustrated, they can say to themselves a phrase like "I just need to do my best," "Every day I'm getting a little better," "I can do it; I'm determined!" or "This is going to need my best work." Define success as believing you gave it your best effort.
   * Teach your teens how to tell the difference between harmful and helpful stress. Help them realize that how they think about stress affects their reactions. When they see stress as an opportunity to grow, they are able to reappraise the situation, change their mind-set, and increase their opportunities for success.
   * Be careful not to overpraise or push kids in ways that make them afraid to risk making mistakes. Short-term disappointments are perfect opportunities for learning and building resilience. Mastery almost always comes after a few stumbles, and these stumbles provide great opportunities for learning (Dweck, 2007).

7. **#GetTechSmart.**

   * Set limits on screen time. Acknowledge how difficult it is to limit screen time. Set an example yourself by limiting your screen time while the kids are up. Parents often admit how much of a time stealer surfing the Internet can become; it's the same temptation for our teens.

   * Find a balance and try not to do anything extreme. We don't recommend taking away technology items for extended periods. This may have a negative effect; some teens may hide their online lives even more or feel socially isolated. There are many good ways to create boundaries, such as limiting laptops, phones, and tablets in your teens' bedroom; setting curfews on their use; and creating a digital break. Figure out which method works best for your family.

   * Talk to your teens about the lack of privacy online. Let them know that everyone has access to their profile, including teachers, other parents, coaches, college admission officers, future employers, and police. Advise them not to post anything online without imagining it appearing on the front page of your local newspaper or a billboard on your front lawn.

   * Impress upon them the permanence of what they post and how a future employer may judge their obscene language or a photo of them drunk at a party while half-dressed. Remind them that there are no "backsies" online—what is posted can't be taken back. Even if something is deleted, there can easily be a screenshot of the post floating around. Yesterday's post can be recalled today and tomorrow. There is no absolute privacy on the Internet, not even if they restrict their settings to "friends only," and when you have 1,000 friends, they have immediate access to everything about you.

   * Teach them online etiquette. Talk about online manners; while texting is fast and impersonal, there's still room for "pls" and "ty." Just like you teach social cues, let them know that many emotional nuances also exist in social media.

* Be knowledgeable and in touch. Know what your teens are doing online. Become familiar with the social media sites your children use. Today it's Instagram, Facebook, WhatsApp, texting, and Snapchat, but rest assured this is in constant flux. Today's cool site may be tomorrow's has-been. You may want to limit your teens' friend lists to people they actually know. As a prerequisite to Facebook, you may ask to be included as one of your teens' friends. Know your children's passwords.
* Promote online literacy. Teach about privacy settings—their importance and their limits. While more rare than is hyped, there are online predators. Let your children know that there are people who create false personas online. They should trust their gut when something feels wrong. Encourage them to let you know when they sense something uncomfortable online. You can empower them by helping them to report abusive online behavior to the site.
* Tell them online actions have consequences. Your teens may experience unwanted consequences offline from the images posted and the words written online.
* Use the Internet to bring the family and friends together. Create a family book of photos together. Sit with your teens and/or have them teach you about their favorite sites or software. Show interest in what they're passionate about. Meet them where they are.
* Understand the value of social networking. Various social media sites help teens to keep up with friends from camp or other schools and can decrease their feelings of isolation.

8. **Prevent sexual harassment, bullying, and cyberbullying.**
    * Talk honestly with your teens about their behavior. Calling behaviors what they are helps us educate our children about their rights, affirms their realities, encourages more complex and meaningful solutions, opens up a dialogue, invites children to participate in social change, and ultimately protects them.

* Ask good questions. Who? What? Where? When? How? Listen more than talk. Try not to react until your children have finished describing things. Bullying and harassment tend to happen a little under the radar (bathrooms, hallways, on the bus or walking to school, teasing, and texting).
* Treat bullying behavior seriously. Don't dismiss or trivialize hurtful or bullying behavior, which only encourages this type of behavior.
* If your children are bullied, let them know that you will be there to help them. Give them advice on how to react to bullying, including speaking up when bullying occurs, walking away, trying not to cry out or lash out in front of the bully, and telling a trusted adult.
* Every school district should have an antibullying policy and an adult identified as in charge. However, you can speak with a teacher or counselor—whomever you or your teens trust. Document and report bullying.
* Work with other parents to stop bullying. A group has power and provides you with support if your children are bullied.
* If your teens experience cyberbullying, they should not respond. Instead, they should block the sender, save or print harmful messages, report cyberbullying to an adult, and contact websites or Internet services to request that the harmful messages be removed.
* If cyberbullying is interfering with school and learning, report it to the school. If you think a crime was committed, contact the police.
* If you find your children are bullies, let them know that this behavior is unacceptable, provide consequences, work with school staff to find out what your teens are doing, and most importantly, model the behavior you want your teens to emulate.
* Teens should understand the role of bystanders in bullying. Review with them helpful responses if they find themselves in a bullying situation: not supporting the bully, supporting the

target in private, or alerting an adult to confront the bully. These actions take courage, and your children will need support from you when attempting some of these behaviors.

* Use legal and educational policies. While certain behavior may be offensive and inappropriate, bullying and sexual harassment are against the law, and your teens should be protected at school and in their neighborhoods!
* Seek help immediately if your teens talk about suicide or seem uncommonly upset. The national Suicide Prevention Lifeline is (800) 273-8255 (http://www.SafeSchools.info).
* You can find additional help with bullying prevention from the U.S. Department of Health and Human Services (http://www .stopbullying.gov) and the Gay, Lesbian & Straight Education Network (http://www.glsen.org).

9. **Provide teens with the skills to navigate popular culture.**
   * Promote media literacy. Teach your teens to develop critical-thinking skills both to know the difference between content and advertising and to question the messages on screen and print. Point out how the main goal of advertisers is to tell us we need their product. Often this means they play on our insecurities to get us to reach into our wallets and buy what they're selling. Give them concrete examples to teach them how ads create insecurity and make us feel insufficient without their product.
   * Tell your daughters that most of the images shown of women have been digitally manipulated. What they see may not exist in nature, so they're comparing themselves with an impossible ideal. Let them know that many girls feel dissatisfied with their bodies when they compare themselves with this phony ideal.
   * Be vigilant and talk to your daughters about the pressure of seeing all these perfect images. Be proactive and educate your daughters about the tricks of using Photoshop to modify images. Show them the videos from responsible advertising

such as the Dove Real Beauty campaign (http://www
.beautyredefined.net).

* Be a role model. Refrain from complaining about your own
body, and keep your personal frustrations to yourself. Stress
health, not thinness.

* Emphasize that your daughters' value and worth are not
defined by how many likes they get when they post a "selfie."

* Offer your daughters the following take-home mantras from
www.beautyredefined.net: "There is more to be than eye candy.
If beauty hurts, we're doing it wrong. Your reflection does not
define your worth, and you are capable of more than being
looked at!" When you praise your daughters' school efforts and
athletic abilities, you give them the message that the important
traits are effort, competence, and intelligence. As one mother
said, "We all should remember this, because your looks fade
faster than your brain."

* Look for healthy images in the media, and point them out to your
daughters. Draw on these examples to build resiliency in your
girls. If you teach your daughters to be critical observers and
consumers, they will learn for themselves the differences between
what feels right to them and what doesn't. They will develop more
confidence in their own opinions, rather than allowing themselves
to be overly influenced by what others may think.

* Talk to your sons about pornography and objectification
(defining a woman's value by her external appearance). Teach
them empathy, and personalize the objectified image of a girl
by reminding them that every girl is someone's daughter and/or
sister. Talk to your sons about what you value in relationships.
Underline the qualities you admire in women other than
physical beauty.

10. **Build communication and connections.**
   * Spend family time and time alone with your children.
   * Be a parent first, not a friend.

* Be willing to negotiate and compromise.
* Be authentic with criticism and praise.
* Enjoy your teens, and keep your sense of humor.
* Communicate early. It's like building a house; it needs a foundation and a first floor before a second floor can be built. Have an open door, an open mind, and an open attitude. Listen to understand, not to advocate a particular position.
* Spend time with your teens. Use the time for conversation, not confrontation. Watch for hints: a child who hangs around usually wants to talk.
* Develop open communication. It is important that you talk with your kids openly and honestly. Use encouragement, support, and positive reinforcement so your kids know that they can ask any question on any topic without fear of consequence. Provide straightforward answers, and if you don't know the answer, admit it, then find the correct information and explore it together.
* Allow negative feelings. It can be difficult for your teens to share feelings of insecurity. Make sure you let them know that these feelings are normal and it's helpful to get them out in the open. That kind of response helps to make the feelings less scary for them. Provide realistic feedback about emotional discomfort and how long it may last.
* Look for teachable moments. Use everyday opportunities to talk. Some of the best talks you'll have with your teens will take place when you least expect them. When they come home after a night out with their friends or while you're cooking dinner are often good opportunities for discussion. And remember, it often takes more than a single discussion for kids to grasp all they need to know. So talk, listen, talk, listen, and talk again.
* Encourage them to talk it out. Children feel better when they talk about their feelings; it lifts the burden of having to face their fears, disappointments, and frustrations alone. Talking about their feelings offers them an emotional release, even if you

don't have all the answers. You offer a safe harbor to air feelings that they may not yet understand or be able to explain fully.

* For boys, initiate a topic while you're engaged in an activity they enjoy. Talk in the car when you're side-by-side, rather than face-to-face. Provide privacy for these conversations, and be ready to listen when they're ready to talk, even if the timing isn't ideal.
* Reveal yourself. Speak honestly to your teens about your thoughts, experiences, ideas, goals, and feelings. Model behavior that you want your teens to adopt; don't contradict what you say by doing the opposite.
* Teach empathy and build strong communication skills. Empathy is a learned skill.

11. Avoid negative stereotypes.
* Begin early to nurture freedom from stereotypes and gender-specific expectations. Help your teens to find their voice, teach tolerance and respect for others, watch how your teens treat others, and don't tolerate exclusionary behavior.
* Support your teens if they identify as nonconforming sexual minorities. Be alert to bias, and encourage and model words and deeds that treat people fairly, including but not limited to LGBTQ teens.
* Let your children know that it isn't OK to say, "That's so gay." Take the time to explain that it means something or someone is bad or stupid. Discuss with your teens why it's hurtful to use this phrase as an insult.
* Be intentional about teaching the language of feelings to boys.
* Help girls to identify the underlying issues that drive their emotions.
* Support girls and boys of color in avoiding having to choose between friends and performance.
* Have high expectations of boys and girls.
* Be aware that girls receive conflicting messages about their worth and place in our culture from television, magazines, music, and the movies.

* Encourage your girls to take risks and be prepared to fail. This is one important way for teens to develop confidence. Girls who have confidence in themselves can have the courage to admit what they don't know and risk making efforts to learn more.
* Talk to your daughters about the advantages of sometimes rocking the boat and how to make decisions that may not make everyone happy. Tell them that you will support their decisions. Starting this early will help your daughters to build confidence in their abilities.
* Keep in mind that many boys are themselves targets of sexual harassment, often in the form of taunts challenging their sexuality. This "culture of cruelty" is as destructive to boys as it is to girls.
* Support your teens' relationships with the opposite sex as friends.

12. Value teen friendship.
* Get to know your children's friends. Create a teen-friendly house where kids feel comfortable. Don't be too intrusive. Form a relationship with them.
* Support your teens to develop and strengthen friendships and activities that encourage acceptance and success for everyone.
* Let your teens know that some friendships are worth the investment, while others are not.
* Don't overreact. Be cautious about judging. If your children see you judging wrongly or based on surface impression, they will devalue your opinion and not trust your judgment. Kids with problems can benefit from a positive peer group and won't necessarily be a bad influence on your children's behavior or character.
* Your children can recognize the good and bad in their friends and not judge them too harshly. It's when the mix of friends is predominantly negative that parents need to be concerned. If most of your children's friends are positive influences, relax and trust your children's judgment.
* Set the stage. Encourage them to get involved in activities and interest groups where they can form friendships. Skills give

them greater self-confidence and more acceptance from others. Some children may need coaching on social skills such as being friendly, talkative, and assertive.

* Keep your lines of communication open. Help your teens when peer relationships go wrong. Be concerned and helpful, and keep your own relationship positive.

* Do things as a family. Enjoy each other's company. Go camping, eat out; family activities provide a good balance to the ups and downs of peer friendships. Teens need a comfort zone of security with family life and with their peer groups at school and in their community.

13. Model cultural competence, not intolerance.

* Teach and model cultural differences as a source of strength.

* Communicate an attitude of inclusiveness and respect that will enable teens to function successfully in today's world.

* Demonstrate positive attitudes toward people who are different from you. This behavior will help your children to develop cultural competence. Teens who develop cultural competence can appreciate their own culture and use this knowledge to understand others'. Cultural competence is an essential ingredient for children to develop self-esteem and will help them to function better as they move into adulthood. It also will contribute to breaking down barriers.

* Our challenge as parents, therefore, is to grow and change with the times while supporting our children by modeling tolerance and speaking out against discrimination.

Please remember that no one expects you to use these strategies perfectly or all at one time. Again, we hope you can use these strategies to smooth—although never eliminate—the inevitable bumps in the road. Stay close, stay connected, and trust your instincts about what is best for your teens. Regardless of what they may say, they look to you for assurance and guidance.

9

Wired to Take Risks

According to Sue Sylvester, the coach from *Glee*, "They [teens] love to be terrified. It's like mother's milk to them."

—*CBS Sunday Morning*, June 15, 2014

"As a society, we both fear teenagers and fear for them," reports Danah Boyd in the *Los Angeles Times* (Boyd, 2014). She says teens suffer from the burden of our fears and obsession with safety when we limit their mobility. At the end of the day, teenagers are doing what their parents are doing. They just want to find a comfortable place for themselves as they grapple with the enormous pressures they face and figure out how they fit in today's world.

We have purposely saved the subjects that create the most anxiety for parents—violence, sex, drugs, and alcohol—until now. Today's reality creates anxieties in adults that are different from those in the past. It's easy to understand the enormous worry many parents have, because the consequences of sex can last a lifetime, and guns can eliminate entire lives. You should anticipate that teens will engage in risky behavior, and while this behavior is expected, the risks have become even more dangerous for our children. Parents fear, justifiably, that if a teenager makes a mistake, it could be fatal.

We have included detailed fact sheets for learning about specific vulnerabilities in the book's Fact Sheets located in the back of the book. They include information about depression and suicide, violence, eating disorders, and drug abuse. We also hope that the strategies provided in Chapter 8 will help you protect your teens.

The mental health of teens affects their vulnerability. Some teens are more prone to anxiety and depression, and some circumstances make it difficult to cope, making them more susceptible to alcoholism, cutting, and drugs. It's especially important to talk to your teens about any family history of alcoholism and other addictions. Your kids may have a genetic disposition to alcoholism and drug addiction, so you owe them this information. All teens need protective mechanisms to help them make better choices, and for more vulnerable teens, this is essential. The best antidotes for abuse and addiction are emotional intelligence, tools for coping with adversity and stress, and having a solid sense of self, with therapy as a constructive option.

Sometimes it's very hard for parents to distinguish among normal adolescent angst, feeling down, and clinical depression. Parental instincts and knowledge are critical in learning to make these distinctions. You are the best judge of your teens' changing behavior. Knowing the early warning signs are key. Specifically, pay close attention to personality changes, fatigue, loss of interest in friends and activities your teens formerly enjoyed, and school behavior and performance. Symptoms of depression include changes in these activities. Any sadness that persists for more than two weeks should be a cause for concern (see Fact Sheet 1, "Depression in Adolescents"). For example, the mother of 16-year-old Danielle said,

> Last month, Danielle started sleeping really late, not just "teenage late." She seemed down, and it was hard for me to sort out what was PMS [premenstrual syndrome], normal teenage behavior, or depression. I asked her if she wanted to see a therapist, and she wasn't opposed. After seeing a counselor, she perked up, and I asked her if she understood why she felt better. She said that she now

understands what made her feel blue and that she finds talking to a therapist helpful.

Before seeing a therapist, Danielle was not in touch with her feelings. After learning to identify what she experienced as the "blahs"—and learning to name and verbalize her feelings—she could effect change. Danielle could now have greater control over her emotions because she was able to label and identify what preceded them. Danielle's depression subsided as a result of her mother's intervention and her sessions with a therapist.

The teen years are when children need and want to interact more with the world than with their family, which can frighten parents, because they aren't in control. Teens also experience a lack of control, which is why it's so important for parents to stay engaged.

Like cultural expectations based on gender, teens' vulnerabilities and risky behaviors are affected by gender, too. As a result, we identify threats to teens for girls, boys, and both.

Girls and Cutting

Cutting is much more common in girls than in boys. Of course, cutting is extremely upsetting, and most parents don't know what to do about it. While both boys and girls experience overwhelming feelings of upset, boys externalize their pain more often by taking it out on others. They get their feelings out by punching walls, getting into fights, and yelling. They don't choose to take it out on their bodies as often as girls do, even though more boys are engaging in cutting today than ever before (Adler & Adler, 2011).

Girls are not expected to express their anger in direct ways, so they learn to be covert or to suppress their anger. Consequently, anger can become depression, manifesting itself in self-mutilation—bingeing, purging, and cutting. When girls can't be their authentic selves and express their anger or sadness, they are more vulnerable and likely to turn their overpowering feelings inward. The act of cutting becomes a coping mechanism that helps girls regulate their unbearable feelings.

Cutting creates a cycle, and the teenage brain adapts quickly to this behavior, creating a pattern: "When I'm upset, I cut." Strange though it is, this action creates relief from the emotional pain. Unfortunately, this creates a circuit that is harder to extinguish over time. As with anorexia, girls teach other girls how to cut. The tendency at this age to mimic the behavior of others is compelling, and sometimes what begins as an experiment becomes a compulsion that's hard to give up. Through self-mutilation, teens communicate that they are hurt but are unable to put their pain into words. Teenagers who are in mental pain find that carving into their flesh and watching it bleed is a release. Teens told us that sometimes when they are feeling emotionally numb, feeling physical pain helps them know that they are alive and real.

The cutting behavior is fueled by too much stress and unhealthy emotional development. If you see these conditions, you need to intercede immediately and help your daughter learn healthier ways to cope with her painful feelings. If you suspect your daughter is engaging in this behavior, seek professional help. Therapy can help her to identify the areas of her life over which she feels she has no control and to gain insight into the emotions she isn't able to access on her own. While insight isn't a panacea, it is your best weapon against your daughter's destructive behavior. Only when she better understands her emotions, knows what she needs, and develops healthier coping skills can she begin to meet those needs and feel more in control of her emotional life.

Boys and Violence

According to sociologist Michael Kimmel,

The belief that violence is manly is not carried on any chromosome, not soldered into the wiring of the right or left hemisphere, not juiced by testosterone. (Half of all boys don't fight, most don't carry weapons, and almost all don't kill: are they not boys?) Boys learn it. Dr. [James] Gilligan writes, violence "has far more to do with the cultural construction of manhood than it does with the hormonal substrates of biology." (Kimmel, 1999, p. 91)

Consequently, some boys act out in highly destructive ways. In 2010, males aged 15–19 were nearly four times more likely to commit suicide, six times more likely to be victims of homicide, and eight times more likely to be involved in a firearm-related death than were females of the same age (Child Trends, 2012).

Parents are acutely aware that their sons are at greater risk. As one parent said, "Keeping my son safe is my top priority. Until he comes home at night, I can't fall asleep." While the boys in our focus groups didn't acknowledge the fear, their parents expressed concern about their sons' being targets of other boys' anger and hostility.

While studying the roots of violence, we realize that emotional language and its expression are absent from many boys' lives. When emotional expression is absent, hostility and impulsive behavior occur. When boys learn that the fastest way to resolve conflict may be with a kick or a punch, it's no wonder they grow up more attuned to and comfortable with combat. When girls feel rejected or ridiculed, they tend to feel ashamed and internalize that feeling of shame. Boys externalize this same feeling into anger. The boys in our focus groups agreed that "fighting somebody" is an acceptable way to resolve an argument. Violence becomes a way of showing strength and dominance, while empathy and caring are seen as weaknesses and are discarded.

Michael Kimmel, author of *Guyland* (2009), believes mistreated boys can lash out to prove their masculinity and see themselves as heroes. Yet, according to Kimmel, some boys who are bullied, picked on, and marginalized become adolescent and college-age school shooters. To the horror of all parents and loved ones, macho school cultures are now a stage for those who have been bullied to turn on everyone, with guns blazing.

The construction of violent masculinity is a cultural norm. Exposure to rock and rap music and videos, Hollywood action films, and professional and college sports can result in violent and abusive men. According to Joseph Pleck, a principal investigator in the National Survey of Adolescent Males, when boys are raised with this attitude about masculinity, they are at higher risk for unsafe sexual behavior, substance use, and educational and legal problems (National Institutes of Health [NIH], 2011; see Fact Sheet 3, "Violence").

Teens and Their Drugs, Alcohol, and Addictions

In a 2013 survey released by the National Center on Addiction and Substance Abuse, the news is not good. For the seventh consecutive year, 60 percent or more of teens reported that drugs are used, kept, or sold at school, and 52 percent said they can always find a place at or near school to use drugs, drink, or smoke cigarettes. One encouraging fact is that teenage use of alcohol is at a historic low, even though alcohol use for girls is increasing (CASAColumbia, 2012). However, it's not the same for drug use.

In 2002, the same survey found that 46 percent of students at public high schools said there was drug use at their schools, compared with 24 percent in private schools. But in 2013, 61 percent of public high-school students said drugs were at their schools, compared with 54 percent in private schools (CASAColumbia, 2012). No one is immune. More middle- and high-school students know how and where to buy drugs, including prescription drugs and alcohol. One high school counselor said, "More kids in my school are willing to risk using drugs at school. There is less of a stigma among them to use drugs, and they seem less fearful about jeopardizing their future."

Drug use is terrifying for parents, and it should be. With drugs like heroin on the rise and stronger marijuana, new "boutique" drugs, and prescription drugs readily available, parents must follow through with consequences if they discover that their teens are substance abusers. Being aware and proactive may save your child's life.

Teens use alcohol more frequently and heavily than all other illicit drugs combined. According to "Make a Difference: Talk to Your Child About Alcohol," a publication of the NIH's National Institute on Alcohol Abuse and Alcoholism (NIAAA), alcohol kills 6.5 times more teens than all other illicit drugs combined. This doesn't even take into consideration the countless life-altering consequences of underage drinking that do not result in death. The statistics are sobering: 5,000 people under age 21 die each year from alcohol-related car crashes, homicides, suicides, alcohol poisoning, and other injuries such as falls, burns, and drowning. Additionally, more than 190,000 people under age 21 visited an emergency room for alcohol-related injuries in 2008 alone (NIAAA, 2009). Many adolescents and young adults are experiencing the consequences of drinking too much, at too early an age. As a result, underage drinking is now a leading public health problem.

It's hard for today's teens to escape the liquor industry's media bombardment and to resist peer pressure. While some parents experience relief that their teens are "only" drinking, rather than taking drugs, this reflects that some parents may not know that alcohol also *is* a drug. When young people try alcohol, they often treat it like a casual rite of passage and don't realize the damaging effects drinking can have on their lives. While teenage alcohol use is down, both boys and girls participate in binge drinking more frequently than in the past. Binge drinking increases significantly with age, from 4 percent in ninth grade to 23 percent of 12th-graders (Peale, 2014).

According to the NIAAA, the rates of drinking for boys and girls are similar in younger age groups; among older teenagers, more boys than girls engage in frequent and heavy drinking, and boys show higher rates of drinking problems (NIAAA, 2006). One mother said, "At Jake's twelfth birthday party, I had a rude awakening. About eight boys and girls sat around my kitchen table pretending to chug down beer, using salad dressing. I had only been out of the kitchen for

15 minutes when I realized that they were playing drinking games." Again, this is not a surprising scene, given that 30 percent of kids admit to binge drinking in high school (NIAAA, n.d.a). Starting young exacerbates the problem.

It's important that you talk to your teens about the dangers of combining drinking and sex. One of the most dangerous things for a girl to do is to drink with a boy she doesn't know well. Blair, an 18-year-old college freshman, told us that she thinks she was date raped after a fraternity party:

> How horrible is it to not even know if I was violated? It haunts me, and I'm not sure what to do. I wasn't conscious enough to trust what I really think went on. I want to confront him, but I'm not sure exactly what happened. I remember passing out while lying on this boy's bed. We were messing around, and I woke up a few hours later half-dressed. I don't know whether to be humiliated or outraged.

Blair's experience is too familiar because excess drinking and sexual assault frequently go together.

Even without trauma, teens can be wounded by the consequences of alcohol consumption. Gabe, a high school senior said,

> I learned the hard way how alcohol can mess you up. The night of my junior prom, I made a fool of myself by being loud and acting out of control. I could tell by the disgusted look on my date's face that she was angry and desperate to get away from me. It got so bad I was escorted out of the school after pushing another guy on the dance floor for dancing too close to my date. My friends kept telling me to lay off the booze, but that night I was too drunk to understand how embarrassing my behavior was. Unfortunately, I got to relive my drunken behavior by watching it on my friend's cell phone video the next day.

Alcohol can cause a group situation to get particularly out of hand. One well-publicized example involved teenage girls who pounded each other during a touch football game that degenerated into a muddy brawl. Five girls were injured in a violent free-for-all that involved 100 students. After this hazing incident at Northbrook High School in Illinois, Kathleen Parker reported in the *Chicago Tribune,*

Girls will be girls, Give them a couple of kegs, some pig intestines and a bucket of human feces and, well, stuff happens. . . . But rules have a funny way of getting broken, especially when alcohol is present and parents are missing. The powder puff ritual was held in a "secret" place and was lubricated with a couple of kegs of beer that police say may have been procured by parents. One parent also may have helped collect the feces, according to early reports. (2003)

The parents who provided the alcohol for this daytime activity were charged with furnishing alcohol to minors.

Parents are responsible for setting limits on their minor children, and teens absolutely need to have boundaries. We know teens fight these limits, but they do need and even want them. Limits help them feel safe and help to contain them while they are experimenting and still developing. Limits communicate to your teens that, while you may act like a friend, you're still very much a parent.

One parent talked about participating in a parent peer group while her children were in high school. Included in this group were discussions of curfews, driving, and drinking. Two of the parents in the group, Sara and Rob, looked at the rest of the group with condescension. They didn't understand what the concern was, because they thought that discussing these issues meant the others couldn't control their own children. Sara said, "I don't know what your problems are, but my son and daughter are in every Friday and Saturday night before midnight."

The rest of the group hid their disbelief at Sara and Rob's naïveté. They knew that virtually every Friday night, those kids were sneaking out of the house, and one father in the group had caught the daughter smoking pot in his kitchen. One of the parents in the group gently told Sara and Rob about the reality of their children's behavior. They then discussed how they could communicate better with their own kids, be clear about expectations, and give them a better sense of control. Sara and Rob decided to extend their kids' curfew with the understanding that they were going to create an environment conducive to more honest and open communication. They also reiterated their values to their children regarding drinking and drugs.

Many teenagers we spoke with said their parents often didn't set clear rules about alcohol and other drugs. It's tough to sort through the mixed messages that society markets about alcohol. Clear, consistent messages have to come from parents. If parents don't set limits, they leave kids to set their own. When rules are broken, consequences are most effective when they are given in real time and match the offense. Parents are also responsible for any underage drinking that takes place in their homes, if for no other reason than if something happens under your watch, you are liable for the consequences.

Each generation has its drug of choice, which depends on affordability and accessibility. Whatever teens' drug of choice, they use these substances to self-soothe and escape uncomfortable feelings. Today the drug of choice might be found for free in their parents' medicine cabinet. Heroin, which was once used primarily in cities, is now more commonly found in rural and suburban communities. One of the reasons heroin is currently popular is that it's less expensive than marijuana. Marijuana is now legal for adults in some cities and may no longer land your teen in jail. Regardless of these changes, the danger remains that abusing drugs will alter the developing brain. This requires serious, ongoing, as-needed, face-to-face conversations between you and your teens. Make sure they are aware that you know what's out there, and if you don't know, find out.

Sexuality: Everything but the Truth

Although teen pregnancy has declined and there is increased awareness of contraception and sexually transmitted diseases (STDs), the rate of HIV diagnosis in teens aged 16–19 has increased (White House Office of National AIDS Policy, 2010). Teens are now coming of age in the era of sexting, when provocative photos are common, pornography sites are accessible to teens, and underwear as outerwear is a fashion statement. Everything, it seems, is sexualized.

In the past, girls fit into one of two ridiculous categories: Madonna or whore, angel or temptress, girl next door or slut. As Liza Mundy writes, these categories are "yet another way of sorting girls, setting them at odds with one another." She continues, "Modern scare tactics have lent a new vocabulary—even a fake veneer of legitimacy—to ancient, pernicious stereotypes" (2000).

Girls with sexual feelings are judged negatively; they learn that finding pleasure in their sexuality is wrong. However, boys who are sexually active have status; they're "players."

Only recently have we begun to explore a more complicated view of girls that accepts their asserting their sexual feelings as normal. Some girls openly pursue sex, brag and lie about sex, and have adopted behavior boys have long taken for granted. Even if your daughters are not sexually active, they are exposed to sexuality in school, at social events, and through the media. Mundy further observes:

> My biggest concern is that girls have taken on the worst of male traits in deciding that they're going to go for sex the way guys have always gone for sex. They are devaluing themselves and limiting their possibility for romance and real intimacy. We have to teach our girls that sometimes power is holding back, not giving everything. It comes in knowing who you are as a person and valuing that and not giving it up so easily. (2000)

Girls are taught to keep a rein on the sexual advances of boys, yet they aren't taught how to acknowledge and manage their own sexual feelings. One mother said, "It seems like girls, on the one hand, aren't supposed to have any sexual feelings, and on the other hand, they are expected to control whether or not they engage in sexual activity with boys." As Deborah Tolman says in *Dilemmas of Desire: Teenage Girls Talk About Sexuality* (2005), society gives a girl the unfair choice between connecting with her body or denying her body pleasure.

Most American parents have a hard time discussing sex with their children. As a result, we give girls and boys many mixed messages. We have a hard time dealing with the fact that our children may be sexually active, just as teens have a difficult time imagining their parents having sex at all! Fathers, particularly, have a hard time with their daughters' sexuality. Many mothers recounted stories of how differently their husbands perceived the way their daughters dressed. Janice, the mother of 14-year-old Alyssa, said,

> This year Alyssa tried on a bathing suit for her dad, and his jaw almost hit the ground. She looked gorgeous. I looked at her wistfully, wishing I could still turn heads like she will. My husband looked at me, puzzled, and said, "You aren't going to let her go out like that, are you?" It was the first time he sounded like a stodgy old father. He was really uncomfortable with her sexuality, realizing that she looked sexy and knowing that boys and men might notice.

On some level, dads more than mothers have a hard time visualizing their daughters being intimate. They don't seem to have the same trouble with sons, however.

As hard as it is for our kids to think that their parents have sex, it's also difficult for us to imagine our children having intimate relationships. Sex is an uncomfortable topic for parents to deal with, regardless of whether we are liberal or conservative; it's just difficult seeing our teens becoming sexual beings. In fact, nearly half of young women surveyed by Katherine Hutchinson and Teresa Cooney (1998) reported feeling somewhat or very uncomfortable discussing sexuality with their parents. However, the same teens reported wishing their mothers and fathers had shared more information with them about sexuality, and we think this may hold true for boys as well.

It makes good sense to discuss sexuality with our daughters and sons. Boys are not immune to STDs or the implications of teenage pregnancy. As Brent Miller (1998) reports, open communication between parents and teenagers has been linked to delaying first intercourse and greater likelihood of contraceptive use. When we keep our heads in the sand, we put our children at risk for unsafe sex. We want both boys and girls to make good choices based on understanding the consequences. (Remember how they are with consequences; you need to be their frontal lobes.) We also want them to be comfortable with their bodies and their development as loving and responsible sexual beings. Girls should have permission to say no, and boys should respect their decisions. In other words, we want our sons to treat girls like they want their sisters to be treated. Girls and boys should be mindful when they make the decision to have sex. To protect your teen, the decision for sex has to be mutual.

Liza Mundy claimed in a *Washington Post Magazine* article that teens "who have a strong, healthy relationship with at least one parent, where they can talk about what's on their mind and what they're dealing with are less likely to have early sexual experiences" (2000). Parents can influence their teenagers' decision making. Sex is about intimacy and is value laden. Each family will set different boundaries around sexuality, and parents must be able to talk about sex with their children and impart their values. If you don't share your opinions with your children, you can be assured that they will get opinions from their friends and the media.

Parental Protective Factors

Even though all parents were once teenagers, most of us seem to lose touch with what this period of development was like. We forget that teens are supposed to make mistakes. As one 14-year-old girl said, "We're teenagers; that's what we do. We make stupid mistakes often and don't know why we made them." Teenage mistakes can be scary, but some risk taking is a developmental necessity and might not be life-threatening. We worry that, as parents, when we encourage their independence, we may inadvertently place our children at risk. But as psychiatrist Dr. Lynn Ponton tells us,

> I have learned, in my roles as psychiatrist and mother, that even though all teenagers engage in a wide range of activities, some of which are potentially destructive, and that they often possess a limited ability to understand the consequences of their actions, not all teenage risk taking is dangerous. In fact, most of it is extremely positive. How they assess or fail to assess risk is the key point, but I believe that risk taking is a vital tool that adolescents use to develop their identities, and that healthy risk taking, for teens and adults, is an extremely valuable experience. (2002)

No matter how many safeguards you put in place, you can't protect your children fully. They drive cars (a legitimate fear), go to parties (why we can't sleep until they get home), or learn a new sport, whether it's skiing or scuba diving. Some risks are worth taking for teenagers to learn new skills, develop self-esteem, learn about and manage consequences, and build resilience. Diverse life experiences, including mistakes, will strengthen their judgment and sense of self. The problem today is that our children live in a much more dangerous world than we did.

Because the world feels more threatening, we are more reluctant to let our children go, and there are more factors to consider with every decision and every act. It's not that we don't want them to have experiences, we just have to work harder at teaching them to use good judgment. You aren't going to prevent them from taking risks, but judgment is about mitigating risks, not eliminating them. You have to ask the hard questions so your children can learn for themselves to lessen the risks and manage their choices successfully. What you also need to consider when making decisions is that your children are individuals, and the advice you give shouldn't be based on gender expectations.

Rather than looking at teenagers "as if adolescence were a vast Bermuda triangle," says Grace Palladino in "A Look at . . . Adolescence," it is our belief that it is "the circumstances of their lives—whether they are neglected or nurtured, encouraged or ignored, exploited or educated—and not their age or their hormones, that puts them at risk. And it is our tendency to demonize teenagers today, to act as if they are aliens with no ancestors and no history, that allows us to shake our heads and wonder what's the matter with kids today." (1998)

10

Preparing for the Next Chapter

The conveyor belt that once transported adolescents into adulthood has broken down.

—Frank Furstenberg, sociologist and researcher

Yes, there is another chapter. It's called extended adolescence, which transitions into emerging adulthood. Nobody knows exactly how long it lasts, but researchers and parent groups agree that in the United States, it goes on into their children's twenties, and in Germany and Italy, possibly into their forties. In the United States, according to the latest findings, one in five people in their twenties and early thirties currently lives at home, and 60 percent of all young adults receive financial support from their parents. This is a huge increase over only one generation ago, when 1 in 10 young adults moved back home and very few received financial support (David, 2014). Apart from cultural issues, neuropsychology explains this. The amygdala (the part of the brain that deals with judgment) is not fully developed until the midtwenties. These young people may not have good judgment and/or fully understand consequences. Once again, when we say, "Parenting is never over; it just changes," we're not kidding. We have written an entire book about this: *Mom, Can I Move Back in with You?* (Gordon & Shaffer, 2004). We felt we had to write that book, because after the soccer games and plays are over, there's no natural chatroom where parents can go to talk about this. Parents are on their own.

Acknowledging this transition from childhood to adulthood and the need for continued parenting can hit like a lightning bolt. Just when you think you're done, you realize you aren't. To accept the concept of extended adolescence, you must recognize that your children aren't quite ready for adulthood. Research tells us that the journey from childhood to adulthood takes longer and is less defined than in previous generations (David, 2014; Gordon & Shaffer, 2004). Parents are fellow travelers in this newly recognized developmental stage.

Our children appear to be more sophisticated at younger ages, but often this is a superficial maturity. They have such easy access to information and are so facile with it that we assume they know more and can do things before they are actually ready. We assume they are adults because they talk somewhat like adults and are physically large. As a result of social change, most colleges have eliminated the rules they had in the past, like curfews, report cards that went to the parents, mandatory meal cards, and single-sex dorms. Students are left to parent themselves before many of them are actually ready.

Having more sophisticated experiences at a younger age doesn't mean a person is more grown-up. Marlene, a five-foot-one-inch mother, is more than a foot shorter than her 22-year-old, six-foot-three-inch son, Robby. She said, "My son looks like he should command authority. Robby is not only tall, he's really big. I have to remind myself he's still the same boy who is scared of spiders. Sometimes he gets the broom and clears the spider webs before he walks through the archway on our porch."

Older teens and young adults still need the encouragement and support required by all children, yet the type of encouragement does differ. Parenting at every stage requires the ability to adapt. The need for these skills is even more important during extended adolescence because parents' role shifts from that of a benevolent dictator to that of a Yoda-like guide. In Chapter 1, we introduced you to the characteristics of adulthood as guideposts for parenting teens. In this chapter, we focus in greater detail on five of them for parenting during the period of extended adolescence and emerging adulthood. As you encourage your children to develop these characteristics, be mindful of the fact that children will integrate the qualities of adulthood incrementally. As one mother said, "Life is not a race." Understanding this will enable you to be more patient with an emphasis on thinking long term.

This transition in parenting continues to require connection as well as a keen sense of restraint. With older teens and adult children, we must stand back, except when it's necessary to ensure that they have learned the characteristics of adulthood. In doing this, we are still going to be perfectly imperfect. The truth is, like all of us, our children are a work in progress. During this period, they may seek advice, and they may need advice, but most important, they must make their own decisions, learn the consequences of these decisions, and build their self-confidence by making good decisions or correcting bad ones.

Parents can help their adult children feel less anxious and less pressured by acknowledging and praising each successful step they take toward independence. At the same time, parents need to continue to be loving and supportive but honest when their adult children stumble or make mistakes. Two questions are important to ask: What can I do to support my teens' development of the characteristics of adulthood and related skills? What do they need to take care of themselves, encourage a sense of well-being, and simultaneously sustain a positive relationship based on respectful and mutual interdependence?

Guideposts for the Transition from the Teenage Years to Adulthood

Based on our professional and personal experience and the wisdom offered by the parents, teens, and adult children in our focus groups, we have identified several characteristics as primary guideposts for parenting during extended adolescence:

* Developing respectful and mutual interdependence
* Becoming personally responsible

* Becoming resilient
* Setting and keeping appropriate boundaries
* Obtaining cultural competence

Every family is different, but these guideposts are essential for all adults and transcend differences in race, gender, culture, language, socioeconomic status, and religion. Consider them when making decisions during these transition years.

Being an Adult Is Developing Respectful and Mutual Interdependence

Albert Einstein spoke of human relationships when he wrote, "Separation is an optical illusion of consciousness, and . . . if we see things only in that framework, we become locked in a prison and lose that capacity to be intimate, compassionate, to know ourselves in the larger sense." Adults understand the importance of being both independent and connected. The goal of parents, therefore, is to encourage our children to use opportunities to be independent and autonomous without disconnecting.

Individuals within a family can remain autonomous and still be connected through dialogue. Family members can demonstrate this by being tolerant of others in the family, without necessarily agreeing, and by being open to different points of view. Love should not be equated with agreement. Families can take pride in being able to discuss controversial subjects openly without children worrying about parents' withholding approval. Independent thinking is essential for our children to become confident adults. Parental openness and ability to communicate advice and opinions, without conditions, contributes to the development of a healthy, interdependent relationship with adult children.

Connections can come in life's small moments in a variety of ways, as evidenced by the following story told by Bob, a 54-year-old father:

> I love talking with my adult children. There is a really big difference
> between saying, "You're wrong," and saying, "I disagree." I have

strong opinions, and so do my kids. My late father always said, "Your judgment is no better than your information." My kids, Sara and Matt, and I can have heated discussions and still respect each other. I don't treat them like little kids because they disagree with me. There is a wide spectrum of ideas that are OK. Most things don't matter in the long run.

Debating ideas is our family's way of staying connected. We love bouncing ideas off one another. Whether it's discussing a movie, debating an issue, or arguing over religion, my wife and I love watching Sara and Matt become independent thinkers yet still wanting to share their ideas with us.

We want our children to flourish as adults, but we also want them to enjoy the connection with their families. This respectful interdependence between adult children and their parents is fuzzy and imprecise and takes on different meanings and challenges for various types of families.

Often when famous people accept awards, they use the occasion as an opportunity to publicly acknowledge the connection they have with their parents. When Sidney Poitier won a Lifetime Achievement Oscar, he said, "My art portrays the dignity of my parents." Accepting his Most Valuable Player award in 2014, Kevin Durant spoke of his connection to his single mother: "I don't think you know what you did; you had my brother when you were eighteen, and three years later I came out. The odds were stacked against us. . . . When something good happens to me, I tend to look back. . . . You made us believe, you sacrificed for us, you're the real MVP" (Schwartz, 2014). These people modeled the idea that being an adult means realizing a sense of family and community as well as independence. As Teddy Roosevelt said, "Connections we make reverberate long after we make them" (Morris, 2001).

Parents must understand that, during extended adolescence, parenting is more about support and respect than about protection. Diane, a 58-year-old mother of two grown sons, said,

> You know, I introduce the idea of a patchwork quilt to the foster children I work with. I tell them I don't want to build a safety net

for them. Instead, I want to make a tapestry, with all the pieces stitched together with love. This quilt will embrace them and provide them with warmth when they need it. For me, this is a more comforting image than a safety net with holes in it.

Mutual interdependence enables both parents and adult children to protect themselves and to state their needs while respecting each other's needs and remaining connected by both giving and receiving assistance when appropriate.

Being an Adult Is Becoming Personally Responsible

When our children are older, indulging them is counterproductive because it doesn't teach personal responsibility. Regardless of circumstances, this is a time for setting limits and encouraging our children to assume responsibility for themselves, including living within their means. The 51-year-old mother of 21-year-old Stuart said,

> Give me a scratched knee anytime; dealing with my son now is much more complicated. Stuart has champagne taste when it comes to eating out. He will fall in love with a trendy new restaurant and think nothing of charging his meals and his drinks to us. It's usually a restaurant that we would think was too expensive for ourselves. Stuart knows that his spending is over the top, but he chooses to act irresponsibly and satisfy his immediate desire, no matter how often we ask him to watch his spending. Last month we canceled his credit card. Now he will have to experience more of the real world by resisting his impulses and adjusting his spending to what his finances can afford. We hope that, in a way, he might feel relieved.

Not all parents can afford to give their children credit cards during this time, but the same principles of fostering personal responsibility apply.

Parents overindulge their children in ways other than giving them money. One father said, "I was furious at my wife when she gave our son, Noah, a wake-up call before a job interview. She was scared he'd sleep though his alarm and miss the appointment. I yelled, 'At some point, he has to care more than we do. It's his job interview, not ours!'" We do a disservice to our emerging adult children when we overdo. Besides creating dependency, we undermine their ability to trust that they can function without us. When parents make decisions based solely on what their children want, the power shifts inappropriately to the children. When children have too much power, they develop a sense of entitlement that may continue into adulthood.

The antidote to a misplaced sense of entitlement and lack of responsibility is to set limits on what we will do for emerging adult children. Many parents talk about making their children happy and are reluctant to set limits. Parents often feel insecure and worry about establishing limits because they don't want to face their children's anger. Young children push against their parents' rules until it may feel as though limits have evaporated. When parents defer to their children, the children suffer because they fail to learn they are not the center of the universe. Some kids resist the process of becoming personally responsible. Parents must be resolute and not overindulge lifestyle, which is different from need. It's one thing to support needs such as health care and some education costs; it's another to pay for expensive restaurants, health clubs, and designer clothing. This discourages personal responsibility and encourages dependence. Accepting personal responsibility means that our older teens and young adults hold themselves accountable and accept limits. Without limits, they have a hard time accepting the world as it is.

Growing Up Is Becoming Resilient

Emphasizing effort rather than outcome early on protects young adults as they manage a challenging and competitive world. We hope focusing on effort will allow you to cope better with your children's disappointments and failures. When children come up short, great antidotes for disappointment include laughter or humor and sharing your own experiences. As comedian Louis C.K. said in an interview with David Letterman, "You aren't going to get what you want most of the time. If you can learn to be OK with disappointment, if you can survive disappointment, then nothing can beat you" (The David Letterman Show, January 5, 2014).

As parents, we can start to encourage resilience at an early age, and this role continues throughout the teen years into early adulthood. However, the challenges are more complicated and have greater consequences as children become adults. Remember, bigger kids, bigger problems. But we can help older teens and emerging adults to cultivate the capacity to better manage their lives. Resilience includes social competence (empathy, caring communications, sense of humor), problem solving (critical thinking, creative planning, asking for help when necessary), independence (self-efficacy, task mastery, self-control/management), and sense of purpose (goal direction, educational aspirations, optimism, connectedness) (Tough, 2012). Practicing these skills needed for long-term resilience begins in childhood, and parents can certainly foster these positive traits. No matter how talented your children are, they have to experience both successes and failures. While successes can build their confidence, that confidence will not be sufficient to lead them to a mature adulthood unless they have practiced coping with obstacles within the safety of their family.

Being an Adult Is Setting and Keeping Appropriate Boundaries

One of the important tasks of growing up is learning to set boundaries. Parents can best teach this by example. Knowing how to maintain appropriate boundaries is essential to becoming a mature adult. This characteristic is integral to creating privacy, building personal integrity, setting protective limits for ourselves, and engaging in appropriate behavior with other people. In dysfunctional families, boundary violations can produce barriers between family members or a complete disregard for privacy and personal space. Parents can demonstrate respect and appropriate boundaries by permitting older teens and adult children to express their opinions freely and by showing consideration for their privacy.

It is difficult for a parent, after having been involved in the details of their children's lives when they were younger, to stay in their own lane. Sometimes we have to learn boundaries before we can teach them. Anna, mother of 23-year-old, Rachel, recalled one such challenge:

> When Rachel moved into an apartment, I automatically offered to help set her up. I had done her previous apartments and every dorm room she had lived in. I just assumed this was my job. My problem is that Rachel assumed this as well. On moving day, I found myself on the floor, scrubbing the grime off of the linoleum in cracks you don't want to know about. I didn't mind pitching in, but I really minded working like a dog when Rachel was making plans with friends for dinner. In the middle of backbreaking Cinderella work, I stood up and decided I was finished, even though the work wasn't done.
>
> I realized that this wasn't my job anymore and that I had contributed to Rachel sitting on her rear while I was on my hands and knees. I had not set appropriate boundaries as the mother of a 23-year-old. How was she ever going to learn to take care of herself, if I didn't stop doing for her?

Parents must also demonstrate the importance of good boundaries by showing respect when their adult children create boundaries for themselves. Josh, a 23-year-old graduate student, said he didn't want his parents to drop by his apartment unannounced. His parents let him know that they understood his request and promised to respect his privacy by calling before they came over. Appropriate boundaries require balance. All mature adults need to establish suitable boundaries for themselves as part of the process of learning to respect the boundaries of others.

Another father said, "My son works as a paralegal in a prominent law firm. He has been there for a few years, and they've never given him a raise. He thinks he's paid fairly and has been highly praised at his annual review. I've been hounding him to ask for more money, and he's told me to back off. It's hard for me, but he's made it clear: this is his job, and any job-related decision is his alone to make."

Boundaries can be set like fences. They can be tight and not let any light through, or they can be loose like lattice. They might be placed too close to the front door or too far away, leaving the occupant feeling open and vulnerable. To be effective, boundaries must be flexible enough to change, depending on the child, period of development, and situation. When they work, boundaries provide limits, and with limits come safety, trust, and privacy for both parents and children.

Being an Adult Requires Obtaining Cultural Competence

One significant skill adult children need to be successful in this diverse, multicultural society is cultural competence, the ability to understand and acknowledge one's own cultural background as well as others'. Becoming knowledgeable about and taking into consideration different standards and operating principles enables older teens and young adults to be successful in the world of work and in the community in which they live. Whether adult children will acquire these skills depends largely on the lessons they learned from their parents. Children will adopt the values of inclusion and appreciation for diversity if their parents model these behaviors at home. One mother of an adult son related the significance of acceptance:

> Yesterday I went to the baptism of a beautiful baby girl. Surrounding this baby were her African American mother and Caucasian father. Also there were multiple friends of their parents, representing diverse backgrounds. This baby girl and others of her generation will grow up in a world much more accepting and tolerant of racial and cultural differences and be enriched by them.

Adulthood and independence may be defined differently in different cultures. For example, European Americans define adulthood in terms of independence significantly more often than do people of color. Other racial and ethnic groups define adulthood in terms of both independence and interdependence: children are expected to assume greater personal responsibility, while at the same time, allegiance to family remains the priority and does not stop with adulthood.

We are aware that different cultures operate under different assumptions, but parents and children have the opportunity to move forward together to create social justice and to celebrate the richness of living in a diverse society. Without the ability to operate in a multicultural society, our children will be less prepared to function well as adults in the workplace and in their interpersonal relationships. These are skills (openness, inclusion, acceptance) that everyone must embody. So we have to parent our teens and emerging adults for *their* future.

Your adult children will probably make different lifestyle or career choices from the ones you made. At this stage, parents must learn to express their uncertainties and anxiety clearly and tactfully. It's important to understand that the manner in which you approach your adult children will influence your relationship positively or negatively. This doesn't mean you can't be upset. Try to ask questions that help you better understand rather than blame. They are growing up in a different world, and so are we.

Strategies for Parents of Older Teens and Young Adults

To meet the challenges associated with this new developmental stage, you may need some additional parenting strategies beyond the ones we offered in Chapter 8. The focus of these additional strategies is the same: building characteristics of adulthood.

1. **Let your older teens and young adults speak. Then have faith they've heard what you've said.**
   * Try not to give advice unless you are asked. Do more listening than talking. Don't react until your child has finished

describing the problem. Suspend judgment. Remember, being invited to give information does not mean your child will use it. As hard as it may be, as parents, we have to learn to let go of the outcome.

* Tell the truth. A certain amount of exploration is appropriate for young adults. Be supportive of and encourage experimenting with new jobs and adventures. It is our job to help our children distinguish the difference between "meandering" and "exploration," but try to remember that it is our children's job to make the choice. This demonstrates mutual respect. Once you have told them the truth as you see it, you should have faith with their decisionmaking, even if you disagree. As emerging adults, it is up to them to make their own choices.

* Don't assume your adult children have not heard you. Many parents feel they are not being listened to because they don't get a timely response from their adult children. But your children do listen, and you may hear about it indirectly in random conversations or see it in decisions they make.

2. **Coach your older teens and adult children, rather than doing for them.**

* Let them do for themselves. By doing things for our older teens and young adults, by always fixing their problems, we run the risk of affirming their lack of confidence. We deny them the opportunity to learn from their own successes and failures and to develop needed skills.

* Be mindful that when you rescue them, making things easier for your adult children doesn't necessarily mean you're making things better for them. If you rescue them, this encourages them to depend on you.

* Teach children about accountability, personal responsibility, and boundaries. Provide children with as many opportunities as possible to practice the skills they need to take care of themselves.

3. **Be the best adult you can be as a parent. Make good decisions in your own best interest, not just your children's, by setting good boundaries.**
   * Continue to feel good about participating in your children's lives while also respecting your own boundaries and their privacy.
   * By all means, remain available. Your older teens and young adults still need you. Be available to listen when they're ready to talk. However, it's important for both parents and kids to set boundaries, because with limits come safety, trust, and privacy for parents and children. You're not required to bend yourself into a pretzel for your adult children.
   * Be clear about what you can and cannot contribute, both financially and emotionally. Come to a mutual understanding that includes your adult children's own responsibilities.
   * Provide only appropriate help. Safety is the overriding consideration when determining whether to get involved in the lives of your adult children when they haven't asked you to do so. If your children are in an abusive relationship or are addicted to drugs or alcohol, you can support your children best by getting them appropriate help and not enabling destructive behavior.

4. **Trust your instincts about what you know is right for your children. Be prepared that, however right you are, they may not agree with you.**
   * Update your parenting advice to match this stage of development. This doesn't mean that you can't continue to rely on guideposts that have worked for you in the past and have faith in what you know about your children. There will be new challenges, so take a breath, give yourself time to regroup, think the problem through, and then respond. If you follow this process, your guidance will be more appropriate for this stage.
   * Be mindful that you can choose to support or not support your children. Expect adult children to live with the consequences

of their decisions and actions, so they can learn from their own mistakes.

* Give "guilt-free" advice or support without conditions. If we choose to give support freely, there shouldn't be any strings or an "I told you so," especially when emerging adult children make decisions with which you disagree.

* Avoid asking loaded questions. One mother said, "My son laughs at me and says, 'Mom, is this something you need to know, or is it another life lesson disguised as curiosity? If it's a life lesson, I'm putting it in my pocket with all the others. You can't stop yourself from asking!'"

5. **Flexibility is better than hard-and-fast rules.**
   * Count on change. Acknowledge that it's normal for parents and children to feel confused during this period. Acknowledging this can normalize this stage of development and help to make this time less overwhelming for parents, older teens, and adult children.

   * Don't misinterpret this transition as a crisis, like a midlife crisis, which is more myth than reality.

   * Try to remember what it was like for you to live with the uncertainties of emerging adulthood. Be mindful that your children have grown up in a world defined by ambivalence.

   * Share concerns about your adult children with friends and family. This can be comforting and increase your capacity to be flexible and respond appropriately to your children's issues. Discussing common experiences will help to lessen the anxiety and self-doubts you and your children may be experiencing.

   * Tolerate differences and be flexible. Parents may help to create adult children who are more self-directed and are not defined by one rigid set of cultural values or expectations.

   * Don't hesitate to treat each of your children differently, as long as you are sensitive and fair. Children take different paths and require different forms of guidance and support.

* Don't sweat the small stuff. One father told us, "I never worried about anything that wasn't permanent. So when my son had his initials carved into his hair by the barber, I couldn't care less. It didn't bother me." Said another parent, "My daughter lives in a pigpen. Just spending time in her apartment could trigger an asthma attack. But it doesn't seem to bother her. I'm tempted to bring my vacuum next time I visit, but I know better!" And from another parent: "I told my son to limit his tattoos to places on his body that won't be visible at work. But I'm braced and ready for when I see one creeping out from his shirtsleeve." This advice works for children of any age.

6. **Have reasonable expectations for their achieving independence.**
   * Expect an extended period of dependence. This transition period will be less problematic, and you can approach it more objectively and diplomatically, if you know it's only temporary.
   * Respect and appreciate that your children have grown up and have the skills to figure things out for themselves. As one parent explained, "Trust that they can figure things out, and be supportive and nonjudgmental when they hit snags."
   * Acknowledge and praise each step toward independence. This will help your older teens and adult children to feel less anxious and less pressured. Try to remember that, even as adults, children tend to seek parental approval.
   * Relax! Understand that the process of becoming independent occurs in stages and takes time.

7. **Prepare your older teens and young adults for the cultural changes they will face in their lifetime.**
   * Accept gender role changes in your children. Mothers no longer are solely responsible for nurturing and taking care of the children, and men are increasingly focusing on their families. In most cases, men and women work outside the

home, so the skill sets of both home and work are critical to
their family's future well-being.

* Adopt the values of inclusion and tolerance, and model these
  behaviors at home. If they lack the ability to operate in a
  diverse society, your children will be less prepared to be
  high-functioning adults in the workplace and in their
  interpersonal relationships.

* Teach tolerance and tell your children about the harm caused by
  the intolerance of others. For children who choose to live with or
  marry someone outside their faith or from a different racial or
  cultural group or choose a same-sex partner, parents do them no
  favor by trying to insulate them from the perils of intolerance. First,
  give them your support. Second, the most you can do is to talk
  honestly about problems they may face and give them a heads-up
  if you see potential conflict with extended family members.

8. **Measure maturity based on the acquisition of emotional characteristics associated with adulthood, rather than the traditional
   milestones of past generations (graduating from college, getting
   married, or owning a home). These characteristics include:**

   * Besides the characteristics defined as guideposts earlier in this
     chapter, characteristics that signal adulthood includes empathy
     for others, the confidence to do things on one's own, financial
     independence, and the establishment of competent marriages
     or partnerships and raising children.

   * Understand the emotional characteristics of maturity. Parents
     can determine the extent to which their children have
     internalized these characteristics by observing whether their
     children have established personal identities, developed
     reasonable and rational judgment, become able to make
     independent decisions, behave in a purposeful and responsible
     manner, and are self-reliant and self-confident.

   * Be patient. Maturity comes in increments and may be
     packaged differently from what we expect. Also, the time frame
     varies from person to person.

* Teach empathy by "holding," which is staying present and communicating that you understand your children's experiences. Holding is unconditional. We have to hold our children in a way that demonstrates we can stay present while they express their discomfort. This is tricky when they're in pain, when it's even more important that we are able to manage our own feelings.

* Don't jump in too early with advice and problem solving. Guide your children to figure out for themselves how to solve their problem, issue, or concern.

* Be responsive to your children's needs and pace. Unlike our relationships with young children, where we direct the process of growing up, our relationships with older teens and adult children require that we be responsive to them.

* Assist in the process of their becoming adults by helping your children understand that they have the competency to take responsibility for their own lives.

9. **Guide your children toward becoming financially literate and independent. This gives them the opportunity to know they can take care of themselves, which builds authentic self-confidence and resilience.**

* Before lending or giving money to your adult children, ask yourself, *Do* you feel comfortable (not *should* you feel comfortable) with this decision? Give assistance when it makes sense to you, such as contributing toward health insurance or augmenting rent to help your children live in a safe neighborhood.

* Teach them to live within *their* means, rather than *your* means. If you continuously subsidize your children's lifestyles or bail them out of debt, you give them false expectations about what they can afford.

* Guide your children toward making a distinction between wants and needs. You might contribute if they ask for help with insurance, rent, and health care but say no if they want help with paying for lifestyle "needs."

10. **Know that they may come back!**

    * If your adult children come home to live for a while, they will do well if they are assured of your love and support during this transition. Know why they're moving back home. If your children don't have any goals, help them to set some.

    * Be explicit about your expectations. Tell them what you need them to do. Mutual respect, cooperation, and compromise are essential. Uphold whatever agreement you reach between yourselves and your children.

    * Reframe the old house rules of childhood and early adolescence to meet the changing needs of an emerging adult.

    * Encourage independence.

    * Distinguish between serious problems and irritations. Some issues require intervention; others don't. If your children seem depressed, sleep all the time, demonstrate dramatic changes in eating habits, or don't experience pleasure from the things that used to please them, they may have a serious problem that requires intervention. Many other things fall under the category of annoyances, however, such as leaving the outside lights on, ignoring dirty dishes in the sink, or keeping Count Dracula's hours. These are irritants that may improve or may not. When your adult children move out, it ultimately is not your business if their electric bill is large or if they run out of clean dishes. Take a deep breath and acknowledge that they won't be living with you forever.

    * Permit yourself to ask your adult children to make "courtesy calls" if they're coming home for dinner or are going to be out exceptionally late. Everyone in the family is expected to do the same; adult children should not be treated any differently.

    * Keep your sense of humor! Enjoy the time you have together.

11. **Convey to your children the value of establishing a community that includes both family and friends.**

    * Connections with family and friends enrich our lives; they don't detract from them.

* Value connection. Avoid making your children embarrassed about feeling a continued need for their family.
* Expect a more mutual and equal relationship. This adult relationship should bring pleasure to both you and your adult child. As one 21-year-old told us, "I don't feel like a little kid in my parents' house anymore. When I go over to their house and I'm cooking dinner, my mom will ask what spice she should put in something. It's a different relationship in a really fun way."
* Enjoy them. One mother suggested, "I think it's very important for us to gather as a family on a regular basis. We do it with family trips, and we do create a lot of hoopla when they come home, even if it's just for the weekend. It's always obvious to them how happy we are to spend time with them."

12. **Communicate, communicate, communicate . . . by email, texting, cell phone, letter, telephone, and visits.**
   * Keep the lines of communication open. How you start the conversation sets the tone for the interaction that follows.
   * Talk to your children as you would talk to a friend. One mother explained, "I always talked to my four sons like I would talk to anybody else. If my friend came into the house with muddy boots, I wouldn't say, 'What are you doing walking around with those muddy boots?' I would use more tact."
   * Stay calm and get a grip on your own intensity and reactivity to pave the path for conversation. Being less reactive gets better results.
   * When you talk to your adult children about your concerns, identify feelings and talk with "I" statements, such as "I am frustrated," rather than "you" statements, such as "You make me nuts."
   * Assume that what your children have to say is as important as what you have to say. Learning is a two-way street. Paying attention to what our children are telling us can help us guide them in a more appropriate way. It also helps us continue to grow.

* Stay in the present and avoid reverting to dated behaviors, rekindling past hurts, and unpacking old baggage.
* Let them know that *you* also need *them*.
* Continue to look for teachable moments.

13. **Don't forget to keep your sense of humor and enjoy them— you've earned it!**

Epilogue

Raising children takes parents on a long and frequently intricate path. Unlike our parents and those of past generations, we still may not know where our children are headed while they're in their twenties. In spite of living with some ambiguity, now is the time to relax a little and reap the benefits. Tricia, a mother of five adult children, recalled,

> My most vivid memory of all those early years was standing, holding a baby, nursing, and scrambling an egg carefully over the stove so that I wouldn't burn the baby's head. The school bus was coming, the lunches were waiting to be assembled, and my husband was out of town. It was unbelievably chaotic.
>
> But they still grew up. They were so close together in age that all of a sudden, they were just older, together. I have a wonderful relationship with my kids, and I love it. It's terrific. I don't begrudge those early years, but I'm really enjoying my kids now.

Having your children as friends can be a joy. One father of older teens said, "Our family went to Vermont for Christmas. At night we sat around and played Scrabble. It was the best family vacation we've ever had. It's so much fun with adult children. We related like friends who really enjoy each other's company." Relationships with adult children finally become more mutual. Not only can you enjoy each other, but you can also depend on each other.

Often we are concerned that there is a danger in being too close to our children as they grow up. This awareness makes us devalue what we think of as normal, healthy closeness and connection. Many parents worry that they shouldn't be supporting their adult children for fear of hindering their independence. This is a reasonable concern; however, we believe that valuing connection is an essential part of health and survival and can be accomplished without interfering with our children's development.

Becoming an adult does not require separating from those who love you. However, this new stage does require negotiating new boundaries and new role definitions. You have to regroup at each stage of your children's development. The beginning of each new stage may seem overwhelming, but you'll eventually find yourself relaxing and feeling more confident.

Parenting is an ongoing process. Launching our children is a timeless experience; so is letting go. With older teens and young adults, the surprise comes because you feel you should have completed all the more complex stages of parenting already. We were led to believe that once our children reached their twenties, our job would be finished. We now understand that we can expect an extended period of involvement in the lives of our children.

Just when you think your children are on smooth and solid ground, it shifts. Today the lives of young adults may be unsettling, but at the same time, it's important to keep in mind that this transitional age is filled with possibilities. This time provides a perfect opportunity for them to explore their world. Young adults have more freedom than at any other time in their lives. As parents, we can provide them with our wisdom and insight as they move forward toward independence.

So what does it take to be a good parent? Love them no matter what.

Depression in Adolescents

Many of the tumultuous moods that we think are normal by-products of adolescence may be signs of depression. Symptoms of depression should not be confused with or dismissed as adolescent mood swings.

When attempts at helping your children are ineffective, then it is advisable to seek professional support, especially if the following symptoms persist for several weeks, become more severe, and/or lead to self-destructive thoughts or behavior. The following symptom list has been developed by the National Institute of Mental Health:

* Persistent sad or "empty" mood, feeling hopeless
* Loss of enjoyment or interest in activities that gave pleasure in the past
* Changes in sleep habits such as insomnia or oversleeping
* Eating disturbances such as decreased appetite or overeating
* Difficulty in concentrating

* Physical aches such as headaches, stomach pain, and chronic pain that have no organic origin
* Low self-esteem
* Decreased energy

Also take into account the following risk factors for adolescent depression:

* Having a family member with depression
* Loss of an important family member or loved one to death
* Abuse or neglect
* Isolation, lack of support from trusted adults
* Harsh or judgmental parents with low tolerance for conflict or disagreements
* Overly permissive parents with few rules and regulation
* Family conflict regardless of parents' marital status

FACT SHEET 2

SUICIDE SIGNS

Certain behaviors are indicators that can help parents or friends recognize the threat of suicide in a loved one. Since mental and substance-related disorders frequently accompany suicidal behavior, many of the cues to look for are symptoms associated with such disorders as depression, bipolar disorder (manic depression), anxiety disorders, alcohol and drug use, disruptive behavior disorders, borderline personality disorder, and schizophrenia.

Some common symptoms of these disorders include:

* Extreme personality changes
* Loss of interest in activities that used to be enjoyable
* Significant loss of or increase in appetite
* Difficulty falling asleep or desire to sleep all day
* Fatigue or loss of energy
* Feelings of worthlessness or guilt
* Withdrawal from family and friends
* Neglect of personal appearance or hygiene
* Sadness, irritability, or indifference
* Having trouble concentrating

* Extreme anxiety or panic
* Drug or alcohol use or abuse
* Aggressive, destructive, or defiant behavior
* Poor school performance
* Hallucinations or unusual beliefs

It is tragic that many of these signs go unrecognized. And while suffering from one of these symptoms certainly does not necessarily mean that one is suicidal, it's always best to communicate openly with a loved one who has one or more of these behaviors, especially if they are unusual for that person.

There are also some more obvious signs of the potential for committing suicide. Putting one's affairs in order, such as giving or throwing away favorite belongings, is a strong clue. And it can't be stressed too strongly that any talk of death or suicide should be taken seriously and paid close attention to. It is a sad fact that while many of those who have committed suicide talked about it beforehand, only 33 percent to 50 percent were identified by their doctors as having a mental illness at the time of their death, and only 15 percent of suicide victims were in treatment at the time of their death. Any history of previous suicide attempts also is reason for concern and watchfulness. Approximately one-third of teens who die by suicide have made a previous suicide attempt. Also, while more females than males attempt suicide, more males are successful in completing suicide.

Recommended Resources

American Academy of Child and Adolescent Psychiatry
3615 Wisconsin Ave., NW
Washington, DC 20016-3007
Phone: 202-966-7300
Fax: 202-966-2891
Website: www.aacap.org

American Association of Suicidology
4201 Connecticut Ave., NW, Suite 408
Washington, DC 20008
Phone: 202-237-2280
Fax: 202-237-2282
Website: www.suicidology.org

American Foundation for Suicide Prevention
120 Wall St., 22nd Floor
New York, NY 10005
Phone (toll-free): 888-333-AFSP (2377)
Phone (local): 212-363-3500
Fax: 212/363-6237
Website: www.afsp.org

Source: National Alliance on Mental Illness, "Teenage Suicide," http://
www.nami.org/Content/ContentGroups/Helpline1/Teenage_Suicide.htm.

FACT SHEET 3

Violence

* Overall, the estimated number of gang-problem jurisdictions in the National Youth Gang Survey study population increased 14 percent between 2002 and 2011. An increase occurred in all areas—large and small urban, rural, and suburban areas. Following a marked decline from the mid-1990s to the early 2000s, the prevalence rate of gang activity significantly increased between 2001 and 2005 and has since remained fairly constant (National Gang Center, 2014).
* Gang problems are most widespread in the largest cities in the United States. Specifically, nearly all law enforcement agencies serving cities with populations of 100,000 or more have reported multiple years of gang problems (National Gang Center, 2014).
* According to the National Youth Gang Survey, total gang homicides averaged more than 1,900 each year from 2007 to 2011. The FBI estimates that there are more than 15,500 homicides each year in the United States, suggesting that gang-related homicides account for about 12 percent of all homicides annually (National Gang Center, 2014).

* Cities account for nearly 70 percent of the gang-related homicides, with Chicago and Los Angeles accounting for about one in five from 2010 to 2011 (National Gang Center, 2014).
* For youth aged 10–24, suicide is the third leading cause of death and accounts for about 4,600 lives lost each year (U.S. Centers for Disease Control and Prevention [CDC], 2014a).
* A survey of public and private high-school students found that 16 percent of students reported having seriously considered suicide, 13 percent reported having created a plan, and 8 percent reported having attempted suicide in the 12 months before the survey (CDC, 2014a).
* Boys are more likely than girls to die from suicide: of the reported suicides for youth aged 10–24, males accounted for 81 percent of the deaths. Girls, however, are more likely to report attempting suicide than boys. Among racial and ethnic groups, Native American/Alaskan Native youth have the highest rates of suicide deaths, and Hispanic youth are more likely to report attempting suicide than their African-American and White, non-Hispanic peers (CDC, 2014a).
* Homicide is the second leading cause of death among 15- to 19-year-olds and accounted for 1,832 deaths in 2010. Among 20- to 24-year-olds, homicide is the third leading cause of death (behind unintentional injury and suicide) but accounts for 2,846 deaths (CDC, 2013a).
* According to a CDC report, "From 1994 to 2010, homicide rates were higher among males than females, regardless of age. Homicide rates for males ages 10 to 24 years declined from 25.4 per 100,000 population in 1994 to 12.7 per 100,000 in 2010, yet were consistently higher than homicide rates for males of all ages combined. Homicide rates for females ages 10 to 24 years declined from 4.5 per 100,000 population in 1994 to 2.1 per 100,000 in 2010" (CDC, 2013a).

* Homicide rates were consistently higher for non-Hispanic African-Americans than for all other racial and ethnic groups from 1994 to 2010. Homicide rates for non-Hispanic African-Americans declined from 60.6 per 100,000 population in 1994 to 28.8 per 100,000 in 2010. In 2010, homicide rates were 10.0 per 100,000 for American Indians, 7.9 for Hispanics, 2.1 for Whites, and 1.9 for Asians (CDC, 2013a).

Related Links

* Injuries by firearms are similarly disproportionate by race and gender: From 2006 to 2012, males experienced 91 percent of the injuries caused by firearms, while females experienced 9 percent. African-American males experienced 41 percent of firearms injuries, and African American females 4 percent. The numbers for Whites and Hispanics were more comparable: 15 percent and 18 percent of firearm injury victims were White and Hispanic males, respectively, while 2 percent and 1.5 percent of victims were White and Hispanic females, respectively (CDC, 2013b).

* Hate crimes declined from 239,400 in 2003 to 148,400 in 2009. Still, nearly 90 percent of hate crime victimizations occurring between 2003 and 2009 were perceived as racially or ethnically motivated (Langton & Planty, 2011).

* In late 2009, the definition of hate crimes was amended to include crimes of prejudice based on gender or gender identity. Before that, the law only included crimes of prejudice based on race, religion, sexual orientation, ethnicity, or disability. Thus, data prior to 2009 do not include information on gender-based hate crimes (Langton & Planty, 2011).

* "The majority of violent hate crimes were interracial while the majority of nonhate violent crimes were intraracial" (Langton & Planty, 2011).

* Males account for 60 percent of hate crime victims, and females for 40 percent. Whites account for 61 percent of hate crime victims, and African-Americans and Hispanics account for 13 percent and 17 percent, respectively. However, persons of two or more races had the highest rate of hate crime violent victimizations, at 4.0 per 1,000 people ages 12 and older. Whites and African-Americans have a rate of 0.6 per 1,000, and Hispanics a rate of 0.9 per 1,000 (Langton & Planty, 2011).

* Violent crimes account for 87 percent of all hate crimes. Of violent hate crimes, 64 percent are simple assault, and 16 percent are aggravated assault (Langton & Planty, 2011).

* In 2012, the national estimate of unique victims of child abuse and neglect was 686,000. The highest rate of victimization, 21.9 per 1,000 children of the same age group, occurred in children under 1 year old. Boys accounted for 48.7 percent of victimization, and girls for 50.9 percent. Forty-four percent of victims were White, 21.8 percent were Hispanic, and 21.0 percent were African-American (Children's Bureau, U.S. Department of Health and Human Services [HHS], 2012).

* For 2011, it is estimated that 1,640 children died from abuse and neglect. Just over 70 percent of all child fatalities involved children younger than three years old, and 80.0 percent of fatalities were caused by one or more parents. Boys had a higher child fatality rate than girls—2.54 per 100,000 boys and 1.94 per 100,000 girls in the population. Whites composed 38.3 percent of the child fatalities, African-Americans 31.9 percent, and Hispanics 15.3 percent (Children's Bureau, HHS, 2012).

* "A 2009 survey of more than 7,000 LGBT middle and high school students aged 13–21 years found that in the past year, because of their sexual orientation, eight of ten students had been verbally harassed at schools, four of ten had been physically harassed at school, six of ten felt unsafe at school, and one of five had been the victim of a physical assault at school" (CDC, 2014b).

＊ According to the National Intimate Partner and Sexual Violence Survey, "Among adult victims of rape, physical violence, and/or stalking by an intimate partner, 22% of women and 15% of men first experienced some form of partner violence between 11 and 17 years of age" (Black et al., 2011).

References

Black, M. C., Basile, K. C., Breiding, M. J., Smith, S. G., Walters, M. L., Merrick, M. T., Chen, J., Stevens, M. R. (2011). The National Intimate Partner and Sexual Violence Survey (NISVS): 2010 Summary report. Atlanta: National Center for Injury Prevention and Control, Centers for Disease Control and Prevention. Retrieved from http://www.cdc.gov/violenceprevention/pdf/nisvs_executive_summary-a.pdf

Children's Bureau, U.S. Department of Health and Human Services (HHS). (2012). *Child maltreatment 2012.* Washington, DC: Administration for Children and Families, Children's Bureau. Retrieved from http://www.acf.hhs.gov/sites/default/files/cb/cm2012.pdf

Langton, L., & Planty, M. (2011). *Special report: Hate crime, 2003–2009.* Washington, DC: Office of Justice Programs, Bureau of Justice Statistics. Retrieved from http://www.bjs.gov/content/pub/pdf/hc0309.pdf

National Gang Center. (2014). *National youth gang survey analysis, 2002–Present.* Retrieved from http://www.nationalgangcenter.gov/Survey-Analysis

U.S. Centers for Disease Control and Prevention (CDC). (2013a). *Youth Violence: National Statistics (Homicide).* Retrieved from http://www.cdc.gov/violenceprevention/youthviolence/stats_at-a_glance/national_stats.html

———. (2013b). *Web-based injury statistics query & reporting system (WISQARS) nonfatal injury reports, 2001–2012.* Retrieved from http://webappa.cdc.gov/sasweb/ncipc/nfirates2001.html

———. (2014a). *Injury center: Violence prevention. Suicide prevention: Youth suicide.* Retrieved from http://www.cdc.gov/violenceprevention/pub/youth_suicide.html

———. (2014b). *Lesbian, gay, bisexual, and transgender health: Youth.* Retrieved from http://www.cdc.gov/lgbthealth/youth.htm.

Source: Jill Salisbury, The Mid-Atlantic Equity Center, Bethesda, MD, April 2014.

FACT SHEET 4

Warning Signs of an Eating Disorder

There are several types of eating disorders, but all share some fundamental features:

* An extreme dissatisfaction with the body
* Body weight, size, or shape being the primary measure of self-worth
* Feelings of guilt or depression after eating
* A tendency to isolate, to withdraw from friends and family
* Preoccupation with weight, food, calories, fat or carbohydrate grams, and diet

For *bulimia nervosa*, also look for:

* Periods of uncontrolled eating, or binges
* Self-induced vomiting or use of laxatives
* Excessive exercise, often used to "undo" the last eating episode

For *binge eating disorder*, also look for:

* Periods of uncontrolled eating, or binges
* Eating often when not hungry
* Eating until uncomfortably full

For *anorexia nervosa*, also look for:

* Dramatic weight loss
* Feeling fat despite dramatic weight loss
* Intense fear of fat
* Excessive exercise
* Odd food rituals such as counting bites, cutting food into tiny pieces, etc.
* Loss of menstrual periods, fainting, or irregular pulse

A Note About Dieting

Many eating disorders begin as a diet. Going on a diet is often the gateway to a full-blown eating disorder, because it introduces unhealthy ideas about food and because it fosters excessive focus on the body. Popular culture is overflowing with dangerous misinformation about nutrition and the body, and nearly all of it can contribute to the development of eating-disordered beliefs and behaviors. If your daughter is dieting, using diet pills or diuretics, or eating under food rules such as "no carbohydrates" or "no eating after 5 p.m.," she is at risk.

Healthy Eating Gone Awry

Sometimes people can become fixated on healthy eating to the point of obsession, a condition called *orthorexia*, similar to an eating disorder. Orthorexia begins in ways that at first can seem healthy:

choosing foods that are good for the body and avoiding ones that aren't. Over time, this interest in health becomes a preoccupation, and the person focuses on what and how much to eat to the exclusion of other important parts of life. Eating rules become increasingly rigid and difficult to maintain, and those who try to maintain them respond to slips with guilt, self-hatred, or increased strictness. Some may be obsessed with the idea of toxins in food or body and may engage in juice fasting or other "cleanses." The end result is a diet so restrictive that it impairs physical health.

If You Feel Concerned That Your Daughter Is "Fat" or "Getting Fat"

It's normal for preadolescents and adolescents to accumulate fat; their bodies are just storing up for the tremendous amount of energy they will need to develop physically into adulthood. This is most often a temporary state, and children should not interfere with it through diets or extra exercise. It is also important to remember that when an adolescent is transitioning from a girl's body to a woman's body, she gains more fat. This is a biological reality that is made more difficult by a society that fears even normal amounts of fat.

Despite what the diet industry tells us, each of us has a set body weight that is predetermined; we can do very little to change it. This is why diets never bring lasting weight loss and why some people spend their entire lives fighting those "last few pounds." Look at both sides of your children's biological family to get a sense of what their set body type might be. If your children are bigger or heavier than they want to be, they may need support in learning to accept their natural bodies despite a culture that overvalues the underweight look. Remember that beginning a diet can set your children up for a demoralizing, lifelong and, most important, losing battle. As long as your children are reasonably active and making thoughtful nutritional choices most of the time, you shouldn't need to worry. However, if your children are inactive or making poor food choices, they are at risk for obesity and other health problems. If you're concerned, it may be helpful for you and your children to go to a nutritionist together to get guidance in making these lifestyle changes.

Eating disorders can be deadly, and over time they usually get worse and more difficult to treat. But when you recognize them early and get proper treatment, your children have an excellent chance for recovery. If your children are showing any warning signs, it is important that you seek professional help as soon as possible. When looking for treatment, be sure that both the therapist and the nutritionist have had special training in treating eating disorders; don't be afraid to ask.

Recommended Resources

National Eating Disorders Association
Information and referral help line: 1-800-931-2237
www.nationaleatingdisorders.org

Gürze Books
Specializing in publications and education about eating
    disorders
1-800-756-7533
www.gurze.com

Source: Kimberly Lawrence Kol, PsyD, Clinical Psychologist/Eating Disorder Specialist

Drug Use in Adolescence

Adolescents experiment with drugs or continue taking them for several reasons, including the following:

* **To fit in:** Many teens use drugs "because others are doing it"—or they *think* others are doing it—and they fear not being accepted in a social circle that includes drug-using peers.
* **To feel good:** Abused drugs interact with the neurochemistry of the brain to produce feelings of pleasure. The intensity of this euphoria differs by the type of drug and how it is used.
* **To feel better:** Some adolescents suffer from depression, social anxiety, stress-related disorders, or physical pain. Using drugs may be an attempt to lessen these feelings of distress. Stress especially plays a significant role in starting and continuing drug use as well as returning to drug use (relapsing) for those recovering from an addiction.
* **To do better:** Ours is a very competitive society in which the pressure to perform athletically and academically can be intense.

Some adolescents may turn to certain drugs like illegal or prescription stimulants because they think those substances will enhance or improve their performance.

* **To experiment:** Adolescents are often motivated to seek new experiences, particularly those they perceive as thrilling or daring.

DRUGS (OTHER THAN TOBACCO AND ALCOHOL) MOST COMMONLY ABUSED BY HIGH-SCHOOL SENIORS

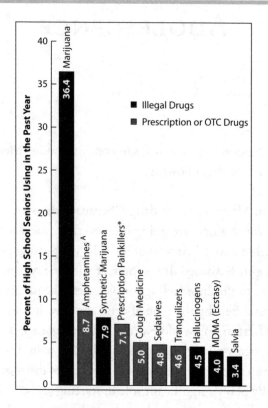

*The top drug used in this category is Adderall (used by 7.4 percent).

†The top drugs used in this category are Vicodin (5.3 percent) and OxyContin (3.6 percent).

Source: *Monitoring the Future: National Results on Adolescent Drug Use: Summary of Key Findings, 2013.*

Alcohol and tobacco are the drugs adolescents most commonly abuse, followed by marijuana. The next most popular substances differ among age groups. Young adolescents tend to favor inhalant substances (such as breathing the fumes of household cleaners, glues, or pens; see "The Dangers of Inhalants" on the National Institute on Drug Abuse's website, www.drugabuse.gov/publications/drugfacts/inhalants). Older teens are more likely to use synthetic marijuana ("K2" or "Spice") and prescription medications—particularly opioid pain relievers like Vicodin and stimulants like Adderall. In fact, the *Monitoring the Future* (2012) survey of adolescent drug use and attitudes revealed that prescription and over-the-counter medications account for a majority of the drugs most commonly abused by high-school seniors.

Signs of Drug Use in Adolescents

If adolescents start behaving differently for no apparent reason—such as acting withdrawn, frequently tired or depressed, or hostile—it could be a sign that they are developing a drug-related problem. Parents and others may overlook such signs, believing them to be a normal part of puberty. Other signs include any of the following:

* A change in peer group
* Carelessness with grooming
* Decline in academic performance
* Missing classes or skipping school
* Loss of interest in favorite activities
* Changes in eating or sleeping habits
* Deteriorating relationships with family members and friends

At the same time, a wide range of genetic and environmental influences that promote strong psychosocial development and resilience (positive self image, communication skills, emotional intelligence) may work to balance or counteract risk factors. Therefore, it ultimately is hard to predict who will develop substance-use disorders and who won't.

Parents' Role in Getting Treatment

Parents tend to underestimate the risks or seriousness of drug use. The symptoms listed here suggest a problem that may already have become serious and should be evaluated to determine the underlying cause—which could be a substance-abuse problem or another mental-health or medical disorder. Parents who are unsure whether their children are abusing drugs can enlist the help of a primary-care physician, school guidance counselor, or drug-abuse treatment provider.

Parents seeking treatment for an adolescent child are encouraged to see the National Institute on Drug Abuse's booklet *Seeking Drug Abuse Treatment: Know What to Ask* (available at the institute's website, www.drugabuse.gov) and the Treatment Referral Resources section of this guide.

Relationship of Other Mental-Health Conditions to Substance Use by Adolescents

Drug use in adolescents frequently overlaps with other mental-health problems. For example, a teen with a substance-use disorder is more likely to have a mood, anxiety, learning, or behavioral disorder, too. Sometimes drugs can complicate the process of accurately diagnosing these other problems. The influence can go in both directions: adolescents may begin taking drugs to deal with depression or anxiety, for example, or frequent drug use may cause or precipitate those disorders.

Adolescents entering drug-abuse treatment should undergo a comprehensive mental-health screening to determine if other disorders are present. Effectively treating a substance-use disorder requires addressing drug abuse and other mental-health problems simultaneously.

Source: National Institute on Drug Abuse, "Frequently Asked Questions," in *Principles of Adolescent Substance Use Disorder Treatment: A Research-Based Guide* (NIH Publication No. 14-7953, January 2014), http://www.drugabuse.gov/publications/principles-adolescent-substance-use-disorder-treatment-research-based-guide/frequently-asked-questions.

REFERENCES

Introduction: Whose Life Is It Anyway?

Davidson, A. (2014, June 22). Hi mom, I'm home. *New York Times Magazine*, pp. 22–31, 46.

Dickler, J. (2012, May 15). Boomerang kids: 85% of college grads move home. *CNNMoney*. Retrieved from http://money.cnn.com/2010/10/14/pf/boomerang_kids_move_home/index.htm

Dweck, C. (2007). *Mindset: The new psychology of success*. New York: Ballantine Books.

U.S. Chamber of Commerce Foundation. (2012, November 14). *The millennial generation research review*. Retrieved from http://www.uschamber foundation.org/millennialsreport

1. Resisting the Entitlement Trend

Bronson, P. (2007, August 3). How not to talk to your kids. The inverse power of praise. *New York Magazine.* Retrieved from http://nymag.com/news /features/27840/

Bruni, F. (2013, November 24). Are kids too coddled? *New York Times.* Retrieved from http://www.nytimes.com/2013/11/24/opinion/sunday /bruni-are-kids-too-coddled.html?_r=0

Duckworth, A. (2013, April). The key to success? Grit. *TED Talks.* Retrieved from http://www.ted.com/talks/angela_lee_duckworth_the_key_to_ success_grit

Goleman, D. (1995). *Emotional intelligence: Why it can matter more than IQ.* New York: Bantam.

Gottlieb, L. (2011, June 7). How to land your kid in therapy. *The Atlantic.* Retrieved from http://www.theatlantic.com/magazine/archive/2011/07 /how-to-land-your-kid-in-therapy/308555/

Gottman, J., & DeClaire, J. (1997). *The heart of parenting: Raising an emotion- ally intelligent child.* New York: Simon & Schuster.

Kolbert, E. (2012, July 2). Spoiled Rotten: Why do kids rule the roost? *New Yorker.* Retrieved from http://www.newyorker.com/arts/critics /books/2012/07/02/120702crbo_books_kolbert?printable=true&current Page=all

Miller, A. (2014). How to teach a teen to have impulse control. *Global Post.* Retrieved from http://everydaylife.globalpost.com/teach-teen-impulse -control-11045.html

Mogel, W. (2004, November 18). Lecture. Washington Hebrew Congregation, Washington, DC.

———. (2010) *The blessing of a B minus.* New York: Scribner.

Ritter, M. (n.d.). Experts link teen brains' immaturity, juvenile crime. *ABCNews.* Retrieved from http://abcnews.go.com/Technology/story?id =3943187

Rousseau, J. J. Rousseau, Jean Jacques. *On the Inequality among Mankind.* Vol. XXXIV, Part 3. The Harvard Classics. New York: P. F. Collier & Son, 1909–14; Bartleby.com, 2001. www.bartleby.com/34/3/. 1/23/15

Shellenbarger, S. (2013, October 15). Teens are still developing empathy skills. *Wall Street Journal,* D3.

Shulte, B. (2014, March 23). In McLean, a crusade to get people to back off in the parenting arms race. *Washington Post.* Retrieved from http://www .washingtonpost.com/lifestyle/style/in-mclean-a-crusade-to-get-people -to-back-off-in-the-parenting-arms-race/2014/03/23/9259c6a2-a552 -11e3-a5fa-55f0c77bf39c_print.html

Taffel, R. (2006, July/August). The divided self: Inside the world of 21st century teens. *Psychotherapy Networker.* Retrieved from http://www .psychotherapynetworker.org/magazine/populartopics/413-the-divided -self--inside-the-world-of-21st-century-teens

Tough, P. (2013). *How children succeed: Grit, curiosity, and the hidden power of character.* New York: Houghton Mifflin Harcourt.

Wiseman, P. (2006, April 10). Ward spins biracial roots into blessing. *USA Today.* Retrieved from http://usatoday30.usatoday.com/sports/football /nfl/steelers/2006-04-09-ward-focus_x.htm

2. Psychology: Lost in Translation

Erikson, E. (1963). *Childhood and society.* New York: Norton.

———. (1994). *Identity, youth, and crisis.* New York: Norton.

Giedd, J. (2000). White House Conference on Teenagers, Washington, DC.

Gilligan, C. (1982). *In a different voice.* Cambridge, MA: Harvard University Press.

Hedaya, R. (2010, June 3). The teenager's brain. *Psychology Today.* Retrieved from http://www.psychologytoday.com/blog/health-matters/201006 /the-teenagers-brain

Siegel, D. (2014, June 1). Brainstorm: The power and purpose of the teenage brain. *Diane Rehm Show.* Retrieved from http://thedianerehmshow.org /shows/2014-01-06/daniel-siegel-brainstorm-power-and-purpose -teenage-brain

Snyderman, N. (2002). *Girl in the mirror.* New York: Hyperion.

Taffel, R. (2006, July/August). The divided self: Inside the world of 21st century teens. *Psychotherapy Networker.* Retrieved from http://www .psychotherapynetworker.org/magazine/populartopics/413-the-divided -self--inside-the-world-of-21st-century-teens

Wallin, D. (2007). *Attachment in psychotherapy.* New York: Guilford.

3. Reality Check: How Do We Raise Our Sons and Daughters?

American Psychological Association (2011). Guidelines for psychological practice with lesbian, gay, and bisexual clients. Retrieved from http://www .apa.org/pi/lgbt/resources/guidelines.aspx

Day of the Girl–US. (2013, October). Negative media images of girls and teens. Retrieved from http://dayofthegirl.org/girls-issues/negative-media -images-of-girls-and-teens/

Ehrensaft, D. (2012, July 11). An interview with Diane Ehrensaft, author of "Gender born, gender made." *The Experiment.* Retrieved from http: //theexperimentpublishing.com/2012/01/an-interview-with-diane -ehrensaft-author-of-gender-born-gender-made/

Eliot, L. (2009). *Pink brain blue brain: How small differences grow into troublesome gaps—and what we can do about it.* New York: Houghton Mifflin Harcourt.

Fivush, R. (1989). Exploring sex differences in the emotional content of mother-child conversation about the past. *Sex Role, 20*(11/12), 675–669.

Garbarino, J. (1999). *Lost boys: Why our sons turn violent and how we can save them*. New York: Free Press.

Greytak, M., Kosciw, J., & Diaz, E. (2009). *Harsh realities: The experiences of transgender youth in our nation's schools*. New York: Gay, Lesbian & Straight Education Network (GLSEN). Retrieved from http://www.umass.edu/stonewall/uploads/listWidget/25125/trans%20youth%20in%20schools.pdf

Grinberg, E. (2012, August 28). When kids play across gender lines. *CNN Living*. Retrieved from http://www.cnn.com/2012/08/27/living/harrods-gender-neutral-toys

Kepple, K., Page, S., & Gainer, D. (2012, December 5). Poll: Attitudes toward gays changing fast; USA's shifting attitudes toward gay men and lesbians. *USA Today*. Retrieved from http://www.usatoday.com/story/news/politics/2012/12/05/poll-from-gay-marriage-to-adoption-attitudes-changing-fast/1748873/

Kosciw, J. G., Greytak, E. A., Bartkiewicz, M. J., Boesen, M. J., & Palmer, N. A. (2012). *The 2011 National School Climate Survey: The experiences of lesbian, gay, bisexual and transgender youth in our nation's schools*. New York: GLSEN.

Ryan, C. (2010). *Supportive families, healthy children: Helping families with lesbian, gay, bisexual and transgender children*. San Francisco: Marian Wright Edelman Institute, San Francisco State University. Retrieved from https://sait.usc.edu/lgbt/files/Supportive%20Families%20Healthy%20Children.pdf

Sadowski, M. (2010). Beyond gay-straight alliance: Research shows why family support is critical to helping LGBT students succeed. *Harvard Education Letter, 26*(2), 3–5.

Sandberg, S. (2013). *Lean in: Women, work, and the will to lead*. New York: Alfred A. Knopf.

Stout, H., & Harris, E. G. (2014, March). Today's girls love pink bows as playthings, but these shoot. *New York Times*, p. 20.

4. Media Takes on Teen Culture

Brown, J. (2001, September 10). Trash mags with training wheels. *Salon.* Retrieved from http://www.salon.com/2001/09/10/teen_mags/

Cromie, W. (2005). East doesn't meet west. *Harvard University Gazette.* Retrieved from http://www.news.harvard.edu/gazette/2005/02.10/11 -bodyimage.html

Cuban, B. (2014, July 6). Shattered image: My triumph over body dysmorphic disorder. *Huffington Post.* Retrieved from http://www.huffingtonpost .com/brian-cuban/men-eating-disorders_b_4150441.html

Deak, J. (2002). *Girls will be girls.* New York: Hyperion.

Katz, J., & Jhally, S. (1999, May 2). The national conversation in the wake of Littleton is missing the mark. *Boston Globe,* p. E-1.

Keegan, R. (2011, May 28). Muscle summer—The men of "Captain America," "Thor" and "Conan." *Hero Complex.* [Blog.] *Los Angeles Times.* Retrieved from http://herocomplex.latimes.com/movies/muscle-summer-the-men -of-captain-america-thor-and-conan/

MailOnline. (2013, August 21). "Anorexia blogs nearly killed me": Even when Grainne, 17, was starving to death, "thinspiration" sites encouraged her to lose more weight. [Video.] Retrieved from http://www.dailymail .co.uk/health/article-2398749/Pro-ana-Anorexia-blogs-nearly-killed -Starving-girl--17-says-thinspiration-sites-encouraged-her.html

Morgan, C. (2010, April 2). I'm bulimic: The true story of a fifteen year struggle with bulimia. Yahoo Voices. [Blog.] Retrieved from http://voices .yahoo.com/im-bulimic-true-story-fifteen-year-struggle-5762544 .html?cat=51

Morrison, Jim. (n.d.) BrainyQuote. Retrieved from http://www.brainyquote .com/quotes/keywords/media.htpl

NewsOne. (2014, February 28). Lupita Nyong'o delivers powerful speech on colorism, self-love. [Video.] Retrieved from http://newsone.com/2932538 /lupita-nyongo-delivers-powerful-speech-on-colorism-self-love-video/

Pollack, W. (1998). *Real Boys: Rescuing our Sons from the Myths of Boyhood.* New York: Random House.

Poncelet, B. (2014, May 30). Male body image: Your son and his body. *About .com: Teen Health.* Retrieved from http://teenhealth.about.com/od /bodyimage/a/malebodyimage.htm

Quenqua, D. (2012, November 19). Muscular body image lures boys into gym, and obsession. *New York Times.* Retrieved from http://www .nytimes.com/2012/11/19/health/teenage-boys-worried-about-body -image-take-risks.html

The Representation Project. (2014a). Statistics from *Miss Representation.* Retrieved from: http://therepresentationproject.org/resources/statistics/

————. (2014b). The mask you live in. [Video.] Retrieved from: http://the representationproject.org/films/the-mask-you-live-in/

Ross, C. (2012). Why do women hate their bodies? *PsychCentral.* [Blog.] Retrieved from http://psychcentral.com/blog/archives/2012/06/02/why -do-women-hate-their-bodies/

Russell, C. (2013, January). Looks aren't everything: Believe me, I'm a model. TED Talks. [Video.] Retrieved from http://www.ted.com/speakers/ cameron_russell

Self-esteem and young women. (n.d.) Retrieved from Office of Juvenile female offenders: A Status of the States Report http://www.ojjdp.gov /pubs/gender

Snyderman, N. (2002). *Girl in the mirror.* New York: Hyperion.Unilever. (2004). The Dove® Campaign for Real Beauty. Dove: Social Mission; Articles and Advice. Retrieved from http://www.dove.us/social-mission /campaign-for-real-beauty.aspx

————. (2006). Evolution. [Video.] Posted in The evolution video: How images of beauty are manipulated by the media. Dove Self-Esteem Project. Retrieved from http://selfesteem.dove.us/Articles/Video /Evolution_video_how_images_of_beauty_are_manipulated_by_the_ media.aspx

———. (2011). Surprising self-esteem statistics. Dove: Social Mission. Retrieved from http://www.dove.us/Social-Mission/Self-Esteem -Statistics.aspx

Weaver, J. (2013, July 24). Tech and gadgets: Teens tune out TV, log on instead. *NBC News.com*. Retrieved from http://www.nbcnews.com /id/3078614/ns/technology_and_science-tech_and_gadgets/t/teens -tune-out-tv-log-instead/#.Uw-9snkQ7wJ

Wilmore, L. (2012, September 12). Does the muscle make the man? *The Representation Project Blog*. Retrieved from http://therepresentation project.org/search/wilmore

Yadagaren, J. (2013, May 9). Minding the "thigh gap": Social media drive teen body-image obsession. *Minneapolis StarTribune*. Retrieved from http: //www.startribune.com/lifestyle/health/206645461.html

5. Screenagers

Baird, D. (2013, July 4). MTV Study: 57% of millennials like to take a break from technology to make things with their hands. *Barking Robot*. [Blog.] Retrieved from http://www.debaird.net/blendededunet/2013/07/mtv -study-57-of-millennials-like-to-take-a-break-from-technology-to-make -things-with-their-hands.html

Belkin, L. (2012, October 24). Have I failed my children by loving technology? *Huffington Post*. Retrieved from http://www.huffingtonpost.com /lisa-belkin/limits-on-kids-technology_b_2010851.html?view=screen

Berry, C. (2004). Berry on Plato. In web ring (online discussion) for Technol-ogy of the Book course at Purdue University. Retrieved from http://www .cla.purdue.edu/english/theory/webring/berryPlato.html

Boyd, D. (2013, October 22). Keeping teens "private'" on Facebook won't protect them. *Time*. Retrieved from http://ideas.time.com/2013/10/22 /keeping-teens-private-on-facebook-wont-protect-them/

Gay, Lesbian & Straight Education Network (GLSEN). (2013, July 10). GLSEN's "Out online: The experiences of lesbian, gay, bisexual and transgender youth" first national report to look in-depth at LGBT youth experience online. Retrieved from http://glsen.org/press/study-finds-lgbt -youth-face-greater-harassment-online

Goleman, D. (2013, November 5). Focus on how you connect. LinkedIn. Retrieved from http://www.linkedin.com/today/post/article/2013 1105173430-117825785-focus-on-how-you-connect?_msplash=1

Kaiser Family Foundation. (2010, January 10). Daily media use among children and teens up dramatically from five years ago. Retrieved from http: //kff.org/disparities-policy/press-release/daily-media-use-among -children-and-teens-up-dramatically-from-five-years-ago/

Li, A. (2012, August 21). Half of teens couldn't live without their phone for a week (study). *Mashable.* Retrieved from http://mashable.com/2012/08/21 /teens-mobile-phones/

Lublin, N. (2013, October 24). DoSomething.org makes the world suck less. [Video.] FORA.tv. Retrieved from http://fora.tv/2013/10/24/nancy_ lublin

Madden, M., Lenhart, A., Duggan, M., Cortesi, S., & Gasser, U. (2013, March 13). Teens and technology 2013. Pew Research Internet Project. Retrieved from http://www.pewinternet.org/2013/03/13/teens-and -technology-2013/

Moyers, B. (2013, October 18). Segment: Sherry Turkle on being alone together. [Video.] *Moyers & Company.* Retrieved from http://billmoyers .com/segment/sherry-turkle-on-being-alone-together/

MTV. (2013, June 18). New MTV study shows sharp differences between younger and older millennials. [News release.] Retrieved from http://the pub.viacom.com/sites/mtvpress/Pages/New_MTV_Study_Shows_ Sharp_Differences_Between_Younger_and_Older_Millennials .aspx#sthash.8poIAzfg.dpuf

Price-Mitchell, M. (2012, November 14). Generation tech: The good, bad, and scary. *The moment of Youth.* [Blog.] *Psychology Today.* Retrieved from http://www.psychologytoday.com/blog/the-moment-youth/201211 /generation-tech-the-good-bad-and-scary

Richtel, M. (2010, November 21). Growing up digital, wired for distraction. *New York Times.* Retrieved from http://www.nytimes.com/2010/11/21 /technology/21brain.html?pagewanted=all&_r=2&

Taylor, J. (2012). *Raising generation tech: Preparing your children for a media-fueled world.* Chicago: Sourcebooks.

Zickuhr, K. (2010, December 16). Generations 2010. Pew Research Internet Project. Retrieved from http://pewinternet.org/Reports/2010 /Generations-2010.aspx.

6. Your Daughters and Sons at School

American Psychological Association. (2014). Single-sex education unlikely to offer advantage over coed schools, research rinds [Press release.] Retrieved from http://www.apa.org/news/press/releases/2014/02/single-sex -education.aspx

American Psychological Association (APA). (2013). One in three U.S. youth report being victims of dating violence [News release.] Retrieved from http://www.apa.org/news/press/releases/2013/07/dating-violence.aspx

Bloom, B., Jones, L. I., & Freeman, G. (2013). Summary health statistics for U.S. children: National health interview survey, 2012. National Center for Health Statistics, *Vital Health Statistics, 10*(258). Retrieved from http://www.cdc.gov/nchs/data/series/sr_10/sr10_258.pdf

Bohm, A. (2012, May 21). Teach kids, not stereotypes. *Blog of Rights.* [ACLU blog.] Retrieved from https://www.aclu.org/blog/womens-rights/teach -kids-not-stereotypes

Boykin, A.W., & Noguera, P. (2011). *Creating the opportunity to learn: Moving from research to practice to close the achievement gap.* Alexandria, VA: ASCD.

Byrk, A., Sebring, P. B., Allensworth, E., Luppescu, S., & Eason, J. Q. (2010). *Organizing schools for improvement: Lessons from Chicago.* Chicago, IL: University of Chicago Press.

Center for Civil Rights Remedies. (2013). A summary of new research closing the school discipline gap: Research to policy. Los Angeles: The Civil Rights Project. Retrieved from http://civilrightsproject.ucla.edu/events/2013/summary-of-new-research-closing-the-school-discipline-gap-research-to-policy/Research_Summary_Closing_the_School_Discipline_Gap.pdf

Conlin, M. (2003, May 25). The new gender gap. Bloomberg Businessweek. Retrieved from: http://www.businessweek.com/stories/2003-05-25/the-new-gender-gap

Domangue, E. A., & Solmon, M. A. (2009). A feminist poststructuralist examination in the President's challenge physical fitness awards program. *Gender and Education, 21*(5), 583–600. doi: 10.1080/09540250802467943

Fergus, E., Noguera, P., & Martin, M. (2014). *Schooling for resilience: Improving the life trajectory of Black and Latino boys.* Cambridge, MA: Harvard Education Press.

Hill, C., & Kearl, H. (2011). *Crossing the line: Sexual harassment at school.* Washington, DC: American Association of University Women (AAUW). Retrieved from http://www.aauw.org/files/2013/02/Crossing-the-Line-Sexual-Harassment-at-School.pdf

Ho, H., Tomlinson, H. A., & Whipple, A. D. (n.d.). *Individual differences: Gender equity and schooling.* Retrieved from http://education.stateuniversity.com/pages/2083/Individual-Differences-GENDER-EQUITY-SCHOOLING.html

Holcomb-McCoy, C. (2011). The middle/high years: A smoother transition for black teens. *Educational Leadership, 68*(7), 59–63.

Kadaba, L. (2014). *The reverse gender gap.* Bethlehem, PA: Leigh University College of Education. Retrieved from http://www4.lehigh.edu/news/newsarticle.aspx?Channel=%2FChannels%2FNews+2013&WorkflowItemID=642d68b2-95f8-47c5-b8bd-94dacadeeee5

Kantrowitz, B., & Kalb, C. (2012, September). *Boys will be boys.* StudyMode. Retrieved from http://www.studymode.com/essays/Boys-Will-Be-Boys-1083480.html Katz, J. (2013). An interview with educator, activist, and author Jackson Katz. *American Men's Studies Association Newsletter, 3*(1). Retrieved from http://www.jacksonkatz.com

Mapp. K. L., & Kuttner, P. J. (2013). *Partners in education: A dual-capacity building framework for family-school partnerships*. Austin, TX: SEDL. Retrieved from: http://www.sedl.org/pubs/framework/FE-Cap-Building.pdf

Matthews, J. (2014, March 17). I used to be terrified of the SATs: This is why I'm not anymore. *Washington Post*, p. B2.

Mattson, S. (2010). Family engagement in education. Tennessee Comptroller of the Treasury, Offices of Research and Education Accountability, Legislative Brief. Retrieved from http://www.comptroller.tn.gov/repository /RE/FamilyEngagement.pdf

National Women's Law Center. (2012). The next generation of Title IX: STEM—Science, Technology, Engineering, and Math. *Title IX 40 years and counting*. Retrieved from http://www.nwlc.org/sites/default/files /pdfs/nwlcstem_titleixfactsheet.pdf

Niederle, M., & Vesterlund, L. (2010, Spring). Explaining the gender gap in math tests scores: The role of competition. *Journal of Economic Perspectives, 24*(2), 129–144.

Obama, M. (2013). Remarks by First Lady Michelle Obama at Education Event with DC High School Sophomores. Retrieved from http://www .whitehouse.gov/the-press-office/2013/11/12/remarks-first-lady-education -event-dc-high-school-sophomores

Office for Civil Rights. (2013). *Civil rights data collection, 2009–2010: National and state estimations*. Washington, DC: U.S. Department of Education. Retrieved from http://ocrdata.ed.gov/StateNational Estimations/Projections_2009_10

Pellegrini, A. D., (2011, August–September). In the eye of the beholder: Sex bias in observations and ratings of children's aggression. *Educational Researcher, 40*(6), 281–286. American Educational Research Association. doi:10.3102/0013189X11421983

Poteat, V. P., O'Dwyer, L. M., & Mereish, E. H. (2012). Changes in how students use and are called homophobic epithets over time: Patterns predicted by gender, bullying, and victimization status. *Journal of Educational Psychology, 104,* 393–406.

Rosenberg, J., & Wilcox, W.B. (2006). *The importance of fathers in the healthy development of children* (Child Abuse & Neglect User Manual Series). Washington, DC: Office on Child Abuse and Neglect, U.S. Children's Bureau, and U.S. Department of Health and Human Services, Administration for Children and Families. Retrieved from https://www.child welfare.gov/pubs/usermanuals/fatherhood/fatherhood.pdf

Sherwin, G. (May 15, 2014). "Busy boys, little ladies"—wait, what decade are we in again? ACLU Women's Rights Project. Retrieved from https://www.aclu.org/blog/womens-rights/busy-boys-little-ladies-wait-what -decade-are-we-again

STEMConnector & My College Options. (2013). Where are the STEM students? What are their career interests? Where are the STEM jobs? Washington, DC: Author.

Taffel, R. (2005). *Breaking through to teens: Psychotherapy for the new adolescence and the second family.* New York: Guilford.

Thompson, M. (2007). *Caring for boys versus girls.* Community Television of Southern California. Retrieved from http://aplaceofourown.org/print.php

Tough, P. (2012). *How children succeed: Grit, curiosity, and the hidden power of character.* New York: Houghton Mifflin Harcourt.

U.S. Department of Education, Institute of Education Sciences, National Center for Education Statistics. (2012). *Digest of Education Statistics: Postsecondary Education.* Retrieved from http://nces.ed.gov/prgrams /digest/d12

U.S. Department of Education, Institute of Education Sciences, National Center for Education Statistics. (2013). *The Nation's Report Card, A First Look: 2013 Mathematics and Reading (NCES 2014451).* Washington, DC: Author. Retrieved from http://nces.ed.gov/nationsreportcard/reading

U.S. Department of Education, Institute of Education Sciences, National Center for Education Statistics. (2013). The Nation's Report Card, A First Look: 2013 Mathematics and Reading (NCES 2014451). Washington,

DC: Author. Retrieved from http://nces.ed.gov/nationsreportcard /mathematics

Weiss, H. B., Lopez, M. E., & Rosenberg, H. (2010). *Beyond random acts: Family, school and community engagement as an integral part of education reform.* Boston: National Policy Forum for Family, School, & Community Engagement. Retrieved from http://www.nationalpirc.org/engagement_ forum/beyond_random_acts.pdf

White House. (2014). *Fact sheet and report: Opportunity for all: My Brother's Keeper blueprint for action* [News release.] Retrieved from http://www.whitehouse .gov/the-press-office/2014/05/30/fact-sheet-report--opportunity-all-my -brother-s-keeper-blueprint-action

White House Council on Women and Girls. (2011). *Women in America: Indicators of social and economic well-being.* Washington, DC: U.S. Department of Commerce Economics and Statistics Administration and the Executive Office of the President Office of Management and Budget. Retrieved from http://www.whitehouse.gov/sites/default/files/rss_viewer /Women_in_America.pdf

7. "The Good, the Bad, and the Ugly" of Teenage Friendships

American Educational Research Association (AERA). (2013). Prevention of bullying in schools, colleges and universities. Retrieved from http://www .aera.net/Portals/38/docs/News%20Release/Prevention%20of%20 Bullying%20in%20Schools,%20Colleges%20and%20Universities.pdf

Bender, D., & Lösel, F. (2011). Bullying at school as a predictor of delinquency, violence and other anti-social behaviour in adulthood. *Criminal Behavior & Mental Health, 21*(2), 99–106. doi:10.1002/cbm.799

Farrington, D. P., Ttofi, M. M., & Lösel, F. (2011). School bullying and later criminal offending. *Criminal Behavior & Mental Health, 21*(2), 77–79. doi:10.1002/cbm.807

Gay, Lesbian & Straight Education Network (GLSEN) & Harris Interactive. (2012). Playgrounds and prejudice: Elementary school climate in the United States, A survey of students and teachers. New York: GLSEN. Retrieved from http://www.glsen.org/binary-data/GLSEN_Atachments /file000/002/2027-1.pdf

Ginsburg, K. R. (2011). *Building resilience in children and teens: Giving kids roots and wings.* Elk Grove Village, IL: American Academy of Pediatrics.

Kosciw, J. G., Greytak, E. A., Bartkiewicz, M. J., Boesen, M. J., & Palmer, N. A. (2012). *The 2011 National School Climate Survey: The experiences of lesbian, gay, bisexual and transgender youth in our nation's schools.* New York: GLSEN.

Long, C. (2013, July 12). The geeks shall inherit the earth. *NEA Today.* Retrieved from http://neatoday.org/2013/07/12/conquering-cliques-in-school/

Michigan State University. (2010, August 16). Boys and girls not as different as previously thought. *ScienceDaily.* Retrieved from www.sciencedaily .com/releases/2010/08/100816114823.htm

National School Climate Council. (2010). *National school climate standards: Benchmarks to promote effective teaching learning and comprehensive school improvement.* New York: Author. Retrieved from http://www.school climate.org/climate/documents/school-climate-standards.pdf

Nobullying.com. (2014). Cyber bullying statistics 2014. Retrieved from www .Nobullying.com/cyber-bullying-statistics-2014

Olweus, D. (2005). A useful evaluation design, and effects of the Olweus bullying prevention program. *Psychology, Crime & Law, 11*(4), 389–402. doi:10.1080/10683160500255471

Poteat, V. P., O'Dwyer, L. M., & Mereish, E. H. (2012). Changes in how students use and are called homophobic epithets over time: Patterns predicted by gender, bullying, and victimization status. *Journal of Educational Psychology, 104*(2), 393–406. doi: 10.1037/a0026437

Real, T. (1997). *I don't want to talk about it: Overcoming the secret legacy of male depression.* New York: Fireside.

Robers, S., Zhang, J., Truman, J., & Snyder, T.D. (2012). Indicators of school crime and safety: 2011. Washington, DC: U.S. Department of Education, and Office of Justice Programs, United States Department of Justice. Retrieved from http://www.bjs.gov/content/pub/pdf/iscs11.pdf

Robinson, J. P., & Espelage, D.L. (2011). Inequities in educational and psychological outcomes between LGBTQ and straight students in middle and high school. *Educational Researcher, 40*(7), 315-330. doi: 10.3102/0013189X11422112

Sheridan, J.W. (2010, July 06). School bullying statistics: The ABC's of harassment. *Ezine Articles.* Retrieved from http://EzineArticles.com/?expert=John_W_Sheridan.

Tough, P. (2012). *How children succeed: Grit, curiosity, and the hidden power of character.* New York: Houghton Mifflin Harcourt.

U.S. Department of Health and Human Services (HHS). (2014a). Who is at risk: Effects of bullying. Retrieved from http://www.stopbullying.gov/at-risk/effects/

———. (2014b). LGBT Youth: Bullying and LGBT youth. Retrieved from http://www.stopbullying.gov/at-risk/groups/lgbt/index.html

———. (2014c). Youth with special needs: Bullying and youth with disabilities and special health needs. Retrieved from http://www.stopbullying.gov/at-risk/groups/special-needs/index.html

U.S. Department of Justice, Bureau of Justice Statistics. (2007). School Survey on Crime and Safety. Table 14. Retrieved from http://nces.ed.gov/surveys/ssocs/tables/scs_2007_tab_14.asp

Wang, J., Iannotti, R. J., & Nansel, T. R. (2009). School bullying among adolescents in the United States: Physical, verbal, relational, and cyber. *Journal of Adolescent Health, 45*(4), 368–375. doi:10.1016/j.jadohealth.2009.03.021.

Way, N. (2013, winter). Boys as human. *Contexts.* [American Sociological Association blog.] Retrieved from http://contexts.org/articles/winter-2013/the-hearts-of-boys/

Way, N., Pascoe, C. J., McCormack, M., Schalet, A., & Oeur, F. (2013). The hearts of boys. *Contexts, 12*(1). [American Sociological Association blog.] Retrieved from http://contexts.org/articles/winter-2013/the-hearts-of-boys/

8. The Parenting Road Map to Communication and Connection

Albom, M. (1997). *Tuesdays with Morrie: An old man, a young man and life's greatest lesson.* New York: Broadway Books.

Colbert, S. (2007). *I am America (and so can you!).* New York: Grand Central Publishing, Hachette.

Dweck, C. (2007). *Mindset: The new psychology of success; How we can learn to fulfill our potential.* New York: Ballantine.

Join Together. (2014, April 2). Parents influence teen's drinking decisions: Survey. Partnership for Drug Free Kids. Retrieved from http://www.drug free.org/join-together/parents-influence-teens-drinking-decisions-survey/

Students Against Destructive Decisions (SADD). (2000, September 13). Parents: Do your teens think "You don't have a clue"? They may be right [News release.] Retrieved from http://www.sadd.org/teenstoday /teenstodaypdfs/survey.pdf

Will, G. (2003, September 21). Disconnected youth. *Washington Post,* p. B7.

9. Wired to Take Risks

Adler, P., & Adler, P. (2011, September 23). Do men self-injure? Male and female patterns of self-harm. *Psychology Today.* [Blog.] Retrieved from http://www.psychologytoday.com/blog/the-deviance-society/201109 /do-men-self-injure

Boyd, D. (2014, April 11). Whether it's bikes or bytes, teens are teens. *Los Angeles Times.* Retrieved from http://articles.latimes.com/2014/apr/11 /opinion/la-oe-boyd-kids-and-technology-20140413

CASAColumbia. (2012). National survey on American attitudes on substance abuse XVII: Teens. Retrieved from http://www.casacolumbia .org/addiction-research/reports/national-survey-american-attitudes -substance-abuse-teens-2012

Child Trends. (2012).Teen homicide, suicide and firearm deaths. Child Trends Data Bank. Retrieved from http://www.childtrends.org/?indicators=teen -homicide-suicide-and-firearm-deaths

Hutchinson, M. K., & Cooney, T. M. (1998). Patterns of parent-teen sexual risk communication: Implications for intervention. *Family Relations, 47*, 185–194.

Kimmel, M. (1999, October/November). What are little boys made of? *Us*, 88–91.

———. (2009). *Guyland: The perilous world where boys become men*. New York: Harper Perennial.

Miller, B. C. (1998). *Families matter: A research synthesis of family influences on adolescent pregnancy*. Washington, DC: National Campaign to Prevent Teen Pregnancy.

Mundy, L. (2000, July 16). Sex sensibility. *Washington Post Magazine*, pp. 17–30.

National Institutes of Health (NIH), Center for Adolescent Health. (2011). National Survey of Adolescent Males (NSAM). Retrieved from https: //sites.google.com/site/cahjhsph/national-survey-of-adolescent-males

National Institutes of Alcohol Abuse and Alcoholism (NIAAA). (2009). Alcohol alert. Alcohol and sexual assault. Retrieved from http://pubs.niaaa .nih.gov/publications/arh25-1/43-51.htm

———. (n.d.b). Special populations and co-occurring disorders: Underage drinking. Retrieved from http://www.niaaa.nih.gov/alcohol-health/ special-populations-co-occurring-disorders/underage-drinking

———. (2006). Why do adolescents drink, what are the risks, and how can underage drinking be prevented? *Alcohol Alert*, no. 67. Retrieved from http://pubs.niaaa.nih.gov/publications/AA67/AA67.htm

Palladino, G. (1998, June 28). A look at . . . adolescence. *Washington Post*, p. C3.

Parker, K. (2003, May 14).What are little girls made of? How about pig guts and beer? *Chicago Tribune*. Retrieved from http://www.chicagotribune.com/news/showcase/chi-0305140141may14,1,3683597.story

Peale, C. (2014, March 11). Survey: Teens' drug, alcohol use declining. *USA Today*. Retrieved from http://www.usatoday.com/story/news/nation/2014/03/11/survey-teens-drug-alcohol-use-declining/6312127/

Ponton, L. (2002, September 17). It's all good. *Salon*. Retrieved from http://www.salon.com/2002/09/17/ponton1/

Tolman, D. (2005). *Dilemmas of desire: Teenage girls talk about sexuality*. Cambridge, MA: Harvard University Press.

White House Office of National AIDS Policy. (2010, July). National HIV/AIDS strategy for the United States. Retrieved from http://www.whitehouse.gov/sites/default/files/uploads/NHAS.pdf

10. Preparing for the Next Chapter

David, A. (2014, June 22). Hi, mom, I'm home. *New York Times Magazine*, pp. 22–30, 46.

Gordon, L. P., & Shaffer, S. M. (2004). *Mom, can I move back in with you? A survival guide for parents of twentysomethings*. New York: Penguin.

Louis C.K., David Letterman Show, Jan. 5, 2014

Morris, E. (2001). *The rise of Teddy Roosevelt*. New York: Modern Library.

Schwartz, N. (2014, May 6). Watch Kevin Durant's powerful, emotional MVP acceptance speech. [Video.] *USA Today*. Retrieved from http://ftw.usatoday.com/2014/05/kevin-durant-mvp-speech-mom

Tough, P. (2012). *How children succeed: Grit, curiosity, and the hidden power of character*. New York: Houghton Mifflin Harcourt.

INDEX

ABOUT THE AUTHORS

Susan Morris Shaffer is the president of the Mid-Atlantic Equity Consortium, Inc., an educational non-profit, and director of the Mid-Atlantic Equity Center. For more than four decades, Shaffer has been a nationally recognized expert for her transformational work in public schools with the development of comprehensive technical assistance and training on educational equity and multicultural gender-related issues. She has published extensively on gender equity, family engagement, civil rights, multicultural education, and disability. Shaffer serves on several boards, including the National Association of Family, School and Community Engagement (co-founder), the School of Education, Bowie State University, Maryland, the Maryland Women's Heritage Center, and Harmony through Education. She holds an undergraduate degree in history and a graduate degree in education from the University of California, Berkeley. Shaffer is the recipient of numerous awards for her service, leadership, and significant contribution to curricular materials on women.

Linda Perlman Gordon, M.S.W., M.Ed., is a psychotherapist in private practice in Chevy Chase, Maryland. She is a graduate of the Family Therapy Practice Center in Washington, DC and has advanced degrees in both social work and education. Her private practice specializes in treating individuals, couples, and families. Gordon has taught seminars on the subject of families and developed programs concerning mental health issues for children. She has been invited to speak at several judicial institutes on issues related to children and family. She has also been included in *Washingtonian* magazine's list of Best Mental Health professionals.

Gordon and Shaffer are the coauthors of *Too Close for Comfort: Questioning the Intimacy of Today's New Mother-Daughter Relationship* (September 2009, Berkley Publishing Group/Putnam), *Why Girls Talk and What They're Rea*' *A Parent's Surv*   005, McGraw   *le for Parents of*   ). As a result of   oups and educ   ter- views an   to participa